A Guide to
NATURAL AREAS
of NORTHERN INDIANA

INDIANA NATURAL SCIENCE

Gillian Harris, *editor*

Part 4

SUPPLEMENTARY MATERIALS

Species List

The following plant and animal species are mentioned in *A Guide to Natural Areas of Northern Indiana*. This is not an exhaustive list of the flora and fauna that live in or pass through the area, broadly defined as north of Interstate 70. It represents what the areas' land stewards— most significantly Indiana Department of Natural Resources Division of Nature Preserves—prioritized when describing the places.

Rankings for species that are endangered, threatened, or otherwise of conservation concern were drawn from Indiana Department of Natural Resources lists with the following designations:

FE: federally endangered Any species that is in danger of extinction throughout all or a significant portion of its range.

FT: federally threatened Any species that is likely to become endangered within the foreseeable future throughout all or a significant portion of its range.

SE: state endangered Any animal species whose prospects for survival or recruitment within the state are in immediate jeopardy and are in danger of disappearing from the state. This includes all species classified as endangered by the federal government that occur in Indiana.

SC: special concern Any animal species requiring monitoring because of known or suspected limited abundance or distribution or because of a recent change in legal status or required habitat. These species do not receive legal protection under the Nongame and Endangered Species Conservation Act.

SR: state rare Any plant species that is vulnerable in the state due to restricted range, relatively few populations, recent and widespread declines, or other factors making it vulnerable in the state.

WL: watch list Any plant species about which some problems of limited abundance or distribution in Indiana are known or suspected and should be closely monitored.

Animals

COMMON NAME	SCIENTIFIC NAME	CONSERVATION STATUS
Amphibians and Reptiles		
Blue racer	*Coluber constrictor foxii*	
Cave salamander	*Eurycea lucifuga*	
Gray tree frog	*Hyla versicolor*	
Leopard frog	*Rana pipiens*	
Long-tailed salamander	*Eurycea longicauda*	
Pickerel frog	*Rana palustris*	
Smallmouth salamander	*Ambystoma texanum*	
Spring peeper frog	*Pseudacris crucifer*	
Tiger salamander	*Ambystoma tigrinum*	
Western chorus frog	*Pseudacris triseriata*	
Wood frog	*Lithobates sylvaticus* or *Rana sylvatica*	
Zigzag salamander	*Plethodon dorsalis*	
Birds		
Acadian flycatcher	*Empidonax virescens*	
Alder flycatcher	*Empidonax alnorum*	
American coot	*Fulica americana*	
American bittern	*Botaurus lentiginosus*	SE
American golden plover	*Pluvialis dominica*	SC
American goldfinch	*Spinus tristis*	
American redstart	*Setophaga ruticilla*	
American woodcock	*Scolopax minor*	
Bald eagle	*Haliaeetus leucocephalus*	SC
Baltimore oriole	*Icterus galbula*	
Barred owl	*Strix varia*	
Bell's vireo	*Vireo bellii*	
Belted kingfisher	*Megaceryle alcyon*	
Black tern	*Chlidonias niger*	SE
Black-and-white warbler	*Mniotilta varia*	SC
Black-capped chickadee	*Poecile atricapillus*	
Black-crowned night-heron	*Nycticorax nycticorax*	SE
Blue jay	*Cyanocitta cristata*	
Blue-gray gnatcatcher	*Polioptila caerulea*	
Blue-winged teal	*Anas discors*	

Species List (continued)

COMMON NAME	SCIENTIFIC NAME	CONSERVATION STATUS
Blue-winged warbler	*Vermivora cyanoptera*	
Bobolink	*Dolichonyx oryzivorus*	
Brown creeper	*Certhia americana*	
Buff-breasted sandpiper	*Calidris subruficollis*	SC
Canada goose	*Branta canadensis*	
Canada warbler	*Cardellina canadensis*	
Canvasback	*Aythya valisineria*	
Carolina chickadee	*Poecile carolinensis*	
Cerulean warbler	*Setophaga cerulea*	SE
Common gallinule	*Gallinula galeata*	
Common loon	*Gavia immer*	
Common redpoll	*Acanthis flammea*	
Common tern	*Sterna hirundo*	
Common yellowthroat	*Geothlypis trichas*	
Connecticut warbler	*Oporornis agilis*	
Dickcissel	*Spiza americana*	
Downy woodpecker	*Picoides pubescens*	
Eastern bluebird	*Sialia sialis*	
Eastern meadowlark	*Sturnella magna*	
Eastern towhee	*Pipilo erythrophthalmus*	
Eastern wood-pewee	*Contopus virens*	
Field sparrow	*Spizella pusilla*	
Golden-winged warbler	*Vermivora chrysoptera*	SE
Grasshopper sparrow	*Ammodramus savannarum*	
Great blue heron	*Ardea herodias*	
Great egret	*Ardea alba*	SC
Great horned owl	*Bubo virginianus*	
Great crested flycatcher	*Myiarchus crinitus*	
Greater prairie chicken	*Tympanuchus cupido*	
Green heron	*Butorides virescens*	
Hairy woodpecker	*Leuconotopicus villosus*	
Henslow's sparrow	*Ammodramus henslowii*	SE
Hooded merganser	*Lophodytes cucullatus*	
Hooded warbler	*Setophaga citrina*	SC
Hudsonian godwit	*Limosa haemastica*	

COMMON NAME	SCIENTIFIC NAME	CONSERVATION STATUS
Indigo bunting	*Passerina cyanea*	
Kentucky warbler	*Geothlypis formosa*	
Lark sparrow	*Chondestes grammacus*	
Least bittern	*Ixobrychus exilis*	SE
LeConte's sparrow	*Ammodramus leconteii*	
Lesser scaup	*Aythya affinis*	
Lesser yellowlegs	*Tringa flavipes*	
Little blue heron	*Egretta caerulea*	
Long-eared owl	*Asio otus*	
Long-tailed jaeger	*Stercorarius longicaudus*	
Louisiana waterthrush	*Parkesia motacilla*	
Mallard	*Anas platyrhynchos*	
Marbled godwit	*Limosa fedoa*	
Marsh wren	*Cistothorus palustris*	SE
Mourning dove	*Zenaida macroura*	
Mourning warbler	*Geothlypis philadelphia*	
Northern bobwhite	*Colinus virginianus*	
Northern cardinal	*Cardinalis cardinalis*	
Northern flicker	*Colaptes auratus*	
Northern harrier	*Circus cyaneus*	SE
Northern parula	*Setophaga americana*	
Northern rough-winged swallow	*Stelgidopteryx serripennis*	
Northern saw-whet owl	*Aegolius acadicus*	
Olive-sided flycatcher	*Contopus cooperi*	
Orange-crowned warbler	*Vermivora celata*	
Orchard oriole	*Icterus spurius*	
Osprey	*Pandion haliaetus*	SE
Ovenbird	*Seiurus aurocapilla*	
Palm warbler	*Setophaga palmarum*	
Parasitic jaeger	*Stercorarius parasiticus*	
Peregrine falcon	*Falco peregrinus*	SC
Pileated woodpecker	*Hylatomus pileatus*	
Piping plover	*Charadrius melodus*	FE
Pomarine jaeger	*Stercorarius pomarinus*	

Species List *(continued)*

COMMON NAME	SCIENTIFIC NAME	CONSERVATION STATUS
Prairie warbler	*Setophaga discolor*	
Prothonotary warbler	*Protonotaria citrea*	
Quail	*Coturnix coturnix*	
Red crossbill	*Loxia curvirostra*	
Red knot	*Calidris canutus*	
Red-bellied woodpecker	*Melanerpes carolinus*	
Red-eyed vireo	*Vireo olivaceus*	
Red-headed woodpecker	*Melanerpes erythrocephalus*	
Red-shouldered hawk	*Buteo lineatus*	SC
Red-tailed hawk	*Buteo jamaicensis*	
Red-winged blackbird	*Agelaius phoeniceus*	
Ring-necked duck	*Aythya collaris*	
Ring-necked pheasant	*Phasianus colchicus*	
Rose-breasted grosbeak	*Pheucticus ludovicianus*	
Rough-legged hawk	*Buteo lagopus*	
Sandhill crane	*Grus canadensis*	SC
Scarlet tanager	*Piranga olivacea*	
Sedge wren	*Cistothorus platensis*	SE
Short-eared owl	*Asio flammeus*	SE
Snowy owl	*Bubo scandiacus*	
Song sparrow	*Melospiza melodia*	
Sora	*Porzana carolina*	
Spotted sandpiper	*Actitis macularius*	
Summer tanager	*Piranga rubra*	
Swamp sparrow	*Melospiza georgiana*	
Tufted titmouse	*Baeolophus bicolor*	
Turkey vulture	*Cathartes aura*	
Upland sandpiper	*Bartramia longicauda*	SE
Virginia rail	*Rallus limicola*	SE
Warbling vireo	*Vireo gilvus*	
Whimbrel	*Numenius phaeopus*	
White-eyed vireo	*Vireo griseus*	
Whooping crane	*Grus americana*	FE
Wild turkey	*Meleagris gallopavo*	
Willow flycatcher	*Empidonax traillii*	

COMMON NAME	SCIENTIFIC NAME	CONSERVATION STATUS
Wilson's phalarope	*Phalaropus tricolor*	SC
Wilson's snipe	*Gallinago delicata*	
Winter wren	*Troglodytes hiemalis*	
Wood duck	*Aix sponsa*	
Wood thrush	*Hylocichla mustelina*	
Worm-eating warbler	*Helmitheros vermivorum*	SC
Yellow-bellied flycatcher	*Empidonax flaviventris*	
Yellow-billed cuckoo	*Coccyzus americanus*	
Yellow-breasted chat	*Icteria virens*	
Yellow-throated vireo	*Vireo flavifrons*	
Yellow-throated warbler	*Setophaga dominica*	
Fish		
Bluegill	*Lepomis macrochirus*	
Brook trout	*Salvelinus fontinalis*	
Brown trout	*Salmo trutta*	
Channel catfish	*Ictalurus punctatus*	
Cisco	*Coregonus artedi*	SC
Common carp	*Cyprinus carpio*	
Crappie	*Pomoxis annularis*	
Goldfish	*Carassius auratus*	
Lake herring. *See* cisco.		
Lake trout	*Salvelinus namaycush*	
Lake whitefish	*Coregonus clupeaformis*	SC
Largemouth bass	*Micropterus salmoides*	
Longnose sucker	*Catostomus catostomus*	SC
Rainbow trout	*Oncorhynchus mykiss*	
Red-ear sunfish	*Lepomis microlophus*	
Rock bass	*Ambloplites rupestris*	
Slimy sculpin	*Cottus cognatus*	SC
Smallmouth bass	*Micropterus dolomieu*	
Walleye	*Sander vitreus*	
White bass	*Morone chrysops*	
Yellow perch	*Perca flavescens*	

Species List (continued)

COMMON NAME	SCIENTIFIC NAME	CONSERVATION STATUS
Invertebrates		
Acadian hairstreak butterfly	*Satyrium acadica*	
Baltimore checkerspot butterfly	*Euphydryas phaeton*	SR
Black dash butterfly	*Euphyes conspicua*	
Black swallowtail butterfly	*Papilio polyxenes*	
Clamp-tipped emerald dragonfly	*Somatochlora tenebrosa*	
Cobweb skipper butterfly	*Hesperia metea*	
Dusted skipper butterfly	*Atrytonopsis hianna*	
Eastern-tailed blue butterfly	*Cupido comyntas*	
Eyed brown butterfly	*Satyrodes eurydice eurydice*	
Giant swallowtail butterfly	*Papilio cresphontes*	
Grey petaltail dragonfly	*Tachopteryx thoreyi*	SC
Monarch butterfly	*Danaus plexippus*	
Mottled duskywing butterfly	*Erynnis martialis*	
Persius duskywing butterfly	*Erynnis persius*	
Red admiral butterfly	*Vanessa atalanta*	
Viceroy butterfly	*Limenitis archippus*	
Mammals		
American bison	*Bison bison*	
Badger	*Taxidea taxus*	
Beaver	*Castor canadensis*	
Big brown bat	*Eptesicus fuscus*	
Black bear	*Ursus americanus*	
Bobcat	*Lynx rufus*	
Chipmunk	*Tamias striatus*	
Coyote	*Canis latrans*	
Eastern cottontail rabbit	*Sylvilagus floridanus*	
Elk	*Cervus canadensis*	
Franklin's ground squirrel	*Poliocitellus franklinii*	
Groundhog	*Marmota monax*	
Mink	*Neovison vison*	
Muskrat	*Ondatra zibethicus*	
Opossum	*Virginia opossum*	

COMMON NAME	SCIENTIFIC NAME	CONSERVATION STATUS
Plains pocket gopher	*Geomys bursarius*	SC
Raccoon	*Procyon lotor*	
Red fox	*Vulpes vulpes*	
River otter	*Lontra canadensis*	
Skunk	*Mephitis mephitis*	
Star-nosed mole	*Condylura cristata*	SC
Western harvest mouse	*Reithrodontomys megalotis*	
White-tailed deer	*Odocoileus virginianus*	

Reptiles

Copperhead snake	*Agkistrodon contortrix*	
Eastern box turtle	*Terrapene carolina*	SC
Eastern hognose snake	*Heterodon platirhinos*	
Glass lizard	*Ophisaurus ventralis*	
Grass lizard	*Takydromus sexlineatus*	
Six-lined racerunner lizard	*Aspidoscelis sexlineata*	
Slender grass lizard	*Ophisaurus attenuatus*	

Plants

Alderleaf buckthorn	*Rhamnus alnifolia*	WL
American basswood	*Tilia americana*	
American beech	*Fagus grandifolia*	
American black elderberry	*Sambucus canadensis*	
American bladdernut	*Staphylea trifolia*	
American elm	*Ulmus americana*	
American golden-saxifrage	*Chrysosplenium americanum*	ST
American hazelnut	*Corylus americana*	
American pinesap	*Monotropa hypopithys*	WL
American wintergreen	*Pyrola rotundifolia var. americana*	SR
Amur honeysuckle	*Lonicera maackii*	Invasive
Appendaged waterleaf	*Hydrophyllum appendiculatum*	
Atlantic sedge	*Carex atlantica ssp. atlantica*	ST
Autumn olive	*Elaeagnus umbellata*	Invasive
Autumn willow	*Salix serissima*	ST
Beach sumac	*Rhus aromatica var. arenaria*	SR

Species List (continued)

COMMON NAME	SCIENTIFIC NAME	CONSERVATION STATUS
Bearberry	*Arctostaphylos uva-ursi*	
Bebb's sedge	*Carex bebbii*	ST
Beech drop	*Epifagus virginianais*	
Big bluestem grass	*Andropogon gerardi*	
Bird's-foot violet	*Viola pedata*	
Bishop's cap	*Mitella diphylla*	
Bitternut hickory	*Carya cordiformis*	
Black ash	*Fraxinus nigra*	
Black cherry	*Prunus serotina*	
Black-eyed Susan	*Rudbeckia hirta*	
Black-fruited spike rush	*Eleocharis melanocarpa*	ST
Black gum	*Nyssa sylvatica*	
Black haw	*Viburnum prunifolium*	
Black huckleberry	*Gaylussacia baccata*	
Black maple	*Acer nigrum*	
Black oak	*Quercus velutina*	
Black sedge	*Carex arctata*	SE
Black walnut	*Juglans nigra*	
Black willow	*Salix nigra*	
Blue beech	*Carpinus caroliniana*	
Blue cohosh	*Caulophyllum giganteum*	
Blue-eyed Mary	*Collinsia verna*	
Blue flag iris	*Iris virginica*	
Blue joint grass	*Calamagrostis canadensis*	
Blue phlox	*Phlox divaricata*	
Blue violet	*Viola sororia*	
Bog rosemary	*Andromeda glaucophylla*	SR
Bog yelloweyed grass	*Xyris difformis*	ST
Boxelder maple	*Acer negundo*	
Bracken fern	*Pteridium aquilinum*	SX
Branching bur-reed	*Sparganium androcladum*	ST
Bristly-stalked sedge	*Carex leptalea*	WL
Broadwing sedge	*Carex alata*	WL
Brown-fruited rush	*Juncus pelocarpus*	SE
Brownish sedge	*Carex brunnescens*	SE

Common name	Scientific name	Conservation Status
Buckbean	*Menyanthes trifoliata*	WL
Buckeye. *See* Ohio buckeye		
Bur oak	*Quercus macrocarpa*	
Burning bush	*Kochia scoparia*	Invasive
Butterfly milkweed	*Asclepias tuberosa*	
Butterfly weed. *See* butterfly milkweed		
Butternut	*Juglans cinerea*	WL
Buttonbush	*Cephalanthus occidentalis*	
Canada buffaloberry	*Shepherdia canadensis*	SX
Canada goldenrod	*Solidago canadensis*	
Canada mayflower	*Maianthemum canadense*	
Canada wild rye	*Elymus canadensis*	
Canada wood nettle	*Laportea canadensis*	
Canada (American) yew	*Taxus canadensis*	SE
Cardinal flower	*Lobelia cardinalis*	
Carolina rose	*Rosa carolina*	
Carey's smartweed	*Polygonum careyi*	ST
Catbird grape	*Vitis palmata*	SR
Chamomile grape-fern	*Botrychium matricariifolium*	SR
Chinquapin oak	*Quercus muehlenbergii*	
Cinnamon fern	*Osmundastrum cinnamomeum*	
Clasping milkweed	*Asclepias amplexicaulis*	
Clustered sedge	*Carex cumulata*	SE
Common boneset	*Eupatorium perfoliatum*	
Common milkweed	*Asclepias syriaca*	
Common privet	*Ligustrum vulgare*	Invasive
Compass plant	*Silphium laciniatum*	
Cream wild indigo	*Baptisia leucophaea*	WL
Creeping St. John's-wort	*Hypericum adpressum*	SE
Cuckoo flower	*Cardamine pratensis var. palustris*	WL
Culver's root	*Veronicastrum virginicum*	
Cup plant	*Silphium perfoliatum*	
Cut-leaved toothwort	*Cardamine concatenata*	
Cyperus-like sedge	*Carex pseudocyperus*	SE

Species List (continued)

COMMON NAME	SCIENTIFIC NAME	CONSERVATION STATUS
Dame's rocket	*Hesperis matronalis*	Invasive
Deam's mercury	*Acalypha deamii*	SR
Dogtooth violet	*Erythronium americanum*	
Doll's eyes	*Actaea pachypoda*	
Drooping trillium	*Trillium flexipes*	
Drummond hemicarpha	*Hemicarpha drummondii*	SE
Dutchman's breeches	*Dicentra cucullaria*	
Dwarf birch	*Betula pumila*	
Dwarf cinquefoil	*Potentilla canadensis*	
Dwarf dandelion	*Krigia virginica*	
Dwarf ginseng	*Panax trifolius*	WL
Dwarf umbrella-sedge	*Fuirena pumila*	ST
Eastern cottonwood	*Populus deltoides*	
Eastern hemlock	*Tsuga canadensis*	WL
Eastern red cedar	*Juniperus virginiana*	
Eastern redbud	*Cercis canadensis*	
Eastern white pine	*Pinus strobus*	SR
Elderberry. *See* American black elderberry		
Elliptical-leaf wintergreen	*Pyrola elliptica*	WL
False asphodel	*Tofieldia glutinosa*	SR
False hop sedge	*Carex lupuliformis*	SR
False mermaid	*Floerkea proserpinacoides*	
False smooth foxglove	*Aureolaria flava*	
False Solomon's seal	*Maianthemum racemosum*	
Fewflower spike rush	*Eleocharis pauciflora*	WL
Fineberry hawthorn	*Crataegus chrysocarpa*	SE
Finely-nerved sedge	*Carex leptonervia*	SE
Fire cherry	*Prunus pensylvanica*	SR
Firepink	*Silene virginica*	
Flatleaf pondweed	*Potamogeton robbinsii*	SR
Flax-leaved aster	*Ionactis linariifolius*	
Flowering dogwood	*Cornus florida*	
Flowering spurge	*Euphorbia corollata*	
Forbe's saxifrage	*Saxifraga forbesii*	SE

COMMON NAME	SCIENTIFIC NAME	CONSERVATION STATUS
Forked aster	*Aster furcatus*	SR
Forked bluecurl	*Trichostema dichotomum*	SR
Foxtail sedge	*Carex alopecoidea*	SE
Fries' pondweed	*Potamogeton friesii*	ST
Fringed brome grass	*Bromus ciliatus*	
Fringed gentian	*Gentianopsis crinita*	
Fringed puccoon	*Lithospermum incisum*	SE
Garlic mustard	*Alliaria petiolata*	Invasive
Glade mallow	*Napaea dioica*	SR
Globe-fruited false-loosestrife	*Ludwigia sphaerocarpa*	SE
Goat's rue	*Tephrosia virginiana*	
Golden ragwort	*Packera aurea*	
Golden seal	*Hydrastis canadensis*	WL
Golden sedge	*Carex aurea*	SR
Goldie's fern	*Dryopteris goldiana*	
Goldthread	*Coptis trifolia var. groenlandica*	WL
Grass-of-parnassus	*Parnassia glauca*	
Gray birch	*Betula populifolia*	SE
Gray dogwood	*Cornus racemosa*	
Gray-headed coneflower	*Ratibida pinnata*	
Great St. John's-wort	*Hypericum pyramidatum*	ST
Green ash	*Fraxinus pennsylvanica*	
Green brier	*Smilax glauca*	
Green dragon	*Arisaema dracontium*	
Green-fringed orchid	*Platanthera lacera*	WL
Green-keeled cotton grass	*Eriophorum viridicarinatum*	SR
Ground juniper	*Juniperus communis*	SR
Grove meadow grass	*Poa alsodes*	SR
Hackberry	*Celtis occidentalis*	
Hairy puccoon	*Lithospermum caroliniense*	
Hairy valerian	*Valeriana edulis*	SE
Hairy woodrush	*Luzula acuminata*	SE
Hall's bulrush	*Schoenoplectus hallii*	SE
Harbinger-of-spring	*Erigenia bulbosa*	
Harebell	*Campanula rotundifolia*	

Species List *(continued)*

COMMON NAME	SCIENTIFIC NAME	CONSERVATION STATUS
Hay-scented fern	*Dennstaedtia punctilobula*	WL
Heartleaf willow	*Salix cordata*	ST
Hepatica	*Hepatica nobilis*	
Herb-robert	*Geranium robertianum*	ST
Hickey's clubmoss	*Lycopodium hickeyi*	SR
Hidden-fruited bladderwort	*Utricularia geminiscapa*	SE
Highbush blueberry	*Vaccinium corymbosum*	
Highbush cranberry	*Viburnum opulus var. americanum*	SE
Hispid green brier	*Smilax hispida*	
Hoary puccoon	*Lithospermum canescens*	
Honey locust	*Gleditsia triacanthos*	
Hooker orchis	*Platanthera hookeri*	SX
Hop hornbeam	*Ostrya virginiana*	
Horned bladderwort	*Utricularia cornuta*	ST
Horse-tail spike rush	*Eleocharis equisetoides*	SE
Hydrangea	*Hydrangea arborescens*	
Hydrilla	*Hydrilla verticillata*	Invasive
Indian cucumber-root	*Medeola virginiana*	
Indian grass	*Sorghastrum nutans*	
Indian paintbrush	*Castilleja coccinea*	
Jack pine	*Pinus banksiana*	SR
Jack-in-the-pulpit	*Arisaema triphyllum*	
Japanese stiltgrass	*Microstegium vimineum*	Invasive
Jewelweed	*Impatiens capensis*	
Jointed rush	*Juncus articulatus*	SE
June grass	*Koeleria macrantha*	
Kentucky coffee tree	*Gymnocladus dioicus*	
Lady fern	*Athyrium filix-femina*	
Large cranberry	*Vaccinium macrocarpon*	WL
Large marsh St. John's-wort	*Triadenum tubulosum*	WL
Large-flowered trillium	*Trillium grandiflorum*	
Largetooth aspen	*Populus grandidentata*	
Leadplant	*Amorpha canescens*	
Leatherleaf	*Chamaedaphne calyculata*	
Ledge spike-moss	*Selaginella rupestris*	ST

Common name	Scientific name	Conservation Status
Leiberg's witchgrass	*Panicum leibergii*	ST
Lesser bladderwort	*Utricularia minor*	ST
Lily-of-the-valley	*Convallaria majalis*	Invasive
Calamint	*Satureja glabella var. angustifolia*	SE
Little bluestem grass	*Schizachyrium scoparium*	
Little prickly sedge	*Carex echinata*	SE
Log sedge	*Carex decomposita*	ST
Long sedge	*Carex folliculata*	SR
Long-beaked baldrush	*Psilocarya scirpoides*	ST
Longstalk sedge	*Carex pedunculata*	SR
Lowbush blueberry	*Vaccinium angustifolium*	
Maple-leaved viburnum	*Viburnum acerifolium*	
Marginal shield fern	*Dryopteris marginalis*	
Marsh bellflower	*Campanula aparinoides*	
Marsh blazing star	*Liatris spicata*	
Marsh marigold	*Caltha palustris*	
Marsh phlox	*Phlox glaberrima*	
Marsh valerian	*Valeriana uliginosa*	SE
Mayapple	*Podophyllum peltatum*	
Meadow beauty	*Rhexia virginica*	
Miami mist	*Phacelia purshii*	
Michaux's stitchwort	*Arenaria stricta*	SR
Michigan lily	*Lilium michiganense*	
Mild water pepper	*Persicaria hydropiperoides*	
Missouri rockcress	*Arabis missouriensis var. deamii*	SE
Montgomery hawthorn	*Crataegus arborea*	SE
Mountain holly	*Ilex mucronata*	
Mud sedge	*Carex limosa*	SE
Muehlenberg's nutrush	*Scleria muehlenbergii*	SE
Narrow-leaved cattail	*Typha angustifolia*	
Narrow-leaved cotton grass	*Eriophorum angustifolium*	SR
New Jersey tea	*Ceanothus americanus*	
Nodding ladies' tresses	*Spiranthes cernua*	
Northeastern smartweed	*Polygonum hydropiperoides var. opelousanum*	ST

Species List (continued)

COMMON NAME	SCIENTIFIC NAME	CONSERVATION STATUS
Northern bedstraw	*Galium boreale*	
Northern pin oak	*Quercus ellipsoidalis*	
Northern pitcher plant	*Sarracenia purpurea*	WL
Northern St. John's-wort	*Hypericum boreale*	
Northern white cedar	*Thuja occidentalis*	SE
Northern wild-raisin	*Viburnum cassinoides*	SE
Northern witchgrass	*Panicum boreale*	SR
Nuttall pondweed	*Potamogeton epihydrus*	SE
Obedient plant	*Physostegia virginiana*	
Ohio buckeye	*Aesculus glabra*	
Orange coneflower	*Rudbeckia fulgida var. fulgida*	WL
Orange-fringed orchid	*Platanthera cillaris*	
Osage orange	*Maclura pomifera*	
Ostrich fern	*Matteuccia struthiopteris*	SR
Pale corydalis	*Corydalis sempervirens*	ST
Pale dogwood	*Cornus obliqua*	
Partridgeberry	*Mitchella repens*	
Pawpaw	*Asimina triloba*	
Pennsylvania sedge	*Carex pensylvanica*	
Periwinkle	*Vinca minor*	Invasive
Philadelphia fleabane	*Erigeron philadelphicus*	
Pickerel weed	*Pontederia cordata*	
Pignut hickory	*Carya glabra*	
Pin oak	*Quercus palustris*	
Pipewort	*Eriocaulon aquaticum*	SE
Pitcher stitchwort	*Minuartia patula*	
Plains muhly	*Muhlenbergia cuspidata*	SE
Poison ivy	*Toxicodendron radicans*	
Poison sumac	*Toxicodendron vernix*	
Porcupine grass	*Hesperostipa spartea*	
Post oak	*Quercus stellata*	
Prairie blazing star	*Liatris pycnostachya*	ST
Prairie dock	*Silphium terebinthinaceum*	
Prairie fleabane	*Erigeron strigosus*	
Prairie gray sedge	*Carex conoidea*	ST

COMMON NAME	SCIENTIFIC NAME	CONSERVATION STATUS
Prairie lily	*Lilium philadelphicum*	
Prairie phlox	*Phlox pilosa*	
Prairie sundrop	*Oenothera pilosella*	
Prairie trillium	*Trillium recurvatum*	
Pretty sedge	*Carex woodii*	WL
Prickly ash	*Zanthoxylum americanum*	
Prickly pear cactus	*Opuntia humifusa*	
Primrose	*Primula vulgaris*	
Primrose-leaf violet	*Viola primulifolia*	ST
Purple avens	*Geum rivale*	SE
Purple bladderwort	*Utricularia purpurea*	SR
Purple coneflower	*Echinacea purpurea*	
Purple creeper	*Euonymus fortunei*	Invasive
Purple cress	*Cardamine douglassii*	
Purple milkweed	*Asclepias purpurascens*	
Rattlesnake master	*Eryngium yuccifolium*	
Red baneberry	*Actaea rubra*	SR
Red clover	*Trifolium pratense*	
Red maple	*Acer rubrum*	
Red oak	*Quercus rubra*	
Red osier dogwood	*Cornus sericea*	
Red pine	*Pinus resinosa*	
Red trillium	*Trillium erectum*	
Reed canary grass	*Phalaris arundinacea*	Invasive
Reticulated (netted) nutrush	*Scleria reticularis*	ST
Rice cut grass	*Leersia oryzoides*	
Riddell's goldenrod	*Solidago riddellii*	
Robbins spike rush	*Eleocharis robbinsii*	SR
Rose turtlehead	*Chelone obliqua var. speciosa*	WL
Rough dropseed grass	*Sporobolus compositus*	
Rough rattlesnake-root	*Prenanthes aspera*	SR
Rough sedge	*Carex scabrata*	SE
Rough-leaved dogwood	*Cornus drummondii*	
Round-headed bush clover	*Lespedeza capitata*	
Roundleaf dogwood	*Cornus rugosa*	SR

Species List (continued)

COMMON NAME	SCIENTIFIC NAME	CONSERVATION STATUS
Royal fern	*Osmunda regalis*	
Rue anemone	*Thalictrum thalictroides*	
Running euonymus	*Euonymus obovatus*	
Running pine	*Lycopodium clavatum*	WL
Running serviceberry	*Amelanchier humilis*	SE
Rushlike aster	*Aster borealis*	SR
Sand cherry	*Prunus pumila*	
Sandplain yellow flax	*Linum intercursum*	SE
Sanicle	*Sanicula europaea*	
Sassafras	*Sassafras albidum*	
Scotch pine	*Pinus sylvestris*	
Sea rocket	*Cakile edentula var. lacustris*	WL
Seabeach needlegrass	*Aristida tuberculosa*	SR
Sessile-leaved bugleweed	*Lycopus amplectens*	SE
Sessile trillium	*Trillium sessile*	
Shagbark hickory	*Carya ovata*	
Sharp-scaled manna-grass	*Glyceria acutiflora*	SE
Shining clubmoss	*Lycopodium lucidulum*	WL
Shooting star	*Dodecatheon meadia*	
Short-point flatsedge	*Cyperus acuminatus*	WL
Showy goldenrod	*Solidago speciosa*	
Shrubby cinquefoil	*Dasiphora fruticosa*	
Shumard's oak	*Quercus shumardii*	
Siberian elm	*Ulmus pumila*	Invasive
Side-oats grama grass	*Bouteloua curtipendula*	
Silver maple	*Acer sacclwrinum*	
Skunk cabbage	*Symplocarpus foetidus*	
Slender cotton grass	*Eriophorum gracile*	ST
Slender gerardia	*Agalinis tenuifolia*	
Slenderleaf false foxglove. *See* slender gerardia		
Slim-spike three-awn grass	*Aristida intermedia*	SR
Slippery elm	*Ulmus rubra*	
Small bristleberry	*Rubus setosus*	SE
Small cranberry	*Vaccinium oxycoccos*	ST

COMMON NAME	SCIENTIFIC NAME	CONSERVATION STATUS
Small sundrop	*Oenothera perennis*	SR
Smith's bulrush	*Schoenoplectus smithii*	SE
Smooth gooseberry	*Ribes hirtellum*	WL
Snow trillium	*Trillium nivale*	
Softleaf arrow-wood	*Viburnum molle*	SR
Sparse-lobe grape-fern	*Botrychium biternatum*	WL
Speckled alder	*Alnus rugosa*	WL
Spicebush	*Lindera benzoin*	
Spindle tree	*Euonymus europaeus*	Invasive
Spotted coralroot	*Corallorhiza maculate*	
Spotted wintergreen	*Chimaphila maculata*	WL
Spring beauty	*Claytonia virginica*	
Squirrel corn	*Dicentra canadensis*	
Staghorn sumac	*Rhus typhina*	
Starflower	*Trientalis borealis*	
Stiff dogwood	*Cornus foemina*	
Straight-leaf pondweed	*Potamogeton strictifolius*	ST
Straw sedge	*Carex straminea*	ST
Sugar maple	*Acer saccharum*	
Swamp cottonwood	*Populus heterophylla*	
Swamp goldenrod	*Solidago patula*	
Swamp loosestrife	*Decodon verticillatus*	
Swamp milkweed	*Asclepias incarnata*	
Swamp rose	*Rosa palustris*	
Swamp thistle	*Cirsium muticum*	
Swamp white oak	*Quercus bicolor*	
Sweet cicely	*Osmorhiza claytonii*	
Sweet coneflower	*Rudbeckia subtomentosa*	
Sweetfern	*Comptonia peregrina*	WL
Switchgrass	*Panicum virgatum*	
Sycamore	*Platanus occidentalis*	
Tall beaked-rush	*Rhynchospora macrostachya*	SR
Tall coreopsis	*Coreopsis tripteris*	
Tamarack	*Larix laricina*	WL
Thicket sedge	*Carex abscondita*	WL

Species List (continued)

COMMON NAME	SCIENTIFIC NAME	CONSERVATION STATUS
Thinleaf sedge	Carex sparganioides var. cephaloidea	SE
Three-seed sedge	Carex trisperma	WL
Torrey's bulrush	Schoenoplectus torreyi	SE
Tree clubmoss	Lycopodium obscurum	SR
Tree-of-heaven	Ailanthus altissima	Invasive
Trout lily. See Dogtooth violet		
Tufted hairgrass	Deschampsia cespitosa	SR
Tulip poplar	Liriodendron tulipifera	
Tussock sedge	Carex stricta	
Twinleaf	Jeffersonia diphylla	
Two-leaf toothwort	Dentaria diphylla	WL
Vasey's pondweed	Potamogeton vaseyi	SE
Velvetleaf blueberry	Vaccinium myrtilloides	SE
Virginia bluebell	Mertensia virginica	
Virginia chainfern	Woodwardia virginica	
Virginia creeper	Parthenocissus quinquefolia	
Virginia pine	Pinus virginiana	WL
Virginia waterleaf	Hydrophyllum virginianum	
Warty panic-grass	Panicum verrucosum	ST
Water bulrush	Scirpus subterminalis	SR
Waterleaf	Talinum fruticosum	
Weak stellate sedge	Carex seorsa	SR
Weakstalk bulrush	Scirpus purshianus	SR
Western rockjasmine	Androsace occidentalis	ST
Western silvery aster	Aster sericeus	SR
White oak	Quercus alba	
White (paper) birch	Betula papyrifera	WL
White ash	Fraxinus americana	
White camas	Zigadenus elegans var. glaucus	SR
White trillium	Trillium grandiflorum	
White violet	Viola canadensis	
White water lily	Nymphaea alba	
White wild indigo	Baptisia alba	
White-edge sedge	Carex debilis var. rudgei	SR
White-stem pondweed	Potamogeton praelongus	ST

COMMON NAME	SCIENTIFIC NAME	CONSERVATION STATUS
Whorled milkweed	*Asclepias verticillata*	
Whorled water-milfoil	*Myriophyllum verticillatum*	SR
Wild bergamot	*Monarda fistulosa*	
Wild columbine	*Aquilegia canadensis*	
Wild geranium	*Geranium maculatum*	
Wild ginger	*Asarum canadense*	
Wild hyacinth	*Camassia scilloides*	
Wild lettuce	*Lactuca canadensis*	
Wild lupine	*Lupinus perennis*	
Wild quinine	*Parthenium integrifolium*	
Wild sensitive plant	*Cassia nictitans*	WL
Winterberry	*Ilex verticillata*	
Wintergreen	*Gaultheria procumbens*	
Witch hazel	*Hamamelis virginiana*	
Wolf bluegrass	*Poa wolfii*	SR
Wood (celandine) poppy	*Stylophorum diphyllum*	
Woodland strawberry	*Fragaria vesca var. americana*	SE
Woodland sunflower	*Helianthus divaricatus*	
Yellow birch	*Betula alleghaniensis*	
Yellow pimpernel	*Taenidia integerrima*	
Yellow sedge	*Carex flava*	ST
Yellow star grass	*Hypoxis hirsuta*	
Yellow violet	*Viola pubescens*	
Yellow water lily	*Nuphar lutea*	
Yellow wild indigo	*Baptisia tinctoria*	WL

Glossary

Backbone A rocky ridge with steep sides.

Backdune A dune that is detached from the shoreline by other dunes, referred to as foredunes.

Barren A small area of prairie surrounded by forest; an area of land where plant growth is sparse, stunted, and/or contains limited biodiversity.

Beach An area of sand or pebble that is washed by waves and does not grow plants; usually on large lakes, occasionally on smaller lakes or streams.

Biodiversity A basic environmental value based upon the number and variety of life forms present in particular habitats or ecosystems, or in the world.

Blowout A sandy depressions in a sand dune ecosystem caused by wind.

Bog A wetland or depression, often with a floating mat of vegetation, typically acidic, rich in accumulated plant material, frequently surrounding a body of open water.

Boreal forest Coniferous forests of the north or northern regions, dominated by spruce and fir; especially relating to or characteristic of the climatic zone south of the Arctic.

Borrow pit A pond created when material (usually soil, gravel, or sand) has been dug for use at another location, for example, highways and bridges.

Calcareous Calcium-rich.

Controlled burn/fire Intentionally set fire to meet specific land management objectives, such as reducing flammable fuels, restoring ecosystem health, recycling nutrients, or preparing areas for new vegetation.

Convex waterfall A waterfall that curves outward rather than falling straight down.

Deciduous forest A forest of predominantly broad-leaved trees that lose their leaves each year, usually during cold or dry seasons.

Driftless A region that was never glaciated.

Dune A hill, mound, or ridge of sand or other loose sediments formed by blowing wind.

Ecological succession. *See* **Succession.**

Ephemeral Lasting for a brief period of time; plants that quickly grow, flower, and die; or waterbodies that dry up in summer.

Escarpment A long cliff or steep slope that separates two comparatively level or more gently sloping surfaces, that is, plateaus or uplands, one of which is lower; typically marks a boundary between physiographic regions.

Esker A long ridge of gravel and other sediments, deposited by meltwater from retreating glaciers, usually in a winding course.

Exotic A nonnative species, originating in or characteristic of other areas or countries.

Extinct The condition of a species that is no longer in existence; having no living members anywhere; may exist in fossil or other preserved forms.

Extirpated The condition of a species that ceases to exist in a geographic area but still exists elsewhere.

Fallow Farmland plowed and harrowed but left unsown for a period of time.

Fen A sloping wetland community where water flows to the surface in a diffused manner, commonly through organic substrates, such as peat, muck, or marl; soils are usually neutral to calcium-rich.

Flatwoods Relatively level forests that have water tables at or above the surface for part or all of a year.

Forb An herbaceous (nonwoody) plant that is not a fern, grass, sedge, shrub, or, generally, a flowering plant.

Foredune The part of a sand dune system on the side nearest to the water.

Glacial depression A sunken or depressed area caused by retreating glaciers.

Glacial erratics Randomly deposited rocks and boulders that were transported long distances south by glacial ice.

Glacial sluice A channel created by melting glaciers that conduct water.

Glacial till Sediments deposited by a glacier that are nonsorted or stratified.

Glacier A massive block of ice, formed at least partly on land by compacted snow, constantly moving as a result of its weight, surviving year to year.

Herbaceous Flowering plants whose stems do not produce woody tissues and generally die back at the end of the growing season.

Honeycomb A type of weathering that leaves rock surfaces with pock-marked patterns.

Indigenous Originating or occurring naturally in a particular place; native to a particular place.

Interdunal wetland A water-filled depression that lies between coastal sand dunes.

Interdune Situated between dunes.

Interglacial (interstadial) A geological interval of warmer global average temperature that separates glacial periods within an ice age, during which revegetation of glaciated landscapes occur.

Kame An isolated ridge of gravel, sand, or other till-like sediments formed by glacial drift, when meltwater streams plunged from glacial surfaces; usually deposited in fanlike forms and left in relief.

Kettle A lake formed when a glacial ice block melted and filled a depression, usually rather circular.

Lagoon A small lake near a larger lake or river.

Marl Unconsolidated sedimentary rock or soil consisting of clay and lime; mostly clay mixed with calcium carbonate, often from shells of marine creatures.

Marsh An area of low-lying land that is seasonally flooded and typically remains waterlogged at all times; shallow wetlands with emergent herbaceous plants, such as cattails, sedges, reeds, and rushes.

Meadow A piece of grassland.

Mesophytic A plant that grows in an environment having a moderate amount of moisture.

Moat A deep, wide trench, usually filled with water, that surrounds an object, such as a mat of sphagnum moss or animals in a zoo; usually the rampart of a fortified place, such as a castle.

Moraine Sedimentary material of sand, gravel, or loam-type soils that was deposited by a glacier near its margin.

Muck Highly decomposed soil in which the original plant materials cannot be recognized.

Natural regions/sections Major, generalized units of landscape where distinctive assemblages of natural features are present, including climate, soil, glacial history, topography, exposed bedrock, presettlement vegetation, species composition, physiography, and flora and fauna. Natural regions are subdivided into sections when sufficient differences warrant separate recognitions.

Outwash Materials washed out from a glacier and deposited beyond its edge.

Outwash plain A large, mostly level area composed of glacial outwash that is not confined to a river valley.

Panne A shallow pond in the flatlands between sand dunes.

Pasture Land covered with grass and other low plants on which animals graze.

Peat Slightly decayed plant material that accumulates in water.

Plate tectonics A theory that explains the structure of the earth's crust and associated phenomena that result from the interaction of rigid plates on the earth's crust that move slowly over the underlying mantle.

Pothole A circular or cylindrical hole in a riverbed produced by swirling water carrying small pebbles and sediment that wear away a rock surface.

Prairie A large open area of grassland that is dominated by grasses and wildflowers, especially the species that once covered much of central North America.

Punchbowl A pothole formed by pieces of bedrock caught in swirling backwash.

Puncheon A short upright framing timber.

Ravine A small, deep gorge or valley with steep sides, usually carved out by running water.

Riffle An area of rough water on a rocky or shallow part of a stream or river, usually caused by underwater rocks.

Sandflat An extended, flat area of sand, with little or no vegetation.

Sand prairie A dry native grassland community dominated by grasses such as little bluestem and June grass.

Savanna A predominantly prairie area, usually sandy, with scattered trees or groves of trees and drought-resistant undergrowth.

Sedge A grasslike plant with triangular stems, typically growing in wet ground.

Sedge meadow An open area dominated by grasslike plants called sedges.

Sediment Material that settles to the bottom of water, such as stones or sand, that is carried onto land or into water by water, wind, or glacier.

Seep A place where water slowly oozes out of the ground.

Shrub A low, woody plant, usually with multiple stems.

Sluice A channel that carries off excess water.

Strand plain A belt of sand along a shoreline whose surface exhibits well-defined parallel or semiparallel sand ridges separated by swales.

Succession The process by which the composition of a biological community evolves over time; a natural change sequence during which one plant or animal species slowly replaces another.

Swale A slight, low, or hollow place on generally level land; especially a moist or marshy depression between ridges, usually a trough between ridges on a beach that carries water during rainstorms and snowmelts.

Swamp A shallow wetland dominated by trees; a bog or marsh with emergent woody vegetation.

Terrace A steplike level space that was once the bottom of a glacial river.

Thicket A dense groups of bushes or trees.

Till. *See* **glacial till.**

Tip-ups Trees that topple over during windstorms.

Tree graveyard A location where buried trees are being reexposed by wind erosion.

Undissected plain A flat area that has not been cut by erosion into hills or valleys.

Unglaciated An area that was not covered by Ice Age glaciers.

Valley train A deposit of glacial sand and gravel that extends along the floor of a valley, often for some distance.

Vernal pool A temporary pool of water that provides habitat for distinctive plants and animals.

Wildflower A flower of uncultivated varieties; a flower that grows freely without human intervention.

Resources

Print

Deam, Charles C. 1940. *Flora of Indiana*. Indianapolis: Indiana Department of Conservation, Division of Forestry.

Homoya, Michael A. 2012. *Wildflowers and Ferns of Indiana Forests*. Bloomington: Indiana University Press.

Homoya, Michael A., D. Brian Abrell, James R. Aldrich, and Thomas W. Post. 1985. "The Natural Regions of Indiana." *Proceedings of the Indiana Academy of Science*.

Jackson, Marion T. 1997. *The Natural Heritage of Indiana*. Bloomington: Indiana University Press.

Jackson, Marion T. 2003. *101 Trees of Indiana*. Bloomington: Indiana University Press.

Jordan, Christopher, and Ron Leonetti. 2006. *The Nature Conservancy's Guide to Indiana Preserves*. Bloomington: Indiana University Press.

Lindsey, Alton A., Damian V. Schmelz, and Stanley A. Nichols. 1969. *Natural Areas of Indiana and their Preservation: Indiana Natural Areas Survey*. West Lafayette: Purdue University Press.

McPherson, Alan. 1996. *Nature Walks in Northern Indiana*. Hoosier Chapter of the Sierra Club, Indianapolis.

Shepardson, Daniel P. 2016. *A Place Called Turkey Run: A Celebration of Indiana's Second State Park in Photographs and Words*. West Lafayette: Purdue University Press.

Simons, Richard S. 1985. *The Rivers of Indiana*. Bloomington: Indiana University Press.

Yatskievych, Kay. 2000. *Field Guide to Indiana Wildflowers*. Bloomington: Indiana University Press.

Online

ACRES LAND TRUST
https://acreslandtrust.org/

ALLEN COUNTY PARKS
http://allencountyparks.org/

BUFFALO FIELD CAMPAIGN
http://www.buffalofieldcampaign.org/legal/esabackground.html

CENTRAL INDIANA LAND TRUST
http://www.conservingindiana.org/

CIVILIAN CONSERVATION CORPS
http://www.ccclegacy.org/

ECO INDIANA
http://www.ecoindiana.net/naturalareas/index.shtml

FORT WAYNE PARKS & RECREATION
http://www.fortwayneparks.org/parks.html

GOSHEN COLLEGE ENVIRONMENTAL LEARNING CENTER
https://www.goshen.edu/merrylea/

HOOSIER HIKERS COUNCIL
https://www.hoosierhikerscouncil.org/

INDIANA DEPARTMENT OF NATURAL RESOURCES
http://www.in.gov/dnr/

Division of Fish & Wildlife
http://www.in.gov/dnr/fishwild/

Division of Forestry
http://www.in.gov/dnr/forestry/

Division of Nature Preserves
http://www.in.gov/dnr/naturepreserve/

Division of State Parks & Lakes
http://www.in.gov/dnr/parklake/

INDIANA GEOLOGICAL & WATER SURVEY
http://igs.indiana.edu/Surficial/

INDY PARKS AND RECREATION
http://www.indy.gov/eGov/City/DPR/Pages/IndyParksHome.aspx

LAGRANGE COUNTY DEPARTMENT OF PARKS AND RECREATION
http://www.lagrangecountyparks.org/

LAKE COUNTY PARKS AND RECREATION
http://www.lakecountyparks.com/parks.html

LAPORTE COUNTY CONSERVATION TRUST
http://lpcct.org/

LAPORTE COUNTY PARKS DEPARTMENT
http://www.laportecountyparks.org/redmill.html

LITTLE RIVER WETLANDS PROJECT
http://www.lrwp.org/

NATIONAL AUDUBON SOCIETY
https://action.audubon.org/

IMPORTANT BIRD AREAS INDIANA
http://www.audubon.org/important-bird-areas/state/indiana/

NATIONAL NATURAL LANDMARKS
https://www.nps.gov/subjects/nnlandmarks/nation.htm

NATIONAL PARK SERVICE
https://www.nps.gov/index.htm

THE NATURE CONSERVANCY
http://www.nature.org/

THE NATURE CONSERVANCY IN INDIANA
https://www.nature.org/ourinitiatives/regions/northamerica
/unitedstates/indiana/index.htm

NICHES LAND TRUST
http://nicheslandtrust.org/

OUABACHE LAND CONSERVANCY
https://ouabachelandconservancy.org/

RED-TAIL LAND CONSERVANCY
http://www.fortheland.org/

SHIRLEY HEINZ LAND TRUST
http://www.heinzetrust.org/

ST. JOSEPH COUNTY PARKS DEPARTMENT
http://www.sjcparks.org/519/Parks-Trails

Index

Page numbers in *italics* refer to illustrations

Beaver Lake Nature Preserve, 134, 138
Bedrock, Indiana (map), 35
Beechwood Nature Preserve, *174*, 176, 229, 232–34, *233*, 234, 240
Bender Nature Preserve, *174*, 175, 208–10
Bendix Corp., 164
Bendix Woods County Park. *See* Bendix Woods Nature Preserve
Bendix Woods Nature Preserve, *124*, 125, 161, *162–63*, 164–65
Berns-Meyer Nature Preserve, *124*, 125, 149, *150*, 151
Beverly Shores, IN, 85
Bicentennial Woods Nature Preserve, *252*, 254, 368–69, *368*
Big Blue River, 63, 315, 319
Big Blue River Conservancy District, 319
Big Blue River Recreation Area, 319
Big Blue River Valley, 319–20
Big Lake, 60
Big Pine Creek, 73, 284–85
Big Raccoon Creek, 261
Big Squaw, 46
Big Walnut Creek, 63, 73, 276–80, 285
Big Walnut Creek National Natural Landmark, 276–77
Big Walnut Creek watershed, 276
Big Walnut Natural Area, 277, 279–80
Big Walnut Preserve, *252*, 253, 276–80, 277, 279
Birdfoot Barrens, 289
Black Oak Bayou Waterfowl Resting Area, 165, 167
Black Rock Barrens Nature Preserve, *252*, 253, 286, 288–90, *289*, 291
Black Rock Nature Preserve, *252*, 253, 288, 290–92, *291*
Black Swamp Natural Region, vii, ix, 75, *252*, 254, 376, 377
Bloomington, IN, xvii, xix, 5, 35, 37
Blue Cast Springs Nature Preserve, *252*, 254, *376*, 377
Blue Island, Chicago, 50
Blue River, 59, 370
Bluffs of Fall Creek Nature Preserve, 310

Bluffton, IN, 55, 354
Bluffton Till Plain Unit, 66
Bluffton Till Plain Section, vii, ix, 72, 74, *252*, 254, 326
Bob Kern Nature Preserve, *174*, 175, 186–88
bogs. *See* Cowles Bog; Pinhook Bog; Spring Lake Woods and Bog Nature Preserve; Volo Bog; wetlands, types of: bog
Boone County, IN, *252*
Boot Lake Nature Preserve, *174*, 175, 182–84, *183*
borrow pit lake, 359
Bowen Lake, 207
Bower, Alan (IU Press Sponsoring Editor), xvi, xix
Boy Scouts, 249
Bremen, IN, 52
Bristol, IN, 45, 47
Broad Ripple, Indianapolis, 304
Brookville, IN, 40
Browand Woods, 218
Brown County, IN, 42
Buell, Dorothy R., 86
Burns Ditch, 50
Burns Harbor, IN, 85

Cagles Mill Lake, 20
Cairo, IL, 56
Caldwell, Lynton Keith, 24
Calumet Feeder Canal, 49
Calumet Harbor, 49
Calumet River, 48–50
Calumet River System, 48
Calumet-Sag Channel, 50
Cambrian Explosion, 36
Cambrian Period, 36
Camp Glenn, 310
Canada, x, 223, 271
Canada, Eastern, 39
Canada, Northern, 61, 134, 353
Canadian bedrock, 268
canyon, sandstone, 61, 284; steep-walled, 284
Cape Cod National Seashore, 86
Cardinal Greenway, 324, 326
Carroll County, IN, *252*
Catfish Pond, 223
Cathedral Oaks, 368

Coulter Nature Preserve. *See* John
Merle Coulter Nature Preserve
covered bridges, 278
Cowles, Henry Chandler, 50, 88, 96
Cowles Bog: as "birthplace of ecol-
ogy," 88; Cowles Bog: National
Natural Landmark, 50, *78, 79,*
88–90, *89*; Cowles Bog Wetlands
Complex Restoration Project, 89
Crawfordsville, IN, 61, *252*
Cressmoor Prairie Nature Preserve,
xiii, *27, 78*, 79, 102–4, *103*
crinoids, 37
Crooked Creek, 46
Crooked Lake, 46, 152, 201–2
Crooked Lake Nature Preserve, *174,*
175, 201–2, *201*
Crossroads of America, x

Daisy Low Falls, 342
Darke County, OH, 57
Daviess County, IN, 62
Davis, Martha F., 330
Davis Fisher Creek, 373
Davis-Purdue Agricultural Center
Forest, *252*, 254, 329–31, *330*
Deaf Man. *See* Chief Shepoconah
(Deaf Man)
Deaf Man's Village, 332
Deam, Charles C., 108, 291, 358
Dearborn County, IN, xiii, 36
Deer Creek, 257
Deer Creek Fish & Wildlife Area,
252, 253, 257–58
DEET, 8
Defiance, OH, 43
DeKalb County, IN, 44, *174*, 249, *252*
Delaware County, IN, *252*, 324,
326–27
Delaware Indians, 55, 63, 261,
310, 332
Delaware Lake, 308
DeMotte, IN, Town of, xiii, 29, 140
Department of Geography and Tour-
ism Studies, Brock University, St.
Catherines, Ontario, 6
depression, glacial, 72; wet, 107,
149, 242
de Tocqueville, Alexis, 5
Devil's Backbone, 42, 272

Devil's Punchbowl, 272
Devonian Period, 36, 37, 73
Dixon Lake, 52
dolomite, 34, 335; Silurian Age, 335
Dora-New Holland State Recreation
Area, 340
Dorothy Buell Memorial Visitor
Center, 86
Douglas, Paul H. (Illinois Sena-
tor), 86
Douglas Woods Nature Preserve,
174, 176, 249–51, *250*
Drainageways Unit, 66
driftless, 40
Dune Acres, IN, 50, 85, 88
dune-and-swale topography, 95, 98
Duneland Campground, Indiana
Dunes National Lakeshore, xiii
Dunes Creek, 94
Dunes Nature Preserve: National
Natural Landmark, *78, 79*, 92, 94
Dunes Prairie Nature Preserve, *78,*
79, 92, 94
dunes, xi, xvi–xvii, 68, 71, 86, 88,
92, 94, 97, 114, 155, 360; high,
67–68, 86; living, 92; moving, 92;
pine-forested, 87; rolling, 152;
sand, 19, 64, 84, 88, 147, 151, 359.
See also Indiana Dunes National
Lakeshore; Indiana Dunes State
Park
Durham Lake Wildlife Conservation
Area, *174, 175*, 194–96
Dustin, Jane, xix, 25, 370
Dustin, Tom, xix, 25, 370
Dyer, IN, 87
Dygert, Evelyn, 203
Dygert, Wendell, 203
Dygert Nature Preserve, *174, 175,*
202–4, *203*

Eagle Creek Ornithology Center, 298
Eagle Creek Park, *252, 253*, 298–99,
300–301
Eagle Creek Reservoir, 302
Eagle Creek Valley, 303
Eagle Marsh, *252*, 254, 359,
361–63, *362*
Eagle's Crest Nature Preserve, *252,*
253, 298, 299, 302–4, *303*

earthkeeping, 197
earth's crust, 34, 36
earthworks, 63, 321, 323
East Arm Little Calumet, 50
East Branch of the St. Joseph
  River, 44
East-Central Indiana, 28
East Fly Creek, 221
East Pool, 223
Eberhardt, Marion, 245
Ecological Society of America, 23
"Ecological Study of the Sand Dune
  Flora of Northern Indiana, An," 88
Ecologists Union, 24
ecosystems, aquatic, 108; lake plain,
  68; ridge-and-swale, 68
Edgar H. and Lois C. Seward Memo-
  rial Prairie, 324
Edna W. Spurgeon Woodland Re-
  serve, 25, *174*, 175, 210–11, *210*
Eel River, 55, 59, 63
Eel River Valley, 60
Efroymson Restoration at Kanka-
  kee Sands, 133–34, 136. *See also*
  Kankakee Sands
Eli Lilly and Company, 299
Elkhart, IN, City of, 29, 30, 35, 37,
  43, 45, 47, *174*, 182–83
Elkhart County, IN, *174*, 182, 184
Elkhart Forestry Division, 183
Elkhart River, 47, 208–9, 214; North
  Branch of, 47, 209, 211, 214; South
  Branch of, 47, 208–9, 214
Elkhorn Creek, 330
endangered species, confidentiality
  of locations, 18
English Lake, IN, 52–53
Entrenched Valley Section, vii, ix,
  73–74, *252*, 253, 256
equator, 34, 343
esker, 207, 215
European encroachment, 60, 70, 296
European settlement, 101, 293, 304
Evansville, IN, x, 35, 37
"Everglades of the North" (Grand
  Marsh), 41, 170

Fall Branch, 284, 286
Fall Creek, Fall Branch tributary,
  284–86

Fall Creek, White River tributary,
  64, 308–10
Fall Creek Gorge, 285
Fall Creek Gorge Nature Preserve,
  252, 253, 284–86, *285*
Fall Creek Gorge Valley, 285
Fall Creek Trail, 310
Fall Creek Valley, 284, 309
Falls of the Ohio State Park, 19
Farm at Prophetstown, 296
father of ecology. *See* Cowles, Henry
  Chandler
Father of Indiana State Parks. *See*
  Lieber, Colonel Richard
Father of Shades (Joseph W.
  Frisz), 272
Fawn River, 46, *226*
Fawn River, MI, 46
Fawn River Nature Preserve, *174*,
  175, 225–27, *226*
Fayette County, IN, *252*, 312
Fennell, David, 6
fens: alkaline, 322; calcareous, 119,
  237; grass/sedge, 226; grassy, 109;
  prairie, 119; wetland, 240. *See also*
  wetlands, locations of; wetlands,
  types of
Fern Cliff Nature Preserve, 23, *252*,
  253, 258–60, *259*
fire tower, 22, 151, 353, 354
Fish Creek, 248–50
Fisher Creek, 371
Fisher Oak Savanna Nature Preserve, *124*, 125, 141–43, *142*
Fishers, IN, Town of, 306–7
Fish Lake, 221
Flatbelly Indian Reservation, 193
Flatbelly Marsh, 192
Flatrock River, 63
flats: acid, 147; muck, 71–72, 181–82,
  185; mud, 166; peat muck, 182,
  185; pin oak, 130, 141, 143; sand,
  71, 137, 182, 185; wet sand, 72
flatwoods, 73, 114, 141, 307; boreal, 111, 114; northern, 73–74;
  oak-dominated, 377; pin oak, 71,
  141; till plain, 308, 312; wet-
  moist, 355
Flora of Indiana (Deam 1940),
  108, 291

goldfish, 48, 385
Goose Pasture, 145
Goshen College, 29, 197
Gottschalk, Evelyn I., 334
Graham McCulloch Ditch, 361, 363
Grand Calumet River, 48–49, 68, 98
Grande Marsh, Kingsbury Fish and
    Wildlife Area, 172
Grand Kankakee Marsh, 41, 49, 51,
    53, 71, 165–66, 170
Grand Marsh, 170
Grand Prairie Natural Region, vii,
    ix, 69–70, 72, *124*, *125*, *126*
Grand Prairie Section, vii, ix, 70–71,
    124, *125*, *127*
Grand Rapids, MI, 41
Grant County, IN, *252*
Granville Sand Barrens Nature Pre-
    serve, *252*, *253*, 293–94, *293*
grasslands, xiii, 25, 69, 103, 144, 172,
    178, 229
Great Black Swamp, 41, 43, 75
great blue heron rookery, 310
Great Depression, 19, 153, 230, 268,
    323, 338
Greatest Wildlife Laboratory, 353
Great Konomick River, 49
Great Lakes, 3, 40, 51, 53, 84–85,
    231, 318, 361–62
Great Marsh, 41
Great Miami Reserve, 332
Great Mound, 321, 323
Greencastle, IN, *252*, 259
Greencastle Girl Scouts Council, 259
Greene County, IN, 63
Greenfield Mills, IN, 46
Greenland, 36
Greider, Jethro, 193
Greider's Woods Nature Preserve,
    174, *175*, 191, 192–94
Griffith, IN, xv, 102
*Guide to Natural Areas of Southern
    Indiana, A*, 2, 5
Guinness World Records, 164
Gulf Coastal Plain, 147

Hagerstown, IN, 315
Hall Woods Nature Preserve, 253,
    277, 278–80, *279*
Hamilton County, IN, *252*, 306

Hammond, IN, xiii, 50, 98
Handbook of Indiana Geology (Logan
    1922), 64
Hanging Rock and Wabash Reef, 343
Hanging Rock National Natural
    Landmark, *54*, 254, 343–45, *344*
Harden, Congresswoman Cecil
    Murray, 261
Harrison, General William Henry,
    56, 61, 292, 296
Harrison County, IN, 370
Harrison Creek, 297
Hathaway Preserve at Ross Run,
    252, 254, 335–37, *336*
Hawk Lake, 47
Heinze, Dr. Shirley, 26
Hell's Point, 229
Hemlock Ridge Nature Preserve,
    xvii, *252*, *253*, 280–81
Hennepin, Father Louis, 52
Henry County, IN, *252*, 315–16,
    328–29
Heron Pond, 183
Heron Rookery, Indiana Dunes
    National Lakeshore, 85, 106
Highland, IN, 102
Highways, Northern Indiana
    (map), *vi*
Hillsdale, MI, 43, 45
Hiram Sweet Ditch, 248
Historic Forks of the Wabash, 56
Hobart, IN, xiii, 50, 102
Holley, Carroll O., 133
Holley Savanna, *124*, *125*, 131–33, *132*
Homer, MI, 45
Hominy Ridge Lake, 337
Hominy Ridge Shelter House, 338
Homoya, Michael A., xviii, 66
Hoosier Hikers Council, 302
Hoosier Prairie Nature Preserve, xv,
    78, 79, 100–102, *101*
Hopewell Indians, xv, 63, 321, 323
Hoss Hills, 192
Hudson, MI, 411
Hudson Bay, 39
Hudson Lake, 111
Hughes Nature Preserve, *252*, 254,
    326–27
Hultz, Eileen, 277
Hultz, Ralph, 277

Huntertown, IN, 25, 44, 59, 370
Huntington, IN, 54–56, 252, 339
Huntington County, IN, 252, 345
Huntington Lake, 339

Ice Age, 38–39, 42, 86, 206, 284
ice sheet, 38–40, 43, 49, 59, 61, 67,
    72, 74, 87, 116, 152, 206, 210–11,
    229, 234, 240, 276, 287, 306,
    309, 358
Illinoian Glacial, 40
Illinois Basin, 38
Illinois River, 43, 46, 50–51
Illinois River Watershed, 50
Illinois state line, 37, 41, 50–51, 53,
    69, 71, 127, 143
Illinois-Wisconsin state line, 87
Important Bird Areas (IBAs), viii,
    21, 30–31, 85, 127, 134, 138, 145,
    178–79, 182, 222, 276, 298, 308
impoundments, 191, 221, 257,
    345; hydroelectric, 223; man-
    made, 192
incised meanders, 273
Indiana Academy of Science, 16, 66
Indiana banana, 190
Indiana Bedrock (map), 35
Indiana Department of Conserva-
    tion, 19, 153, 207
Indiana Department of Correc-
    tions, 106
Indiana Department of Environ-
    mental Management, xv, xviii
Indiana Department of Natural
    Resources, viii, 3, 15, 66, 380
Indiana Department of Natural
    Resources, Division of Fish &
    Game, 153, 155
Indiana Department of Natural
    Resources, Division of Fish &
    Wildlife, viii, 20, 160, 168, 214,
    244, 257, 345
Indiana Department of Natural
    Resources, Division of Forestry,
    viii, 21–22
Indiana Department of Natural
    Resources, Division of Nature
    Preserves, viii, xviii, 2, 13, 16–18,
    137, 278, 380

Indiana Department of Natural Re-
    sources, Division of State Parks &
    Lakes, viii, 18
Indiana Department of Natural
    Resources, Land Management
    Team, 16
Indiana Department of Natural Re-
    sources, Nongame & Endangered
    Wildlife, 21
Indiana Department of Natural
    Resources, Regulatory Team, 16
Indiana Division of Fish & Game.
    See Indiana Department of Nat-
    ural Resources, Division of Fish
    & Game
Indiana Dunes National Lakeshore,
    13, 50, 78, 79, 83, 84–87, 89–90,
    92–93, 95, 104, 106; visitor center,
    12, 86
Indiana Dunes National Park, xiii
Indiana Dunes State Park, 2, 14, 78,
    79, 81, 84, 86, 91–92, 92, 94
Indiana environmental license
    plate, 22
Indiana General Assembly, 5, 16,
    22, 64
Indiana Geological & Water Survey,
    39–41
Indiana Green, 288
Indiana Harbor Canal, 49
Indiana Heritage Trust, viii, 22, 245
Indiana Historical Society, 53
Indiana-Michigan-Ohio border, 45
Indiana-Michigan state line, 71,
    87, 225
Indiana Native American Indian
    Affairs Commission, 314
Indiana Natural Heritage Data
    Center, xviii, 17
Indiana Natural Resources Commis-
    sion, 16
Indiana-Ohio border, 377
Indianapolis, City of, 299
Indianapolis, IN, vi, x, xiii, 19, 30,
    35, 37, 42, 62–64, 286, 298, 302,
    304, 306, 308, 310
Indianapolis Metropolitan Air-
    port, 306
Indiana State Board of Health, 284

Kokomo, IN, vi, 35, 37, 188, *252*
Koontz Lake Nature Preserve, *124*,
 125, 160–61, *161*
Koontz Lake Wetland Conservation
 Area, *124*, 125, 160–61
Korean War, 172
Kosciusko County, IN, *174*, 188,
 190–91, 195
Krannert School of Manage-
 ment, 287
Kunkel Lake, 351

Labrador, Canada, 39
ladders, 265, 270
Lafayette, IN, vi, 26, 35, 37, 42,
 54–56, 60, *124*, 252, 286, 295
LaGrange County, IN, 46–47, *174*,
 216, 219, 221, 225
LaGrange County Department of
 Parks and Recreation, 29
LaGrange County Nature Preserve,
 174, 175, 219, 220, 221
Lagro, IN, 57
lake, xiii, 18–19, 21–23, 40, 47, 52,
 58, 64, 66, 68–69, 71–75, 84, 127,
 152, 156, 172, 178, 181, 191, 194,
 201, 207, 215–16, 218, 221, 231,
 236–37, 244, 261, 318–19, 324,
 331–32, 337–38, 340–41, 345, 360;
 borrow pit, 359; chain of, 46, 229;
 freshwater, 72, 84; glacial, 43;
 kettle, xiii, 72, 121, 206, 215, 229,
 234, 238, 240; morainal, 46; moraine, 196; natural, xvi, 60, 152,
 192, 204, 229; overlook, 260–61;
 round, 72; spring-fed, 187, 201;
 undeveloped, 216
Lake Calumet, 97
Lake County, IN, xiii, 48, 69, 78, 87,
 95–96, 98–100, 102, 104, *124*
Lake County Parks and Recreation, 96
Lake Erie, 41–43, 55–56, 65, 75, 86,
 250, 360
Lake Erie Basin, 39
Lake Everett, 204–5
Lake Freeman, 60
Lake James, 229
Lake James State Park, 229, *230*, 234
Lake Kankakee, 60

Lake Lonidaw, 231
Lake Manitou, 60, 186, 188
Lake Michigan, xiii, xvi, xvii, 13, 19,
 37–39, 41–43, 45–46, 48–50, 52,
 65, 67–69, 78, 80, 81–82, 84–88,
 91–94, 97
Lake Michigan Border Section,
 67–68
Lake Michigan Border Unit, 65
Lake Michigan Natural Region, viii,
 67, 81
Lake Michigan Watershed, 45
Lake of the Woods, 52
Lake Shafer, 60
lakeshore, xviii, 14, 67, 84, 86–87,
 204; natural, 197
Lake Wawasee, 192
Lake Webster, 60, 152
Lancaster Lake, 121
land of the Indian, Indianapolis, 64
LaPorte, IN, 30, *78*
LaPorte County, IN, 26, *78*, 84,
 107, 109, 111, 117, 119, 122,
 124, 172
LaPorte County Conservation
 Trust, 29
LaPorte County Parks Depart-
 ment, 29
La Salle, Rene-Robert Cavalier,
 Sieur de, 43, 46, 52, 55–56,
 166, 170
LaSalle Fish & Wildlife Area, *124*,
 125, 165–67, *166*
Latonka Lake, 52
Lawrence County, IN, 37
Lawrence Creek Nature Preserve,
 252, 253, 310, 312
Lawrence Creek Trail, 312
Lenape Indians. *See* Delaware
 Indians
Lenhart-Baltzell, Alice, 356
Leo-Cedarville, IN, 366
Leopold, A. Carl, 287
Leopold, Aldo, 287
Le Petite Riviere, 56
Lewis, Randy, 281
Lichtfield, MI, 45
Lieber, Colonel Richard, 19, 230, 265
Lieber, Emma, 268
Lieber, William L., 184

127, 133, 146–47, 151, 160, 165–66,
169–70, 172, 178, 186, 195, 202,
216, 222–25, 229, 234, 240, 302–3,
318, 339, 351, 358–61, 363, 372–73;
cattail, 98, 214, 226, 231, 237;
emergent, 156; floodplain, 98;
open, 244; sedge, 156, 237; shal-
low, 178, 197; shrub, 214
Marsh Lake, *174*, 176, 229, 234,
236–38, *237*
Marsh Lake Nature Preserve, 236, 237
Marsh Lake Wetland Conservation
Area, *174*, 176, 236–38, 240
marshland, 47, 127, 171, 186
Martin Lake, 218
Martinsville, IN, 40, 63
Maumee Lake Plain Region, 64–65
Maumee River, 41–44, 46, 55–56,
361, 376, 377
Maumee River Valley, 65
Maxinkuckee Moraine, 69
McClue, Maurice, 242
McCormick's Creek State Park, 265
McNabb-Walter Nature Preserve,
252, 254, 373–75, *374*
meadow, 197, 233, 280–81, 308, 322,
331, 370; grassy, 365; open, 234,
365; sedge, 72, 97–100, 104, 130,
133, 141, 147, 178, 195, 231, 244,
297, 307, 327, 361; successional,
249; wet, 197; wet sedge, 321–22
Mengerson, Carl, 366
Mengerson, Ursula, 366
Mengerson Nature Preserve, *252*,
254, 365–66, *365*
Meno-aki, 367
Meno-aki Nature Preserve, *252*, 254,
366–68, *367*
Merry Lea Environmental Learning
Center, 197
Merry Lea Nature Preserve, 175,
196, *198–99*
Merry Lea Sustainable Farm, 200
Mesozoic era, 36
Messick Lake, 214
Metea, Potawatomie Indian
Chief, 366
Metea Park, 366–67
Mexico, 103

Mexico, IN, 59
Miami County, IN, 18, 22, *174*,
252, 331
Miami Indians, xv, 44–45, 51, 55–60,
62–63, 207, 259, 261, 272, 331, 337,
340, 353
Miami River, 44
Miami State Recreation Area, 331
Mianus River Gorge, 24
Michigan Central Railroad, 96
Michigan City, IN, 3, 41, 49–51, *78*,
84, 86, 90, 109, 111, 117, 170
Michigan City Harbor, 111
Michigan state line, 3, 37, 71–72, 87,
122, 225
middle life, 36
Miller (area of Gary), 97
Miller Beach, 49
Miller Woods, 84–85
Milwaukee, WI, 41
Mis-chis-in-wah (Mississinewa
River), *58*, 331
Mishawaka, IN, 45
Mississinewa Audubon Club, 334
Mississinewa Lake, 18, 58, 254,
331–33, *332*, 340, 345
Mississinewa River, 55, 57–59, *58*,
331, 339
Mississippian Period, 35–37, 73
Mississippi River, 39, 43, 46, 49, 51,
56, 361–62
moat, 91
Modoc Wildlife Management
Area, 315
Mohawk Indians, 53
Momence, IL, 51
Mongo, IN, xiii, 46–47, 222
Mongo hydroelectric impound-
ment, 223
Mongo Mill Pond, 223
Mongoquinong (Potawatomi for "Big
Squaw"), 46
Mongoquinong Nature Preserve,
174, *175*, 222, *222*, 224–25
Monon Trail, 305
Monroe County, IN, 37
Monroe Lake, xv
Montezuma, IN, 61
Montgomery County, IN, *252*, 270

Studebaker Corporation, 164
Sturgeon Creek, 45
Sugar Creek, 55, 61, 73, 263–64, 263,
  268, 270, 273
Sugar Creek, Lower Valley, 262
Sugar Creek Valley, 61, 270
Summit Lake, 318–19
Summit Lake State Park, 252, 254,
  318–29, 319
Sunset Shelter, Summit Lake State
  Park, 318
swale, xiii, 71, 94, 99–100; wet,
  97, 143
swamp, xiii, 41, 51, 53, 56, 61, 68–69,
  71–75, 84, 88, 92, 94–95, 118, 121,
  178, 188, 197, 208–9, 218, 222, 224,
  227, 229, 238, 250, 358; buttonbush, 92, 97–99, 182; coal, 38; relict, 223; shrub, 94, 115, 121, 226,
  237; spicebush-winterberry-buttonbush shrub, 121; spongy, 51;
  tamarack, 223; tamarack-black
  ash, 231; wooded, 219; yellow
  birch, 231
Swamp Rose Nature Preserve,
  178–79
Swensen, Ben, 241
Swensen, Helen, 241
Sylvan Lake, 47

Tailwater Recreation Area, 340
Tall Timbers Trail, 278
Tall Trees Memorial Grove, 202
Tamarack Bog Nature Preserve, 174,
  175, 222–24
Tamarack Marsh, 172
Teays River, 39–40
tectonic plates, 34
Tefft Savanna Complex, 124, 125, 146
Tefft Savanna Nature Preserve, 124,
  125, 146
teh-yak-ki-ki (Potawatomi word for
  swampy country), 51
Tekonsha, MI, 45
Ten O'Clock Line Treaty (1809), 262
Tenskwatawa. See Prophet, The
Terre Haute, IN, vi, 3, 28, 30, 35, 37,
  40, 42, 55, 143, 256, 258
Territories of Montana, 15

Territory of Wyoming, 15
thicket, 233, 318; brushy, 359; shrub,
  143; willow shrub, 143
Thorntown, IN, 61
Three Rivers, MI, 45
till, 40, 66, 69; glacial, 72, 276, 286
till plain, 40–41, 63, 69, 314
timber harvesting, 16, 22, 277
Tippecanoe, 61
Tippecanoe County, IN, 66, 124, 252,
  293–94, 370
Tippecanoe Lake, 60, 152, 190
Tippecanoe River, 55, 60–61, 151,
  154, 194, 296
Tippecanoe River Nature Preserve,
  124, 125, 151, 153–54
Tippecanoe River State Park, 18, 60,
  124, 125, 151–53, 152, 155
Tippecanoe State Park, 153
Tipton Till Plain, 42, 72
Tipton Till Plain Section, vii, ix, 74,
  252, 253, 298
Tipton Till Plain Unit, 66
tip-ups, 114
toboggan run, Pokagon State Park,
  231–32
Toledo, Ohio, 43
Tolleston dunes, 97
Tolleston Strand Plain, 78, 79, 95,
  97–98
Tom and Jane Dustin Nature Pre-
  serve, 254, 370, 371, 371, 372
Tonti, Henri de, 52
Trail Creek, 110–11
Trail Creek Fen, 78, 79, 109–11, 110
Trail Creek West Branch, 109
Trail of Death, 61
Treaty of St. Mary's (1818), 262,
  272, 310
tree army, 268
tree graveyard, 93–94
tree sign, 164
Tribune-Star, Terre Haute, 256
Tri-County Fish & Wildlife Area,
  174, 175, 191–92, 192, 195–96
Trine, Ralph, 236
Trine, Sheri, 236
Trine State Recreation Area, 174, 176,
  229, 231, 234, 235, 236, 237, 240

tropical sea, 34
Troxel Mill Pond, 223
Turkey Run State Park, 55, 61, 252, 253, 264–65, 266–67, 268, 270
Tuscarora Indians, 53

UN General Assembly, 5
unglaciated, 40, 63
Union City, OH, 45, 57
Union City Moraine, 74
University of Chicago, 50, 88, 96
Upper Great Lake States, 223
Upper Sandusky, Ohio, 41
Upper Wabash Valley, 340, 345
Upstate New York, 53
US Army, 308, 310
US Army Corps of Engineers, 20, 261, 340
US Congress, 14, 15, 49, 86, 285
US Department of Interior, 155
US Fish & Wildlife Service, 21, 249
US War Department, 15

valley train, 72
Valparaiso, IN, 26, 78, 124
Valparaiso Morainal Complex Unit, 65
Valparaiso Moraine, 41, 67–69, 87, 100, 115, 143
Valparaiso Moraine Section, vii, viii, 69, 78, 79, 115
Vandolah Nature Preserve, 252, 254, 372–73, 372
vernal pool, 132, 188, 358
Vigo County, IN, 41, 66, 69, 252, 256
Vincennes, IN, 14, 35, 55, 86
Virginia, 39
Visitors Center, Fort Harrison State Park, 310
Volo Bog, 90

waapaahsiiki (Miami word for pure, shining white) 353
Wabash, 55, 339
Wabash, IN, 55, 57, 252, 333
Wabash and Erie Canal, 56, 283, 377
Wabash County, IN, 21, 174, 252, 331, 333, 335, 337, 339, 341, 343
Wabash River, 3, 29, 38, 40, 43, 53–57, 54, 59–62, 73, 262, 273, 281,

284, 286, 288, 290–91, 293–95, 334–35, 339, 343, 345, 350–51, 350, 354, 361, 363
Wabash River, Lower, 261–62, 332
Wabash River, Upper, 331–32
Wabash River Basin, 340, 345
Wabash River Valley, 30, 66, 69, 289
Wabash River Watershed, 42–44, 55–56
Wabash River Watershed, Lower, 261
Wah-Bah-Shik-Ki (Wabash), 55
Waldron Lake, 214
Waltz, IN, 332
Warbler Woods Nature Preserve, 42, 252, 253, 310, 311
Warren, IN, 57
Warren County, IN, 124, 252, 284–86, 288, 290
Warsaw, IN, 174
Warsaw Moraines and Drainageways Unit, 65
Washington, George, 56
Washington County, IN, 370
Washington Park, 111
waterfall, 268, 269, 282, 284, 284, 286, 335, 337, 342; convex, 270
Wayne, General "Mad Anthony," 45, 63
Wayne County, IN, 36–38, 41, 66, 252
Weaver, Edith, 314
Weaver, Laz, 314
Webster Lake, 152
Weiler, Emanuel, 287
Weiler-Leopold Nature Preserve, 252, 253, 286–88, 287, 288, 289, 290, 291
Wells County, IN, 252, 348, 350, 351, 353
Wells County State Forest and Game Preserve, 353
West Central Indiana, 26, 28, 272, 276, 284
West Central Michigan, 116
West Central Ohio, 58
Western Illinois, 39
Western Indiana, 73
Western Iowa, 100
Weston, Edward, xv
We-thau-ka-mik (Yellow River), 53

Steven Higgs is one of Indiana's senior environmental writers and photographers. He is the author of *A Guide to Natural Areas of Southern Indiana* and *Eternal Vigilance: Nine Tales of Environmental Heroism in Indiana*. His experience includes eleven years as an environmental reporter at the *Bloomington Herald-Times* and four as a senior environmental writer and editor at the Indiana Department of Environmental Management. He is an adjunct lecturer at the Indiana University Media School, where he has taught introductory and advanced classes in information gathering; reporting, writing, and editing; and online journalism. He lives in Bloomington, Indiana.

Jason Kissel declared at age five that his life's vocation would be caring for trees. He stayed true to this vision by earning degrees in forestry and ministry and serving as curator of trees for the North Carolina Zoo and natural resources administrator for the city of Indianapolis. In 2006, he became ACRES' executive director, which means he ensures ACRES' land, funds, members, volunteers, and employees receive the attention and resources they need to thrive. Jason's favorite preserves are the ones that have been undisturbed the longest, providing glimpses into the unique, healthy, and diverse systems that all ACRES' properties will offer forever.

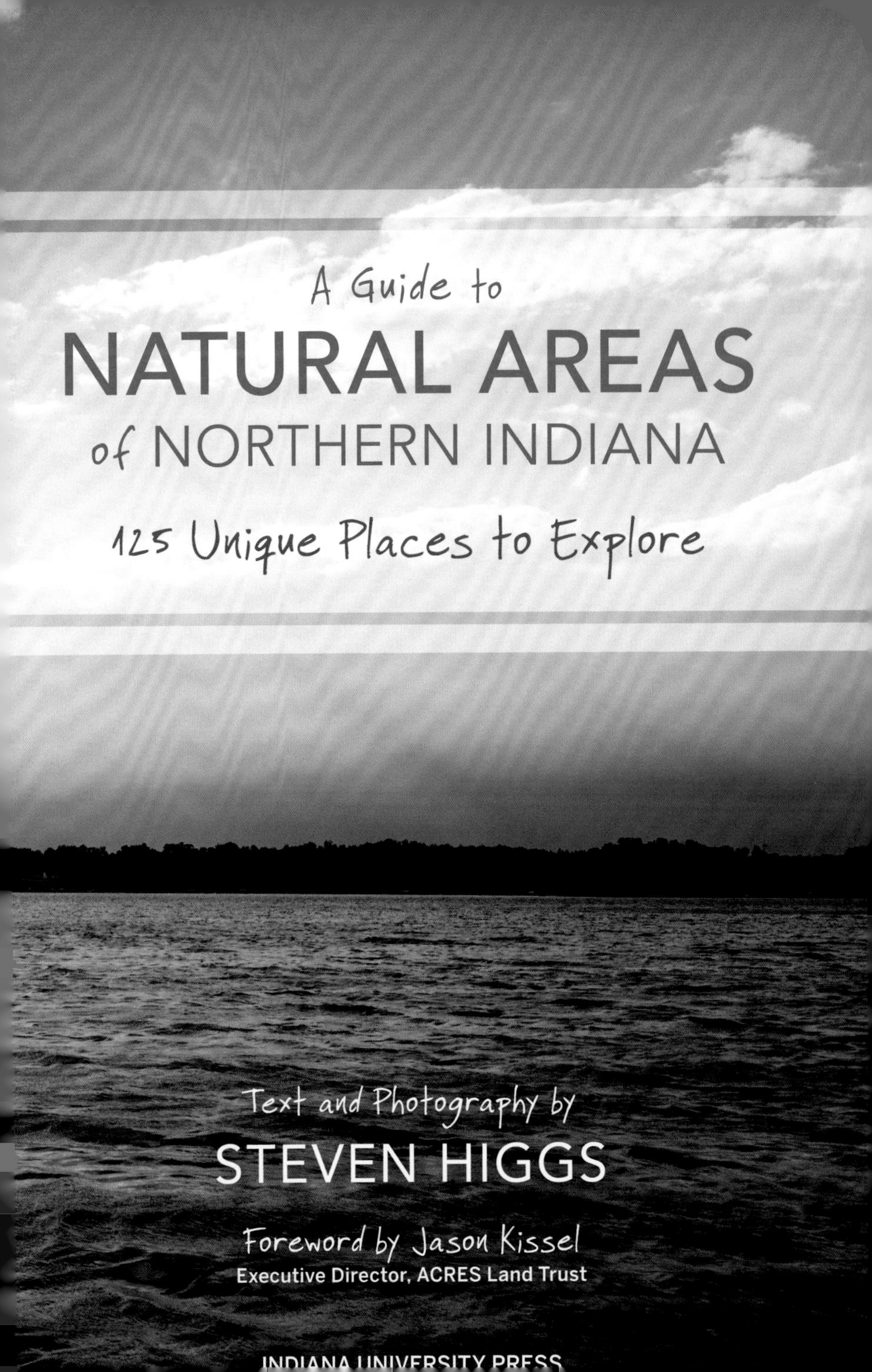

A Guide to

NATURAL AREAS
of NORTHERN INDIANA

125 Unique Places to Explore

Text and Photography by
STEVEN HIGGS

Foreword by Jason Kissel
Executive Director, ACRES Land Trust

INDIANA UNIVERSITY PRESS

This book is a publication of

Indiana University Press
Office of Scholarly Publishing
Herman B Wells Library 350
1320 East 10th Street
Bloomington, Indiana 47405 USA

www.iupress.indiana.edu

This book is printed on acid-free paper.

Manufactured in China

Library of Congress Cataloging-in-Publication Data

Names: Higgs, Steven, [date] author, photographer.
Title: A guide to natural areas of northern Indiana : 125 unique
places to explore / text and photographs by Steven Higgs ; foreword
by Jason Kissel, Executive Director, ACRES Land Trust.
Description: Bloomington, Indiana : Indiana University
Press, [2019] | Series: Indiana natural science |
Includes bibliographical references and index.
Identifiers: LCCN 2018049707 (print) | LCCN 2018050260 (ebook) |
ISBN 9780253039224 (e-book) | ISBN 9780253039217 (pb : alk. paper)
Subjects: LCSH: Natural areas—Indiana—Guidebooks. | Natural
history—Indiana—Guidebooks. | Indiana—Guidebooks.
Classification: LCC QH76.5.I6 (ebook) | LCC QH76.5.I6
H538 2019 (print) | DDC 508.772—dc23
LC record available at https://lccn.loc.gov/2018049707

This book is dedicated to all the visionary souls
who saw the need to preserve what is left
of Indiana's natural heritage and invested
their hearts, minds, funds, and souls
to protect what precious little remains.

Northern Indiana Highways

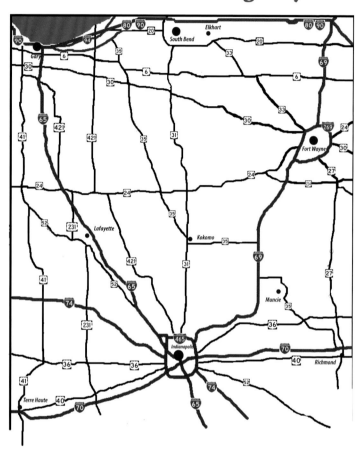

Natural Regions of Nothern Indiana

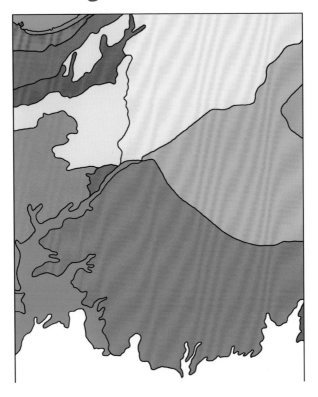

LAKE MICHIGAN NATURAL REGION

NORTHWESTERN MORAINAL NATURAL REGION

Lake Border Section

Chicago Lake Plain Section

Valparaiso Moraine Section

GRAND PRAIRIE NATURAL REGION

Kankakee Sand Section

Grand Prairie Section

Kankakee Marsh Section

NORTHERN LAKES NATURAL REGION

CENTRAL TILL PLAIN NATURAL REGION

Entrenched Valley Section

Tipton Till Plain Section

Bluffton Till Plain Section

BLACK SWAMP NATURAL REGION

Contents

Foreword

My affinity for Indiana was shaped growing up in Southern Indiana, visiting grandparents in Evansville, attending college in West Lafayette, working summers in North Vernon, living in Indianapolis, and, for the past twelve years, living in and exploring Northeast Indiana. I've grown to value each region's unique culture, land ethic, and natural features.

What I appreciate most about Northern Indiana is its diversity of natural systems. The 125 sites that Steven Higgs explored and photographed for this guide represent and provide access to this vast diversity. At the confluence of three major vegetation types—prairie, northern forest, and central hardwood forest—Northern Indiana is the "Crossroads of America" for natural plant communities. The blending of these ecosystems results in an explosion of natural combinations not found elsewhere.

Northwest Indiana is the easternmost range of the short and tallgrass prairie system that extends west to the Rocky Mountains. Indiana's northernmost counties begin the northern forests that continue up through much of Canada, turning more coniferous until the tundra's extreme cold prevents tree growth. The central hardwood forest extends from Northern Indiana east to the Atlantic and south until the southern pine forests begin.

Since nature doesn't divide itself into rigid boundaries, the confluence of these three systems results in diverse and unique landscapes. Northwest Indiana's vast prairies morph into oak savannas, and as you travel further east, trees rather than grass begin to dominate. From the north, tree species such as tamarack and aspen start to infiltrate oak and hickory forests.

This means that in Northern Indiana you can discover plant species from the Rocky Mountains, the tundra's fringe, the

ACRES Land Trust headquarters

Atlantic coast, and the Deep South—all in one place. No matter where you are in Northern Indiana, by driving an hour or two, you arrive in a new natural system.

Within the three major plant communities, you will also find unique, localized systems scattered throughout Northern Indiana, each with its own discoveries: cacti in the dunes communities, orchids in the fens, carnivorous plants in the bogs, and many other local natural systems that Steven highlights. While giving you your bearings, Steven does not overwhelm with information or spoil the surprises you will discover at each place.

Northern Indiana is also home to a vast, diverse cast of animals. As you experience common sightings of white-tailed deer, possums, bald eagles, raccoons, river otters, rabbits, and turkeys, you'll also be rewarded with occasional sightings of badgers, snowy owls, massasauga rattlesnakes, bobcats, osprey, mink, and quail. If you are really lucky, you may spot some of the black bears beginning to return to Northern Indiana.

Rather than just recommend you read this book, I encourage you to experience it. Get outside and into the amazing places Steven has selected. This book is meant to be marked with your observations and questions—to be dog-eared, mud spattered, sweat stained, and well worn. You are holding a guide, a prompt, an invitation to explore the splendors of our Northern Indiana natural areas, teeming with life.

Go, enjoy, explore.

Jason Kissel
Executive Director, ACRES Land Trust

Preface

Never in my wildest campsite visions did I foresee a ten-thousand-mile journey through the Indiana backcountry reaching its conclusion on Interstate 80 in Lake County—during rush hour—en route to a patch of grassland inside the Hobart city limits. The more poetic version would have faded to black at sunset in Indiana Dunes National Park, sandwiched between Lake Michigan and a sandy, grassy foredune.

However, especially in late July, practicality would trump mystique at the end of a four-year excursion that snaked to and through 250 natural areas, from the swamps of Posey County to the kettle lakes of Steuben, from the sloughs of Dearborn County to the swales of Lake County. Logistically, the exploration *had* to end at Cressmoor Prairie Nature Preserve.

Besides, the road itself ended at the national park's Duneland Campground on the Dunes Highway, after Cressmoor, which is poetic enough. And ecologically speaking, Cressmoor was the ideal preserve from which to bid farewell to natural Northern Indiana.

While most of the 125 natural areas in this guide are remote and rugged, many, like Cressmoor, are located near or in urban metropolises, such as Indianapolis, Fort Wayne, South Bend, and Hammond, or small burgs, like DeMotte, Angola, and Mongo. Cressmoor is surrounded by a country club, an apartment complex, an active railroad track, and a residential housing development.

While a Southern Indiana boy like myself was most transfixed by the northland's waters—29 percent of the photographs in the book feature rivers, lakes, and streams—prairie is *the* most precious natural landscape in Indiana, north or south. Of the estimated two million acres of grasslands that occupied Northwest and North Central Indiana in pre-European

Jasper-Pulaski Fish & Wildlife Area

settlement times, only one thousand remain. And 40 percent of those survive at just one site—the Hoosier Prairie Nature Preserve, a Natural National Landmark situated fifteen miles due east of Cressmoor in Griffith, which was the journey's next-to-last stop.

But prairie grass and wildflowers, while critical, are microscopic slices of natural Northern Indiana when it supported the Hopewell, Miami, and other native peoples who inhabited the pre-Hoosier state through the ages. Photographically speaking, water is followed by wildflowers, wildlife, trees, trail scenes, landscapes, bedrock, and grasses in order of the book's visual emphasis. (Speaking of imagery, the photos in this collection represent *only* the best color, form, and light on given days. They do not necessarily represent the sites' unique natural features. Some do. But many do not. In some places, the unique features are best kept secret.)

While Cressmoor was the final stop on a four-year odyssey through all ninety-two Indiana counties for both books, it marked the end of but the latest phase of a lifelong nature quest.

My fondest childhood memories feature an acre of woods across a dead-end road at my aunt's house in the mid-1950s on Indy's East Eighteenth Street. I've explored and photographed natural Indiana since the mid-1970s, when I began adulthood on a ridgetop overlooking Monroe Lake armed with my first Nikon, inspired by a photographic spirit named Edward Weston. My final master's project at the Indiana University School of Journalism in 1985 was titled "Clearcutting the Hoosier National Forest: Professional Forestry or Panacea?" I've spent the past thirty-five-plus years as a newspaper reporter, a senior writer and editor at the Indiana Department of Environmental Management, a newspaper publisher, and an occasional free-lancer—always specializing in environmental issues, from pollution to conservation.

Still, what an illuminating experience the Northern Indiana leg of the trip was.

Between September 2016—when then Indiana University Press sponsoring editor Alan Bower called this Northern Indiana companion guide a "no-brainer"—and the book's completion in December 2017, I navigated more than five thousand road miles, hiked a couple hundred trail miles, and uploaded roughly five thousand digital photographs to the Natural Bloomington and related websites. I plotted and followed routes via Google Earth and refined my use of GPS.

On more than 120 hikes, I only got lost once, and that was momentary. My discombobulation came a couple hundred feet before the trail fork I knew was near. I stepped in muck above my boots a couple times and was forced to sleep in the gravel at a state park (huh?). I awoke in another park campground with a raccoon nibbling on the picnic basket inside the fully screened, but not fully zipped, tent porch. I had to stay in one private campground where teens driving four-wheelers with headlights circled the primitive sites at night.

But I couldn't begin to list all the wonders we experienced. Often with traveling companion and granddaughter Raina, I traversed a six-foot-wide bedrock backbone with one-hundred-foot drops on both sides and paid homage to evergreens that have survived since the last glaciers receded. I literally walked in the footsteps of Tecumseh and focused my Nikon on more than one buffalo's eyelashes. I photographed crystal-clear-blue natural lakes, not to mention Lake Michigan and its dunes, under perfect conditions.

I experienced the largest patch of native prairie left in the state. And we always stopped too soon. Always.

Along the path, I also gathered and perused information from hundreds of websites, relying heavily on those that included property stewards' opinions on what was noteworthy. I shared my experiences with a diverse group of nature lovers, from scientists and property managers to campers and other fellow travelers I encountered on the backroads and trails.

I didn't get to explore all of the preserves included here. Due to time and logistics, I missed two: J. D. Marshall Preserve (in Lake Michigan) and Wintergreen Woods Nature Preserve. A couple—Hemlock Ridge Nature Preserve and Little Cedar Creek Wildlife Sanctuary Nature Preserve—were impassable or closed.

The most common question I answered after telling folks I was writing a guide to Northern Indiana natural areas was, Are there any? The answer, which I reconfirmed through this epic journey, is a resounding yes. In general, the remnants of the northland's natural heritage may not be as grand as their mostly rugged southern counterparts. But many are. The dunes surpass anything nature has to offer south of I-70—crowds notwithstanding. The Entrenched Valley's rock formations are second to none. The tiny fragments of presettlement natural Northern Indiana that remain, like the Hoosier Prairie and Cressmoor Preserves, are every bit as precious as the hills of the south. I could argue even more so.

Acknowledgments

I've told anyone who cared to listen about my journeys through natural Northern and Southern Indiana these past four years that I'm as much editor as I am author of both volumes. While I do offer my own observations from the roads, trails, overlooks, bluffs, valleys, creek beds, lakeshores, and the like, both books are compilations of others' work, which I simply rewrote, reorganized, and embellished with additional research and my own experiences.

So before acknowledging any of the individuals who assisted me directly in this guidebook's preparation, I want to thank the communications folks at the organizations that own and manage the natural areas I included. In some places I simply couldn't say things better than they did and merely tweaked their prose. Informed by serving four years as a senior environmental writer/editor at the Indiana Department of Environmental Management in the late 1990s, I can say from experience that they all performed their jobs admirably.

With all that as prelude, I want to thank Michael A. Homoya (Indiana's state botanist and plant ecologist for the past thirty years), Ron Hellmich (coordinator for the Indiana Natural Heritage Data Center), and their colleagues at the Indiana Department of Natural Resources Division of Nature Preserves, who provided data and reviewed and commented on the manuscript. Mike reviewed the manuscript twice—mostly to ensure I didn't advertise species that are too sensitive to subject to public exposure. They were always available to answer questions. Their insights and expertise were invaluable.

Not only do I owe a debt of gratitude to ACRES Land Trust executive director Jason Kissel for writing the foreword to this guidebook, but also for overseeing perhaps the best system of nature preserves in the state. As we would approach a site in our travels, it became a habit for Raina to ask, "Is this an ACRES site?" If it was, we knew it would be meticulously maintained. Nearly a quarter of the sites in the book are owned and/or managed by ACRES. I confess I have a built-in bias for the group, given that it is headquartered in the former home of Tom and Jane Dustin, whom I was honored to know as friends and inspirations. As part of their groundbreaking work as Hoosier environmental pioneers, they were founding members of ACRES.

For proofing their properties' individual sections, appreciation goes to ACRES Land Trust's Lettie Haver and The Nature Conservancy conservation coordinator Susan MiHalo. Chip Sutton from The Nature Conservancy, Barry Banks and Julie Borgmann from Red-tail Land Conservancy, and Brad Weigel from NICHES Land Trust offered additional guidance and support.

Without former Indiana University Press sponsoring editors Linda Oblack and Alan Bower, neither of my guidebook projects would exist. The Southern Indiana book was Linda's idea; this Northern Indiana follow-up was Alan's. The support and guidance of their successor, Ashley Runyon, has been vital.

Finally, I want to mention the hundreds of friends and followers who have liked, shared, read, and commented on this project through the Natural Bloomington website and social media. Their support and encouragement left no doubt that I was engaged in a worthy pursuit.

It's been an honor working with and learning from them all. This book is much more than it would have been without them—that's for sure.

A Guide to

NATURAL AREAS
of NORTHERN INDIANA

Indiana Dunes State Park

Introduction

Like its predecessor—*A Guide to Natural Areas of Southern Indiana*—this Northern Indiana companion is designed as a tool for fellow travelers who enjoy, desire, or require nature for recreation and inspiration. Its pages provide details on, anecdotes about, and directions to 125 natural areas in the northern half of Indiana, identified ecologically by natural regions and directionally by transportation corridors.

The Indiana Division of Nature Preserves defines a natural area as land or water that has retained or reestablished its natural character, has unusual plants and animals, or has "biotic, geological, scenic, or paleontological features of scientific or educational value." State nature preserves, and most of the individual sites included in this guidebook, are protected against extractive uses—from logging to road building to building building. Hunting and fishing are allowed on some. Prairie sites are periodically burned or otherwise managed to restore and protect native plant species. Other preserves offer developed recreation, lodging, and amenities like pools and tennis courts (in the case of state parks).

Nearly all of the sites—most of which contain rare remnants of the Indiana landscape that existed before the Europeans arrived—lie between Interstate 70 and the Michigan state line. They range from the diminutive Jackson-Schnyder Nature Preserve near Terre Haute to the sprawling Indiana Dunes, from Gary to Michigan City, from Marion's Woods, a tiny urban woodlot in Angola, to the National Natural Landmark at Shrader-Weaver Nature Preserve near Connersville.

The book is organized from northwest to southeast, around Northern Indiana's six natural regions and four major highways—I-70, I-65, US 31, and I-69. It's divided into three parts.

Part 1 tells the story of those who have fought for and now steward the 185,000 acres of land highlighted here. They include the National Park Service, various divisions of the Indiana Department of Natural Resources, local governments, and nonprofit groups like ACRES Land Trust and The Nature Conservancy.

Part 2 provides a brief overview of the Northern Indiana landscape's ever-evolving natural history and features, tracing billions of years of geologic evolution to the land's present state, where every drop of precipitation that reaches its surface ultimately flows southwest toward the Wabash River or north to the Great Lakes.

The natural features section discusses Northern Indiana's six natural regions and their nine sections, each of which is categorized by distinctive assemblages of natural characteristics, including plants, animals, climate, soils, glacial history, topography, bedrock, and physiography.

Part 3 lists the individual natural areas and provides details about them, including ecological characteristics and natural and human histories, as well as anecdotes, activities, and specific directions from the nearest highways with GPS coordinates.

Natural Area Etiquette

Behave Like an Ecotourist

By the time I started researching this guidebook's predecessor—*A Guide to Natural Areas of Southern Indiana*—in early 2014, I was fairly well schooled in the field of ecotourism. I had launched Natural Bloomington Ecotours & More in the spring of 2013 and had read up on the subject, led a few tours, and been a guest speaker at ecotourism and sustainable tourism classes in the Indiana University School of Public Health.

One thing I learned is that ecotourism, defined by the International Ecotourism Society as "responsible travel to natural areas that conserves the environment and improves the well-being of local people," has been advancing for decades. Its roots trace directly to the dawn of the environmental movement in the 1960s and 1970s. My favorite theory actually dates its birth to Alexis de Tocqueville, whose early nineteenth-century American hosts on the Michigan frontier were stunned when the French writer and historian said he wanted to explore the surrounding wilderness—for the sake of curiosity.

Two centuries after de Tocqueville, such responsible travel to natural areas was recognized as a global imperative when the UN General Assembly approved a landmark resolution in December 2012 that declared ecotourism "as key in the fight against poverty, the protection of the environment and the promotion of sustainable development."

So, as a proud, lifelong environmentalist, I knew if I were going to lead or encourage any form of nature-based tourism—through ecotours or guidebooks—I would subscribe to the field's highest ethical standards. Despite my journalistic aversion to clichés, my Natural Bloomington brochures prominently feature the old ecological saw, "Take only photographs. Leave only footprints."

The best way to protect what's left of our wild places, of course, is to practice environmental abstinence—to stay out altogether. I worry about the loving-it-to-death syndrome. But natural noncontact is neither practical nor, perhaps, even desirable. A basic ecotourism tenet is the notion that human beings have innate attractions to other life forms and need to interact with natural living systems.

This book's emphasis on raising awareness of nature reflects the belief that humans must physically experience nature to appreciate its grandeur fully. Preservation is dependent upon sensory interaction. To truly love nature, the theory goes, you must touch it, smell it, hear it, feel it, and see it up close.

To accomplish these goals, the International Ecotourism Society identifies a set of principles for ecotourism that include the following:

- Minimize physical, social, behavioral, and psychological impacts
- Build environmental and cultural awareness and respect
- Deliver memorable interpretative experiences to visitors that help raise sensitivity to host communities' political, environmental, and social climates

According to David Fennell, founder and editor in chief of the *Journal of Ecotourism* and professor in the Department of Geography and Tourism Studies at Brock University, St. Catharines, Ontario: "Ecotourism is a sustainable, non-invasive form of nature-based tourism that focuses primarily on learning about nature first-hand and which is ethically managed to be low-impact, non-consumptive, and locally oriented (control, benefits and scale). It typically occurs in natural areas, and should contribute to the conservation of such areas."

In short, ecotourists know the natural areas and local cultures they visit, leave no adverse trace of their incursions therein, support those who steward the land, and contribute to the local economies in which they are preserved.

An Ecotourist Tip List

PLAN YOUR ADVENTURE

Most of the natural areas included in this guide are not developed. Some are remote—by Midwest standards, anyway—and can be intimidating, even if their most secluded tracts are seldom more than a mile or two from a road. You're not going to get lost for days in the Northern Indiana backcountry, but you can end up disoriented, befuddled, bug bitten, and frustrated. So know your weaknesses and learn everything you can about your destination before you go. Study maps and learn the terrain. Familiarize yourself with timing, trails, and weather.

Nearly all the natural areas in this guide have rules and special concerns that you should likewise research before your exploration. Don't count on information kiosks indicated on property maps. They are often empty or no longer exist.

Wear season- and location-appropriate clothing. Well-fitting hiking boots are a must. Except during hunting season, wear earth tones—browns, blues, and greens—so you are less visible. Reds, oranges, and yellows visually intrude into the spaces and solitude that are part and parcel of the outdoor experience. Wear them during hunting seasons, when you need to stand out.

Be prepared for nature's challenges, extreme weather, and emergencies. Always carry more water than you think you will need, maps, a first aid kit, a compass, and a cell phone (service is available in the most far-flung locales). Make sure someone knows where you are.

Northern Indiana's wild places teem with insects between frosts, and a strategy to combat them is essential; Lyme and other diseases can result from bug bites. Turkey mites, which are the first stage of tick larva, can cause severe itching that lasts for weeks.

An insect-deterrence strategy begins with repellent. To DEET or not to DEET is the question. DEET stands for the active chemical ingredient—N,N-diethyl-meta-toluamide—in the more powerful products. I find non-DEET sprays effective, but I've been surprised by others' choices. Permethrin—actually a synthetic insecticide—is the most powerful insect repellent on the market and should be placed on clothing (including the bill of your hat), not on the skin. It is available online and in outfitter, sporting goods, and other stores. Tucking pant legs into socks and shirttails into pants helps block the path to your skin.

TREAD LIGHTLY, ON THE TRAIL AND IN CAMP

The footprints you leave behind should follow only those that preceded you—on established trails and campsites. That means stick to the trail. Don't take shortcuts or cut switchbacks. Groups should walk single file, in the middle of the path, even when it is wet and/or muddy.

If you must stray from the trail, tread with extreme caution. Photographers are particularly bad about leaving the path in search of light, color, and form. Indeed, one preserve included in this book has specific instructions for photographers. If you must bushwhack to find the optimum camera angle, watch where you plant your feet. And remember, the more plants you come in contact with, the more bugs come in contact with you.

GARBAGE IN, GARBAGE OUT

No respectable nature lover would ever litter on a city street, let alone along a wooded trail or creek bank deep in the wild. But many do, sometimes knowingly—leaving trash behind at campsites, for example—and sometimes unknowingly—discarding trash upstream that washes ashore on downstream lowlands. Whether you are hiking or camping, bring trash bags so you can carry out the trash you generate or find on the trail.

To eliminate waste on the trail and in areas where restrooms are not provided, stay a couple hundred feet from any water supply and camping area. Dig a hole approximately eight inches deep and then cover it with loose soil and leaf litter to promote decomposition and sanitary conditions.

HANDS OFF THE NATURAL GOODS

To preserve the past and conserve the future, you should never touch cultural or historic structures and artifacts, and you should leave rocks, plants, and other natural objects where they are. State law prohibits disturbing or removing anything from dedicated state nature preserves without a special permit. Do not build structures or furniture, or dig trenches.

LET THE CRITTERS BE

Wildlife should be observed from a distance and then left alone. Animals should never be fed. It can harm their health, alter their natural behaviors, and expose them to predators and other dangers. Leave them alone when they are mating, nesting, raising young, or wintering.

Pets should be controlled at all times. Keep all pet waste well away from the trail, and don't allow your dog to bark at or chase other trail users or wildlife. Bring food and water for your dog.

RESPECT YOUR FELLOW TRAVELERS AND NEIGHBORS

Nearly all of the natural areas included in this book are adjacent to or surround private properties. Do not trespass.

You can rest assured that most anyone you encounter in the wilder areas in this guide is a nature lover, almost by definition. You don't sweat, swat, and stumble your way through the Northern Indiana backcountry for long if you're not committed. Be courteous, and respect the quality of their experiences. When you encounter horseback riders, step to the downhill side of the trail.

Stop talking and listen. Let nature's sounds prevail.

Part 1

THE LAND STEWARDS

Indiana Dunes National Lakeshore, Visitor Center

The Land Stewards

The natural destinations in this book are owned and managed by a variety of public and private entities, including federal, state, and local governments and private nonprofit conservation organizations. Some are jointly owned, mostly between Indiana Division of Nature Preserves and nonprofits and other government agencies. Others are contiguous to one another, with separate owners, and are managed under cooperative agreements.

Nearly half are owned by nonprofit land trusts, which protect their properties' natural characteristics by owning them outright or working with private landowners who retain ownership. Land trusts accept land donations, purchase properties from willing sellers, monitor land-use restrictions agreed to by landowners, or enter into partnerships with other organizations and government agencies. Land trusts go by a variety of names, including conservancies, foundations, or projects.

While the 185,000 acres of land highlighted here are stewarded by their owners, management techniques and levels of protection vary. Dedicated state nature preserves and most nonprofit sites prohibit all development—roads, buildings, and so forth. Some allow hunting or fishing, while others do not. State parks and lakes allow limited development. Fish and wildlife areas may include crop plantings like corn and sunflowers that are intended to attract and feed game species. State forests are logged.

National Park Service

The National Park Service owns and manages only one natural area in Northern Indiana—the fifteen-thousand-acre Indiana Dunes National Lakeshore on Lake Michigan. Combined with the 2,182-acre Indiana Dunes State Park that lies within its boundaries, the dunes are the largest contiguous natural area in Northern Indiana. Elsewhere in Indiana, the service owns the twenty-four-acre George Rogers Clark National Historical Park in Vincennes and the two-hundred-acre Lincoln Boyhood National Memorial in Lincoln City.

Nationwide, the Park Service manages 417 parks, which are visited by an estimated 275 million visitors each year. Its mission statement reads: "The National Park Service preserves unimpaired the natural and cultural resources and values of the National Park System for the enjoyment, education, and inspiration of this and future generations. The Park Service cooperates with partners to extend the benefits of natural and cultural resource conservation and outdoor recreation throughout this country and the world."

The Park Service's sites total eighty-four million acres in all fifty states and the District of Columbia, American Samoa, Guam, Puerto Rico, Saipan, and the Virgin Islands. Individual sites range in size from 13.2 million acres at Wrangell–St. Elias National Park and Preserve in Alaska to 0.02 acres at Thaddeus Kosciuszko National Memorial in Pennsylvania. They include one hundred twenty-nine historical parks or sites, eighty-seven national monuments, fifty-nine national parks, twenty-five battlefields or military parks, nineteen preserves, eighteen recreation areas, ten seashores, four parkways, four lakeshores, and two reserves. Altogether the service's sites offer eighteen thousand miles of trails and protect some 250 species of threatened or endangered plants and animals, more than seventy-five thousand archaeological sites, nearly twenty-seven thousand historic and prehistoric structures, and more than 167 million museum items. The National Park Service is a bureau of the US Department of the Interior, whose director is nominated by the president and confirmed by the US Senate.

HISTORY OF THE NATIONAL PARK SERVICE
Congress created the National Park Service in 1916, nearly a half century after Yellowstone National Park became the nation's

and the world's first park in 1872. Located in the Territories of Montana and Wyoming, Yellowstone's mission was to serve "as a public park or pleasuring-ground for the benefit and enjoyment of the people."

When President Woodrow Wilson signed the Organic Act creating the National Park Service and Department of the Interior in August 1916, the system included thirty-five national parks and monuments. The law said the new agency "shall promote and regulate the use of the Federal areas known as national parks, monuments and reservations . . . to conserve the scenery and the natural and historic objects and the wild life therein and to provide for the enjoyment of the same in such manner and by such means as will leave them unimpaired for the enjoyment of future generations."

National parks can only be added to the National Park System through acts of Congress. But the Antiquities Act of 1906 gave presidents the authority to proclaim national monuments on lands already under federal jurisdiction, and twenty-seven years later President Franklin D. Roosevelt transferred fifty-six national monuments and military sites from the US Forest Service and the US War Department to the National Park System via executive order.

In 1970, Congress recognized that "the National Park System . . . has since grown to include superlative natural, historic, and recreation areas in every region . . . and that it is the purpose of this Act to include all such areas in the System."

Indiana Department of Natural Resources

The Indiana Department of Natural Resources (DNR) owns and manages more than two-thirds of the 185,000 acres described in this guide. It is the state government agency entrusted with protecting, enhancing, and preserving the state's natural, cultural, and recreational resources for the public's benefit. These include state nature preserves, parks, forests, and fish and wildlife areas.

The agency is divided into two teams. The Land Management Team oversees the state's natural areas and manages them for preservation, recreation, and extractive activities like timber harvesting. Its divisions include Nature Preserves, State Parks & Lakes, Fish & Wildlife, Outdoor Recreation, and Forestry. The Regulatory Team has authority over entomology and plant pathology, historic preservation, oil and gas, reclamation, and water.

The DNR is overseen by the autonomous twelve-member Indiana Natural Resources Commission (NRC), which is composed of seven citizens chosen on a bipartisan basis, three ex-officio members from state agencies, the chair of the Natural Resources Advisory Council, and a member of the Indiana Academy of Science.

DIVISION OF NATURE PRESERVES

As of late 2017, the DNR Division of Nature Preserves protected and managed more than 280 nature preserves totaling more than fifty-two thousand acres in all areas of the state. Its mission is to preserve natural areas in sufficient numbers and sizes to maintain viable examples of all of the state's natural communities and to provide living museums of natural Indiana as it was before the European settlers arrived.

Established by an act of the Indiana General Assembly in 1967, the Division of Nature Preserves provides permanent protection for natural areas, defined as land or water that has "retained or re-established its natural character, or has unusual flora or fauna, or has biotic, geological, scenic, or paleontological features of scientific or educational value." It also manages and maintains viable populations of endangered, threatened, and rare plant and animal species. The first state preserve—Pine Hills Nature Preserve at Shades State Park—was dedicated in 1969.

Inclusion as a dedicated state nature preserve requires agreement of a site's owner, the DNR, and the NRC. Once dedicated, a preserve is protected in perpetuity from development that would harm its natural character. Dedicated state nature

Shrader-Weaver Nature Preserve

preserves are owned by the DNR Nature Preserves, Parks & Lakes, and Fish & Wildlife divisions, as well as city and county park and recreation boards, universities and colleges, and private conservation organizations.

As part of its management protocol, the Division of Nature Preserves uses controlled burns, removes nonnative plants, and maintains preserve boundaries and trails. It also inventories the state for previously unknown natural areas, keeps a registry of natural areas, and dedicates new preserves. The Indiana Natural Heritage Data Center, a program administered by the Division of Nature Preserves, locates and tracks the state's rarest and most sensitive plants, animals, and natural communities. It maintains a database of this natural diversity to help set priorities for protection.

Dedicated state nature preserves, regardless of ownership, are managed to restore and maintain their natural ecological conditions. With some exceptions, they are open to the public for hiking, nature study, photography, wildlife watching, and, with advance permission, scientific research. Some allow hunting and fishing. Visitors are asked to stay on trails to reduce erosion and damage to the fragile plant communities that thrive on the preserves' grounds.

Some preserves do not have parking lots or hiking trails. The Division of Nature Preserves and the organizations that own the individual sites can answer questions about access and visitation. As the Division of Nature Preserves says on its website, nature, not recreation, is priority number one: "More than any other reason, nature preserves are set aside to protect the plants, animals, and natural communities which are found on them. Visitation is allowed to the extent that the features can tolerate it without deterioration."

State laws prohibit disturbing or removing anything from dedicated state nature preserves without a special permit and protect the locations of the state's most sensitive plant and animal species. No plant or animal species covered by the Confidentiality of Endangered Species Locations section of Indiana Code Title 14 Natural and Cultural Resources are listed in this book.

DIVISION OF STATE PARKS & LAKES

The Division of State Parks & Lakes, the DNR's largest division, manages thirty-four parks, lakes, and recreation areas across the state, seventeen in Northern Indiana. The properties range in size from the 290-acre Mounds State Park in Madison County to the 15,282-acre Mississinewa Lake in Miami County, the largest in Northern Indiana.

The division's mission is to "manage and interpret our properties' unique natural, wildlife, and cultural resources using the principles of multiple use and preservation, while sustaining the integrity of these resources for current and future generations." "Multiple use" means properties are managed for various public uses, from scenic drives, in the case of state parks and lakes, to fishing, camping, hiking, horseback riding, biking, and nature study. State and national forests allow logging and other resource extractive uses under the multiple-use umbrella.

Some Division of State Parks & Lakes properties, like Salamonie and Mississinewa Lakes, have multiple recreation areas under their supervision. Most, like Chain O' Lakes and Tippecanoe River State Parks, have dedicated state nature preserves within their boundaries. Others, like Pokagon State Park, abut other state, federal, and land trust properties to create more expansive natural areas than each provides on its own.

HISTORY OF INDIANA STATE PARKS

The history of Indiana state parks dates to 1916, when Colonel Richard Lieber, an Indianapolis businessman who came to be known as the "father of Indiana state parks," recommended creation of a state park system to coincide with the state's centennial celebration. Lieber became a national leader in the state parks movement and served as the Indiana Department of Conservation's first director for more than a decade.

Under Lieber's direction, the state purchased 350-plus acres in Owen County for $5,250 at auction and established McCormick's Creek as Indiana's first state park on May 25, 1916. In just over a century, the number of parks has grown to twenty-two, ranging from ever-changing sand dunes on Lake Michigan to four-hundred-million-year-old fossil beds at the Falls of the Ohio State Park.

As with national and state forests, parks, and other public properties, Indiana's state park history is inextricably linked to President Franklin D. Roosevelt's New Deal–era Civilian Conservation Corps (CCC). A division of the Works Progress Administration, the CCC hired unemployed workers during the Great Depression to reclaim Hoosier landscapes devastated by overlogging, ill-fated agricultural operations, and other poorly planned development projects. They planted trees. They implemented erosion control. They built lakes, roads, shelters, restrooms, gatehouses, trails, bridges, and other structures, many of which are still in use at state parks and other state and federal properties today.

A stated goal of the Parks & Lakes division is to "give Hoosiers the ability to experience what the Indiana landscape was like prior to settlement . . . mature forests, wetlands and prairies. Additionally, we interpret the historical and archeological context of our state. All of this involves what is known today as resource management."

The lakes side of the Division of Parks & Lakes traces its roots to Cagles Mill Lake, just north of McCormick's Creek in Putnam County, which was built in 1952 as the first US Army Corps of Engineers reservoir in Indiana. While recreation and wildlife management were among the goals for all corps dam projects, the primary reason for the state reservoir system was flood control—impounding water in one area to slow downstream flooding in others. The corps owns the reservoirs and leases the water and surrounding landforms to the DNR for management.

DIVISION OF FISH & WILDLIFE

The Indiana Division of Fish & Wildlife manages Indiana's fish and wildlife populations on more than 150,000 acres of land on twenty-six properties statewide, through research, regulation, and restoration. Thirteen of these properties are located in Northern Indiana. The division's emphasis is on managing game species for hunting, fishing, and trapping, and protecting rare and endangered species. Some, like Jasper-Pulaski, Willow Slough, and Pigeon River Fish & Wildlife Areas, encompass dedicated state nature preserves.

The division's mission is to "professionally manage Indiana's fish and wildlife for present and future generations, balancing ecological, recreational, and economic benefits." Under state law, fish and wildlife areas shall "provide for the protection, reproduction, care, management, survival, and regulation of wild animal populations, regardless of whether the wild animals are present on public or private property."

Among the division's stated values are the following:

- Fish and wildlife resources belong to all the people of Indiana.
- Regulated hunting, fishing, and trapping are important wildlife management tools.
- Fish and wildlife resources enrich the quality of human life.

- Public participation is essential for effective resource management. Regulated hunting, fishing, and trapping are legitimate pursuits when conducted in fair chase.

"Fish and wildlife resources are renewable, and when wisely managed will indefinitely provide numerous public benefits such as hunting, fishing, trapping, and wildlife viewing," the division says on its website. The Fish & Wildlife division also raises and stocks fish in public waters, provides access to public lakes and rivers, and offers advice and incentives to landowners who wish to develop wildlife habitat.

Nongame & Endangered Wildlife

The Nongame & Endangered Wildlife section focuses on the conservation and management of 750 species of nongame, endangered, and threatened wildlife throughout the state. Nongame wildlife includes any species that is not pursued through hunting and fishing, which includes more than 90 percent of the state's mammals, birds, fish, mussels, reptiles, and amphibians.

The nongame program receives no tax support and is funded through citizen donations to the Nongame Fund, which can be made on state tax forms or online through the agency's website. Nongame programs also receive reimbursements through the State Wildlife Grant program from the US Fish & Wildlife Service. Grant funds must be used on species of greatest conservation need.

Many fish and wildlife areas in Indiana have been designated as Important Bird Areas (IBAs) by the National Audubon Society. Northern Indiana's Kankakee and Willow Slough Fish & Wildlife Areas, for example, are designated as Global Important Bird Areas.

DIVISION OF FORESTRY

The Indiana Division of Forestry manages two state forests in Northern Indiana—the 850-acre Salamonie River State Forest in Wabash County and the obscure Frances Slocum State Forest in Miami County. (Slocum is not even listed as a state property on the Division of Forestry's properties list.) State forests are managed for multiple uses that include timber harvesting, recreation, and watershed protection. Timber harvesting in state forests, however, has been one of Indiana's more controversial environmental policy issues since the 1990s. Conflicts over state forest logging in Southern Indiana have led to protests and, in some cases, arrests. The DNR has done minimal timber harvesting at Salamonie State Forest and none at Frances Slocum State Forest.

Statewide the Division of Forestry system is open to the public. This includes remote backcountry areas, campgrounds, trails, fire towers, lakes, shelters, and other amenities. The properties are managed for natural resources, not recreation. "Recreational development will not take precedence over natural resource conservation and protection and will continue to be structured on the natural rather than the 'built' environment," the division says on its website.

District foresters assist private landowners with inspections and forest management stewardship objectives. The Division of Forestry also operates nurseries that provide stock for landscaping, windbreaks, fire control, and other uses.

Indiana Heritage Trust

The DNR's Indiana Heritage Trust does not own any natural areas, but it funds the acquisition of lands that represent outstanding natural resources and habitats or have recreational, historical, or archaeological significance for other DNR agencies to manage. Created in 1992, the Indiana Heritage Trust program generates revenue through Indiana environmental license plate sales. In the fifteen years between its creation in 1992 and 2017, the trust has purchased more than sixty-two thousand acres across the state.

The Indiana Heritage Trust buys land from willing sellers. In addition to the revenue from environmental license plates, General Assembly appropriations and public donations are used for natural area purchases.

Fern Cliff Nature Preserve

The Nature Conservancy

The Nature Conservancy's Indiana chapter protects more than one hundred thousand acres of forests, wetlands, prairies, lakes, and streams on nearly five dozen properties in all twelve of the state's natural regions. Founded in 1951, TNC pursues a mission that is both prodigious and succinct, expressed in a mere ten words: "Conserve the lands and waters on which all life depends." To accomplish that charge, the nonprofit conservation organization protects and preserves ecologically important lands and waters in all fifty states and more than thirty countries. TNC has more than one million members worldwide and has protected more than 103 million acres of land, twenty-one million in the United States.

According to the Our History page on its website, The Nature Conservancy traces its origins to the Ecological Society of America's formation in 1915, which included disagreement about its mission from the get-go: "Should it exist only to support ecologists and publish research, or should it also pursue an agenda to preserve natural areas?" In 1917, the society's activist wing formed the Committee for the Preservation of Natural Conditions that, in 1926, published *The Naturalist's Guide to the Americas*, which attempted to catalog all the known patches of wilderness left in North and Central America.

In 1946, "a small group of scientists formed the Ecologists Union, resolving to take 'direct action' to save threatened natural areas." In 1950, the Ecologists Union changed its name to the Nature Conservancy, which incorporated as a nonprofit on October 22, 1951. Land acquisition has been the organization's primary conservation tool since 1955, when the conservancy purchased a sixty-acre tract along the Mianus River Gorge on the New York–Connecticut border.

In 1970, TNC created a biological inventory of the United States, providing the impetus for the Natural Heritage Network, which includes the Indiana Natural Heritage Database. "Its sophisticated databases provide the most complete information about the existence and location of species and natural communities in the United States," the TNC says on its website. "The methodology becomes the national standard and is adopted by numerous partner organizations and federal and state governments and universities."

INDIANA CHAPTER OF THE NATURE CONSERVANCY

The Indiana chapter formed at a time when conservation was only beginning to take root in Indiana. "The Indiana Chapter of the Nature Conservancy formed in 1959 and struggled for a decade to justify its existence," former Indiana University professor emeritus Lynton Keith Caldwell wrote in the foreword to *The Natural Heritage of Indiana* (Jackson 1997). "Then with unforeseeable rapidity and external funding the Indiana Chapter grew to become one of the most active in the nation."

ACRES Land Trust

Formed in 1960, ACRES Land Trust is Indiana's second-oldest nonprofit land trust and the oldest with a purely local focus. Headquartered in Huntertown, in the home of historic Hoosier environmental activists Tom and Jane Dustin, the conservation organization protects nearly seven thousand acres on 108 preserves across Northeast Indiana, Northern Ohio, and Southern Michigan.

ACRES' properties include working land, forests, wetlands, native grasslands, unique geologic formations, and habitat for rare, threatened, and endangered species. Protecting the natural resources and minimizing human impact are among the management priorities. Almost half of the properties are closed to the public to protect sensitive areas and natural features or because their donors still live on them.

Staff and volunteers seek to maintain native plants and eliminate nonnative invasive species while promoting public knowledge and appreciation of natural areas as living systems to which humans belong. Public education is a key management strategy.

ACRES lists its values as the following:

- A growing awareness of people's place within and responsibility to the natural world
- The intrinsic and diverse benefits of natural places and the life they sustain
- Individuals', families', and communities' compelling desire to preserve our local land
- Owning and managing land as a means to protect it
- A long-term perspective in planning, decision-making, and acting on behalf of future generations

A year after forming, ACRES acquired its first preserve by donation—the Edna W. Spurgeon Woodland Reserve in Noble County. Some of its founding members played key roles in creating the Indiana Nature Preserve Act in 1967, which affords permanent protection to natural areas throughout Indiana. Many ACRES preserves are also dedicated state nature preserves.

NICHES Land Trust

Founded in 1995 and headquartered in Lafayette, NICHES Land Trust manages roughly fifty natural areas in thirteen West Central Indiana counties. NICHES owns most of its properties, which are managed for native species and public education. "With the help of dedicated volunteers and generous donors, NICHES provides public access to high quality natural areas, acquires land for conservation, and stewards the land once acquired," the organization says on its website. NICHES is an acronym for Northern Indiana Citizens Helping Ecosystems Survive.

Shirley Heinz Land Trust

Established in 1981, the Valparaiso-based Shirley Heinze Land Trust protects more than 2,400 acres on eighteen nature preserves in Lake, Porter, LaPorte, and St. Joseph Counties. The organization's mission statement reads: "To protect habitats and ecosystems of Northwest Indiana through acquiring, restoring, and protecting environmentally significant landscapes for present and future generations, and to inspire and educate people of all ages about the value of land conservation to protect our natural world and enrich our lives." The land trust is named in honor of Dr. Shirley Heinze, who, according to the organization's website, "devoted her free time to exploring, restoring, and preserving the Indiana Dunes."

Central Indiana Land Trust

The Indianapolis-based Central Indiana Land Trust (CILT) protects more than four thousand acres of land on twenty-one

Cressmoor Prairie Nature Preserve

nature preserves through conservation easements and management agreements with landowners in Central Indiana. Five CILT preserves are closed to the public, and ten others have limited access.

The organization's mission statement reads: "Through land protection, stewardship and education, the Central Indiana Land Trust preserves natural areas, improving air and water quality and enhancing life in our communities for present and future generations."

Red-tail Land Conservancy

Established in 1999, the Red-tail Land Conservancy protects some twenty-six hundred acres of East Central Indiana landscape on fourteen nature preserves via conservation easements on privately owned lands. Nine of the Red-tail preserves are open to the public. The nonprofit's mission is to preserve, protect, and restore natural areas and farmland in East Central Indiana while increasing awareness of the region's natural heritage. "Red-tail Land Conservancy cares about and works to preserve our natural heritage," the Muncie-based organization says on its website. "Red-tail Land Conservancy plans for a future where the natural beauty and working lands of East-Central Indiana still exist."

Ouabache Land Conservancy

The Terre Haute–based Ouabache Land Conservancy protects more than six hundred acres on six nature preserves in West Central Indiana. Founded in 2007, its management priorities include planting native species, removing invasive species, monitoring threatened species, planting trees to control erosion, cleaning up trash, and building trails. The organization's mission statement proclaims: "The Ouabache Land Conservancy protects, preserves, and restores land in West Central Indiana to provide habitat for wildlife, maintain natural scenic beauty, [and] improve water and air quality, while enhancing the quality of life in our communities for future generations."

Little River Wetlands Project

The Little River Wetlands Project is a land trust focused exclusively on protecting the Little River Watershed in Allen and Huntington Counties. Founded in 1990, the Fort Wayne–based project seeks to restore and preserve landscape on twenty-five thousand acres along the river. In 2017, the project protected more than twelve hundred acres on four preserves. "The mission of the Little River Wetlands Project is to restore and protect wetlands in the historic watershed of the Little River, a major tributary of the Wabash River, and to provide educational opportunities that encourage good stewardship of wetlands and other natural ecosystems," the organization says on its website.

Other Public Stewards

Seventeen of the natural areas in this book are owned or managed by other types of public and private organizations, including local governments, colleges and universities, and conservation trusts, including the following:

- Allen County Parks
- Town of DeMotte
- City of Elkhart
- Fort Wayne Parks and Recreation
- Goshen College
- Indy Parks and Recreation
- LaGrange County Department of Parks and Recreation
- Lake County Parks & Rec
- LaPorte County Conservation Trust
- LaPorte County Parks Department
- Purdue University
- St. Joseph County Parks Department
- Steuben County

National Audubon Society: Important Bird Area Program

Neither the National Audubon Society nor any of its state or regional affiliates in Indiana own any publicly accessible natural areas in Northern Indiana. But Indiana's local Audubon Society chapters have conducted extensive research that helped identify Important Bird Areas across the state.

The IBA program was initiated in Europe in the 1980s by BirdLife International and now identifies bird species of concern in more than eight thousand areas in 178 countries. "Hundreds of these sites and millions of acres have received better protection as a result of the Important Bird Areas Program," according to the IBA page at the National Audubon Society, which administers the program in the United States.

The National Audubon Society is a multilayered conservation organization whose mission is "to conserve and restore natural ecosystems, focusing on birds, other wildlife, and their habitats for the benefit of humanity and the earth's biological diversity." Named after nineteenth-century artist and ornithologist John James Audubon, who lived in Kentucky and painted in Indiana in the early 1800s, the society has more than five hundred state and local affiliates around the nation. Nine chapters—Amos Butler in Indianapolis, Dunes–Calumet in Chesterton, Potawatomie in LaPorte, Robert Cooper in Muncie, South Bend–Elkhart in South Bend, Stockbridge in Fort Wayne, Sycamore in West Lafayette, Tippecanoe in Silver Lake, and Wabash Valley in Terre Haute—are active in Northern Indiana.

The National Audubon Society launched its IBA initiative in 1995, establishing programs in each state. IBAs are designated as either global, continental, or state, and by definition are sites that support wildlife meeting the following criteria:

- Species of conservation concern (e.g., threatened and endangered species)
- Range-restricted species (species vulnerable because they are not widely distributed)
- Species that are vulnerable because their populations are concentrated in one general habitat type or biome
- Species, or groups of similar species (such as waterfowl or shorebirds), that are vulnerable because they occur at high densities due to their congregatory behavior

The Indiana Important Bird Areas Program was launched in 1998 and initially relied on a volunteer coordinator and a technical committee. By 2017, forty-one Indiana sites, totaling more than 750,000 acres, had been designated as IBAs.

Part 2

THE NORTHERN INDIANA LANDSCAPE

The Northern
Indiana Landscape

Sculpted by Rock, Ice, and Water

BILLION-YEAR-OLD BEDROCK

Like the rest of the state, Northern Indiana is underlain with layers of bedrock formed over the ages by the compression of clay, sand, silt, and other sedimentary materials that were deposited here via the wind and water a quarter to a half billion years ago. Depending on the location, the rock at or near the surface in Indiana formed during what geologists call the Paleozoic era, between 570 million and 245 million years ago, when vertebrate life-forms evolved from fish to amphibians and reptiles (*ancient life*).

Indiana's geologic record began a billion years ago on the portion of the earth's crust that today is called the North American Plate. Like the planet's other twelve *tectonic plates*, ours has perpetually merged, diverged, and drifted around the globe through a process known as *plate tectonics*. During the Paleozoic era, Indiana sat where Northern Brazil is now, about five hundred miles south of the equator, under a vast tropical sea that incessantly ebbed and flowed and changed depths through the ages.

Over hundreds of millions of years, sedimentary materials from these ancient seas—including skeletons, clamshells, and other animal remains—settled to the ocean floor and compressed and cemented into the limestone, dolomite, siltstone, sandstone, and shale bedrock that underlie the state today. As detailed in *The Natural Heritage of Indiana* (Jackson 1997), the Paleozoic era is divided into seven periods, with the bedrock nearest the Indiana surface forming during the middle five:

Indiana Bedrock

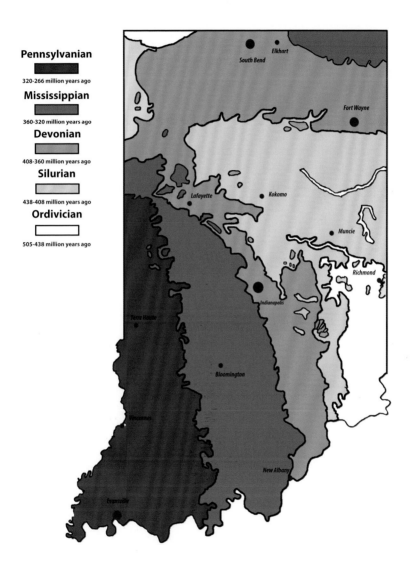

Pennsylvanian

320-266 million years ago

Mississippian

360-320 million years ago

Devonian

408-360 million years ago

Silurian

438-408 million years ago

Ordivician

505-438 million years ago

Elkhart

South Bend

Fort Wayne

Lafayette

Kokomo

Muncie

Richmond

Indianapolis

Terre Haute

Bloomington

Vincennes

New Albany

Evansville

- Cambrian (570–505 million years ago)
- Ordovician (505–438 million years ago)
- Silurian (438–408 million years ago)
- Devonian (408–360 million years ago)
- Mississippian (360–320 million years ago)
- Pennsylvanian (320–266 million years ago)
- Permian (266–245 million years ago)

Cambrian Period rock underlies the other five types but does not approach the surface in Indiana. Most of the earth's major animal life-forms appeared during what is called Cambrian explosion. Because Indiana has been above sea level for millions of years, erosion has washed away the younger rock from the Permian Period, which was the Paleozoic's last. No stones from this period have been found in the state.

Geologic time includes two more recent eras—the Mesozoic and Cenozoic eras. The Mesozoic, 245 million to 66 million years ago, is known as the Age of Reptiles or Age of Dinosaurs (*middle life*). The Cenozoic, which continues today, is known as the Age of Mammals (*recent life*).

Even though the earth's oldest rocks are an estimated four billion years old, and the earliest fossil, discovered in Greenland in 2016, is 3.7 billion years old, physical evidence of Precambrian life is exceedingly rare. Few life-forms had skeletons or other mineralized parts to fossilize. The Greenland fossil is believed to be made up of sediment layers compacted together by microbial communities in shallow water.

The oldest bedrock that reaches the surface in Indiana formed during the Ordovician Period, when invertebrates began diversifying and fish appear in fossil records. A narrow slice of Ordovician rock runs about a hundred miles north and south along the Ohio border from Wayne County, just south of Richmond, to Dearborn County, where the Ohio River marks the state line with Kentucky.

This most ancient, erosion-resistant deposit lies just west of the Cincinnati Arch, where an upheaval in the earth's crust nearly five hundred million years ago slightly elevated the landscape. Despite its surrounding flat to gently rolling farmland, the state's highest elevation is in northern Wayne County farm country—1,257 feet above sea level. Only a few of the fifty miles of Ordovician bedrock are in Northern Indiana—broadly defined in this book as north of Interstate 70—with a couple of east-west-facing, string-like strips a few miles to the north.

Much of Northern Indiana rests on an amoeba-shaped block of Silurian Period bedrock that sprawls northwest from a line between Richmond and Fort Wayne, through Muncie and Kokomo, to the state's far northwest corner at Lake Michigan. During the Silurian Period, this area was a shallow sea that was resplendent with brilliantly colored coral reefs. Elsewhere, fungi, mosses, and other primitive plants were just beginning to take root on the land.

A broad, top-heavy mass of Devonian Period bedrock surrounds the Silurian on all sides and overlies it in the northwest, isolating a tiny slice of Silurian south from Lake Michigan for about forty miles along the Indiana-Illinois state line. Devonian bedrock underlies communities from Fort Wayne west to Gary and then southeast through Lafayette and Indianapolis to New Albany. Fossil records show amphibians appeared during the Devonian Period.

Two separate blocks of Mississippian Period bedrock, formed when crinoids flourished on the sea floor, underlie two portions of Northern Indiana. A small, narrow block runs about seventy-five miles along the Michigan state line from just east of Elkhart to the Ohio state line. A narrow, arrowhead-like swath runs west of Indianapolis and Lafayette a couple hundred miles south through Bloomington, past Corydon, to the Ohio River. The world-famous limestone quarried in Monroe and Lawrence Counties in Southern Indiana is Mississippian.

A similarly sized, pistol-shaped formation from the Pennsylvanian Period parallels the Mississippian bedrock for about fifty miles north from Terre Haute along the Indiana-Illinois state line and south another 150 miles to Evansville and

Ritchey Woods Nature Preserve

the Ohio River. Lizards and other reptiles appeared in the fossil record during the Pennsylvanian, and coal swamps covered the landscape.

Due to the Cincinnati Arch, Indiana's bedrock deposi-tions follow a gentle, on average half-degree slope from that 1,200-foot-plus *peak* in Wayne County to 324 feet where the Wabash meets the Ohio in the Illinois Basin. The landscape is even flatter as it sprawls from the arch toward Lake Michigan's 580-foot elevation.

PROFOUND ICE AGE EFFECTS

Northern Indiana's physical geography began its last and most relevant transformation roughly seven hundred thou-sand years ago during the Pleistocene Epoch, also known as the Ice Age, when sediment-laden ice sheets redirected drain-age patterns in the region and began forming the Ohio River Valley. Prior to that glacial event, rainwater and snowmelt in the Midwest drained north to the preglacial Teays River, which stretched from its North Carolina and Virginia headwaters through Northern Indiana to the Mississippi River in Western Illinois.

As explained on the Indiana Geological & Water Survey website: "No other event since the extinction of the dinosaurs sixty-five million years ago can compare to the Ice Age in terms of the profound effect it had on our landscape and the natural environment in which we live today. In fact, virtually all of societal affairs are in one way or another affected by some facet of the Ice Age."

The Pleistocene Epoch began two million years ago, presumably lasted until ten thousand years ago, and is divided into four periods, each named after the states in which its impacts are most evident:

- Nebraskan glacial (2 million to 770,000 years ago)
- Kansan glacial (770,000–220,000 years ago)
- llinoian glacial (220,000–70,000 years ago)
- Wisconsin glacial (70,000–10,000 years ago)

During this time, snowfall accumulated on large portions of the Hudson Bay and Labrador sections in Northern and Eastern Canada and formed continent-sized ice sheets. Under the pressure of their own weights, influenced by temperature fluctuations to the south, and lubed beneath by surface water, these glaciers repeatedly advanced and retreated from north to south and back. Described by the Indiana Geological & Water Survey as "rivers of ice, slowly flowing outward from their source to their terminus," the last—the Wisconsin glaciers—alternately and repeatedly advanced and retreated from two directions, leaving in their wakes the Lake Michigan and Lake Erie Basins.

While scientists disagree on how big they were and how fast they moved, these ice rivers ground, gouged, and reformed the earth surface beneath them, picking up and redistributing sediments from sand and clay to pebbles, rocks, and giant boulders.

As they ebbed and flowed, they left depressions and holes in the earth surface that filled with water and became lakes, great and small.

As the glaciers melted, they deposited these sedimentary materials in various combinations known as till—in some places as uneven piles or ridges known as moraines, in others as flatlands known as till plains—that reach hundreds of feet deep. Their meltwaters' erosive properties carved valleys and canyons laced with rivers, creeks, and streams.

Geologists estimate there may have been between twelve and eighteen different glacial events, dating back perhaps 2.4 billion years. But it's unclear how many of them impacted Indiana. The Indiana Geological & Water Survey says there were at least eleven.

The first ice sheet known to reach Indiana arrived some seven hundred thousand years ago during the Kansan glacial and came south from Michigan, stopping somewhere around the middle of the state. This slowly creeping glacier's erosive power and resulting sedimentary deposits reconfigured the entire Midwest drainage patterns, blocking the Teays River with glacial debris, forming basins that would become the Great Lakes, and redirecting most of Indiana's water south to the developing Ohio River Valley.

The Illinoian glacial event began nearly five hundred million years after the Kansan. It was the coldest of them all and extended the furthest south. It covered all of Indiana except for an upside-down, funnel-shaped mass in the southwest that stretches from New Albany to Martinsville to the Wabash River just north of the Ohio. This area is referred to as *unglaciated* or *driftless*.

The last and most influential ice sheets in Indiana advanced and retreated during the Wisconsin glacial event, which began in the state about 50,000 years ago, retreated some 13,600 years ago, and was gone 10,000 years ago. These Wisconsin ice sheets stopped north of Martinsville along an uneven line from Brookville to Terre Haute and were largely responsible for

Northern Indiana's flat to gently rolling landscape. Their path and the resulting differences in natural characteristics also mark the boundary between Northern and Southern Indiana in this book.

Even though the glaciers themselves were absent for many tens of thousands of years between the advances—known as *interglacial* or *interstadial* periods depending on length—their reformative work continued unabated. As the Indiana Geological & Water Survey further explains: "Rivers cut great valleys, sediments weathered to form thick soils, and forests and prairies dominated by temperate vegetation pushed the tundra and spruce forests northward."

The ice created several morainal complexes in Northern Indiana that consist of mostly gentle ridges around broad, flat drainageways. The Valparaiso Moraine forms a massive *U* shape around Lake Michigan from west of Milwaukee, around the west side of Chicago, through Northwest Indiana, and past Grand Rapids, topping out at a little more than one hundred feet above Lake Michigan. The Fort Wayne Moraine begins near Upper Sandusky, Ohio, and, following portions of the St. Marys and St. Joseph Rivers, passes through Fort Wayne and Northwest Ohio, to Hudson, Michigan, about forty miles west of Lake Erie.

Much of the region is so flat that massive swamps dominated when the French arrived in the late seventeenth century. The Great Marsh extended miles inland along the Lake Michigan shoreline from the Illinois state line to Michigan City. The Grand Kankakee Marsh to the south, which covered nearly a million acres of Indiana and Illinois, has been called the "Everglades of the North." The Maumee River east of Fort Wayne fed the Great Black Swamp.

From the wetlands south to another ragged line from Vigo through Morgan to Wayne Counties, the melting ice deposited vast till plains atop the bedrock, whose sediments weathered into deep, fertile soils. Drained and converted to agriculture today, the area once supported vast hardwood forests of beech, maple, oak, ash, and elm.

Kankakee River, Kankakee Fish & Wildlife Area

Most of Northern Indiana's rugged topography—and exposed bedrock—is limited to down-cut riverine environments along streams, creeks, and rivers. The trail through Warbler Woods Nature Preserve inside Fall Creek State Park in Indianapolis, deep in the Tipton Till Plain, includes stairs on a seventy-five-foot relief.

The Wabash River Watershed from Lafayette to Terre Haute, while not featuring the three-hundred-food drops at Clifty Falls State Park on the Ohio River, can be as treacherous as many areas in the state's southern hill country. The Devil's Backbone at Pine Hills Nature Preserve in Shades State Park features a sandstone spine that is only six feet wide at one point with precipitous one-hundred-foot drops on either side. Nothing like that exists in Brown County.

THE WATER FLOWS SOUTH AND WEST, MOSTLY

The drainage conduits and landforms that those Ice Age rivers created in Northern Indiana flow in four directions. Three small watersheds along the state's far northern border drain to Lake Erie via the Maumee River, Lake Michigan via the St. Joseph

River, and the Mississippi River via the Kankakee and Illinois Rivers. The rest of the state's watersheds—85 percent—ultimately flow southwest to the Ohio River via the Wabash River.

Two Northern Indiana rivers are named the St. Joseph River: one (of the Maumee) flows into the Maumee River and on to Lake Erie and the other (of Lake Michigan) flows into Lake Michigan. They rise a couple miles apart near the Southern Michigan town of Hillsdale, just north of the tristate junction of Indiana, Michigan, and Ohio. The larger and more forceful of the two bears west, passes through Elkhart and South Bend, and then turns north to Lake Michigan. The smaller feeds the Maumee at Fort Wayne from the northeast.

The Maumee River

The 137-mile Maumee River flows northeast from its origin where the St. Joseph (of the Maumee) and St. Marys Rivers join in Fort Wayne, through Northwest Ohio, to Toledo and its mouth on Lake Erie. That Great Lake's longest inland tributary, the Maumee's path from Fort Wayne, Indiana, to Defiance, Ohio, is so tortuously ribbon-like that settlers estimated the water took 160 miles to travel a hundred.

The Maumee passes through morainal ridges of boulders, gravel, and sand left as the Wisconsin glacier receded some thirteen thousand years ago. At that time, the Glacial Lake Maumee, a one-hundred-mile extension of Lake Erie, spread southwest to Fort Wayne. Prior to the last ice sheet's retreat and resulting sedimentary deposits, the Maumee flowed into the Wabash River Watershed.

By the time the first explorer, Frenchman René-Robert Cavelier, Sieur de La Salle, wrote about the region in 1682, the glacial lake had become the Great Black Swamp, which was fed by the Maumee River. Its tributaries—the St. Joseph and St. Marys Rivers—approached from the northeast and southeast, as they do today, heading in the direction of the Wabash River watershed to the west. But where they meet the Maumee at its headwaters, the water flow reverses direction, taking a sharp turn east. The French initially called the Maumee the Miami after the Indians whose capital village of Kekionga sat near the three rivers' confluence. The name was changed to avoid confusion with the other Miami River that runs through Southwest Ohio.

Due to an easy nine-mile portage from the Maumee to the Wabash River watershed via the Little River, the three-rivers area played key roles in the state's and nation's histories. Because of its strategic position along the most direct route between Quebec and New Orleans, the area became a major North American trading center from the late 1600s on. Multiple forts—including the French Fort Miamis and American Fort Wayne—were constructed along these rivers. From 1747 to 1813, no fewer than seven battles were fought among the Native Americans, French, British, and Americans.

The St. Joseph River (of the Maumee)

The Maumee's St. Joseph, known at its rise as the East Branch of the St. Joseph River, cuts some seventy-five miles south and west through the northwest corner of Ohio to Fort Wayne. It flows between two of several morainal ridges deposited by the last glacier.

The Miami Indians called this St. Joseph the Ko-chis-ah-se-pe, or Bean River. The French called it the St. Joseph or the Little St. Joseph River or St. Joseph of the Maumee to differentiate it from the similarly named westward-flowing waterway.

This St. Joe's largest tributary is Cedar Creek, which flows fourteen miles from Cedar Lake north of Auburn in DeKalb County, past Huntertown, to the confluence northeast of Fort Wayne. Among the state's most pristine waterways, Cedar Creek is one of only three designated as part of Indiana's Natural, Scenic, and Recreational River System.

The St. Marys River

The St. Marys River rises in the flatlands near New Bremen, Ohio, and flows roughly ninety miles northwest to its rendezvous with the St. Joseph in Fort Wayne. The Miami Indians called the St. Marys Mahi-may-i-wah-se-pe-way, or Sturgeon Creek, because of its large population of spawning sturgeon.

While the early French explorers charted the St. Marys River's flow, the level upper reaches were too swampy for exploration. On his way to the decisive Battle of Fallen Timbers in 1794 with the Miami, Shawnee, and other native Indian tribes and the subsequent establishment of Fort Wayne, General "Mad Anthony" Wayne established a smaller Fort Adams by the St. Marys. His plans to connect the two forts through the water failed due to the river's soggy wetlands.

The St. Joseph River (of Lake Michigan)

The 210-mile St. Joseph River is the watery spine of Northern Indiana's Lake Michigan Watershed, rising just north of the Indiana-Michigan-Ohio border near Hillsdale, Michigan. After crossing the Michigan-Indiana state line twice, this St. Joe empties into Lake Michigan at St. Joseph / Benton Harbor some thirty miles to the north.

Along the way, the waters of the St. Joseph River spend less than a quarter of their journey in Indiana. After traversing about half the state of Michigan from its headwaters, the river crosses the state line just north of Bristol and flows roughly forty miles west through Elkhart, Mishawaka, and South Bend. In South Bend, the flow turns north and crosses the state line again on its way to Lake Michigan. South Bend's name is derived from the river's ninety-degree turn at its southernmost point.

This St. Joe's initial route follows every imaginable direction but east, flowing twenty miles north from Hillsdale, skirting the village of Homer before winding west and south through backroad towns with names like Lichtfield, Tekonsha, Union City, and Colon. The largest town on its Michigan route is Three Rivers, population eight thousand. For the first few miles in Indiana, the St. Joseph continues its rural route through the fertile farmland that lies between Bristol and Elkhart. But as it reaches the urban centers from Elkhart west, elegant homes, industries, and downtown commercial centers line its banks. After changing direction in South Bend and recrossing the state line a couple miles north of the city limits, the St. Joseph flows through Southern Michigan fruit-tree country to its mouth.

In 1679, René-Robert Cavelier, Sieur de La Salle, became the first French explorer known to have traveled the St. Joseph River. He and a twenty-nine-man expedition with eight canoes paddled from Lake Michigan to South Bend, where they made the portage to the Kankakee River on their way west to the Mississippi via the Illinois River. As with the three-rivers area at the mouth of the Maumee, control over the western St. Joseph ricocheted among the Indians, French, British, and Americans, though the Revolutionary War cemented this far northern region's status as American earlier than in other parts of Northern Indiana.

The Fawn River

A shallow, marshy tributary, the Fawn River rises near Orland in Steuben County, population 434, and feeds the St. Joseph River some forty miles to the west and north at Constantine, Michigan. Perhaps the wildest stream in the state, the Fawn passes through only two towns—Greenfield Mills, Indiana, and Fawn River, Michigan—both so small the census doesn't even list them.

Along with its tributary Crooked Creek, the Fawn drains nearly forty morainal lakes in the far northeastern portion of the state. In its upper reaches near Pokagon State Park, the creek is fed by a chain of lakes, including the 802-acre Crooked Lake, that extend from south of Nevada Mills to near Angola.

The Pigeon River

The St. Joseph's primary tributary is the thirty-six-mile Pigeon River, which parallels the Fawn River to the south and west by less than a mile in places. It rises among the LaGrange County moraines near the one-hundred-resident town of Mongo, short for *Mongoquinong,* the Potawatomi Indian word meaning Big

Squaw. "The Pigeon Creek, which rises at the Cedar Marsh upstream of Mongo, nearly doubles the flowing water's length. The river, creek, and town are named after Potawatomi chief White Pigeon.

The Pigeon River's flow, which is fed by more than fifty lakes, hugs the state line, slowly angling northwest through LaGrange County and briefly crossing into Michigan on a twisting, arcing route past White Pigeon, Michigan. The mouth feeds the St. Joseph just before it reenters Indiana near Bristol.

The Elkhart River

The forty-eight-mile Elkhart River rises from two branches in northern Noble and southern LaGrange Counties that join just east of Ligonier for a thirty-mile run northwest to the St. Joseph River in downtown Elkhart. The city of Elkhart and the Elkhart River were named by the Indians for one of the river's islands that they thought resembled an elk's heart. This relatively shallow waterway drifts through scenic farms and woodlands. The upper reaches are bordered by marshlands that constitute some of the largest remaining wetlands in the state.

The South Branch of the Elkhart River, once considered for inclusion in Indiana's Natural, Scenic and Recreational River System, originates at the eighteen-acre Hawk Lake in LaGrange County. It passes through Marl, Bartley, and Port Mitchell Lakes and is swollen along the way by other lake-fed streams, including some from Chain O' Lakes State Park.

The North Branch of the Elkhart River begins its flow at Sylvan Lake, where author, photographer, and conservationist Gene Stratton-Porter lived and worked for six years. Also called Limberlost North, her home at "Wildflower Woods" is now the Gene Stratton-Porter State Historic Site. The North Branch's loopy path flows eighteen miles through multiple lakes, including the Indian Lakes Chain in Amish country near Wolcottville in Noble County, to meet the South Branch. The only town on its path, Cosperville, is so small it is not counted in the census.

Art Hammer Wetlands

The Grand Calumet River

The thirteen-mile-long Grand Calumet River is perhaps the most misnamed waterbody in the nation. First, in every regard, the "Grand Cal" is less than grand. It is wholly contained in one county—Lake County. The Little Calumet River to the south, to which the Grand Calumet connects in South Chicago, is wider, deeper, and eight times longer. Second, the Grand Cal has become an industrial sewer that carries toxic waste from steel mills, oil refineries, and other heavy industries to Lake Michigan. Supporting almost no wildlife except for pollution-tolerant species like carp and goldfish, it is among the most polluted waterways in the United States. While cleanup efforts have been underway since 2012, state officials in 2018 still warned against eating any fish from the Grand Calumet River.

The interconnected Grand Cal, Little Cal, and Calumet Rivers comprise the Calumet River System that drains Northwest Indiana and South Chicago into Lake Michigan and, thanks to the canal-building fever of the late nineteenth and early twentieth centuries, the Mississippi River.

Historically speaking, the Grand Cal does live up to its self-important name. A year after Father Jacques Marquette and fur trapper Louis Joliet became the first Europeans to map the Mississippi River, Marquette ventured to Lake Michigan's southwestern reach in late 1674 to establish a mission among the Illinois Indians, a journey recognized as the first visit to Chicago by a Westerner. Some historic sources say that on his return, Marquette camped on the beach at the mouth of the Grand Calumet River, then called the Great Konomick River, which is now the Miller Beach area of Gary. (Other sources place Marquette in the region as early as 1673.)

In the late seventeenth century, the Grand and Little Cal Rivers were the same waterway. The Konomick, a marshy, bayou-like stream, rose a few miles south of Michigan City and bore west to the Chicago suburb of Riverdale. There it made a 180-degree loop back east to the lake at Miller Beach.

The landscape consisted of sand ridges surrounding swampy sloughs, remnants of the Glacial Lake Chicago that formed after the Wisconsin glacial ice sheets retreated from the area some thirteen thousand years ago. The river itself was unnavigable in places due to heavy vegetation clogging its channels. To the south lay the Grand Kankakee Marsh.

In 1820, the Calumet Feeder Canal was cut from the Little Calumet to the Calumet River in South Chicago, redirecting the river flow north to Lake Michigan and starving the Grand Cal's northern stretch of water. A half century later, sandbars covered the old river mouth on Lake Michigan, reversing its flow toward the Calumet Feeder Canal.

In 1869, Congress appropriated funds to build Calumet Harbor in South Chicago at the Illinois-Indiana state line, spawning drainage projects and industrialization on the Indiana side. By 1906, the Grand Cal's channel had been moved and straightened, and the human-made Indiana Harbor Canal and Burns Ditch connected the Grand Cal and Little Cal, respectively, to Lake Michigan.

The Little Calumet River

The sixty-three-mile Little Calumet River may be on the short end for a major Northern Indiana river, and the final quarter or so of its flow is west of the Illinois state line. The Little Cal, however, is anything but small in terms of its role in the region's history.

Today, the Little Cal rises from a tiny stream just east of Round Lake about six miles south of Michigan City, where it is also known as the East Arm Little Calumet or the Little Calumet East Branch. From there the river tracks west to the South Chicago suburb of Blue Island, where it makes a soft hairpin turn east and is intercepted by the Calumet-Sag Channel, which diverts its flow west to the Illinois River Watershed. Five miles east of that merger, the Little Cal meets the Calumet Feeder Channel, which connects the Little Cal with the Calumet River and Lake Michigan in Chicago.

From the time the Little Cal reaches the twin cities of Chesterton and Portage, it drains the most industrialized and populous region in the state. From there on it carries effluent from mills, factories, plants, and the cities of Portage, Hobart, Gary, and Hammond to the state line and South Chicago.

In its upper reaches, however, the Little Calumet has a totally different character, passing through natural areas steeped in history and natural beauty. It rises a little more than a mile outside an isolated parcel of the Indiana Dunes National Lakeshore's eastern edge and flows about five miles through the park's western section. Within those two sections are two protected National Natural Landmarks—Cowles Bog and Pinhook Bog.

The 205-acre Cowles Bog, about a mile north of the Little Cal by the town of Dune Acres, is named after University of Chicago botany professor Henry Chandler Cowles, who was a pioneer in the emerging field of ecology. (See Indiana Dunes National Lakeshore: Cowles Bog section for details.)

The landmark *Natural Areas of Indiana and Their Preservation* (Purdue University 1969) calls Pinhook "the finest bog in Indiana." Its soggy environs lie within a bowl-shaped ice-block depression surrounded by low, wooded, morainal hills. It is located due south of Michigan City, just east of the Little Calumet's rise.

The Kankakee River

The Kankakee River flows some 133 miles from its rise on what is now the southwest side of South Bend, across rural Northwest Indiana, and into Illinois to rendezvous with the Illinois River a few miles southwest of the Chicago suburb Joliet. From there, the water flows southwest through Central Illinois to the Mississippi River just north of St. Louis.

The Kankakee Watershed is flat to moderately rolling, draining about three thousand square miles of river basin, including parts or all of thirteen Northwestern Indiana counties. Once a massive, spongy swamp in its upper Indiana reaches, one explanation for the name links it to the Potawatomi word *teh-yak-ki-ki*, which means "swampy country." Another says it is from the Miami Indian word *m'wha-ki-ki*, "wolf country."

The Kankakee Basin formed after the retreating Wisconsin glacier gouged a ten-mile-wide river valley that flowed south of South Bend from east to west, leaving in its wake one of the most contorted river flows in Indiana, if not in the nation. When French explorers arrived in the 1670s, the river had more than two thousand turns, flowing 250 miles to travel 85 from South Bend to Momence, Illinois, nine miles west of the Illinois state line. After passing through an erosion-resistant rock barrier at Momence, the Kankakee naturally widens, straightens, and picks up the pace.

When the Europeans arrived, the Kankakee River Basin was the Grand Kankakee Marsh and the province of the Potawatomi Indians, a Great Lakes tribe whose name means "Keepers of the Fire." They used the swamps and woodlands not only as hunting grounds but also as barriers against the Iroquois Indians, their enemies to the east, who had warred with them in the

1740s and 1750s and pushed them west from their Michigan homelands.

René-Robert Cavelier, Sieur de La Salle, was the first European to reach the Kankakee, discovering its source during his first venture into Northern Indiana in 1679, a decade after he became the first to paddle the Ohio and reach Indiana soil. After canoeing the St. Joseph River from Lake Michigan to the turn at South Bend, he became separated from his camp and, while looking for them, discovered the portage at a small lake that today bears his name. Other French explorers who charted the region included Pierre Francois Xavier de Charlevoix, Henri de Tonti, and Father Louis Hennepin.

Chiefs from Potawatomi villages ceded claims in Indiana to the Americans in 1832 and 1836, and their forced removal to Kansas began in 1838 on a route that would become known as the Potawatomi Trail of Death.

A six-year channelization project to drain the Kankakee lowland areas for agriculture had straightened the main channel by 1917. Today the river averages 75 to 180 feet in width and 4 to 5 feet in depth, falling roughly 1 foot per river mile. About 75 percent of the basin drains cropland, pastureland, and forestland.

The Yellow River

The sixty-two-mile Yellow River begins its route to the Kankakee in southeastern St. Joseph County, where two agricultural ditches meet about four miles north of Bremen. Its initial flow tracks south through farm fields to Bremen, where it is joined by a feeder creek from the 416-acre Lake of the Woods. From there the path is south and then west through narrow rows of trees flanked by more agricultural fields to Plymouth, the largest city in the valley.

Just outside Plymouth, the Yellow River flows through a morainal valley, where it is fed by a series of lakes with names like Latonka, Pretty, and Dixon, to the town of Knox in Starke County. Beyond Knox, the Yellow's path has been straightened for a five-mile stretch to the Kankakee Fish & Wildlife Area and the Kankakee River near the town of English Lake.

In presettlement times, the Yellow's lower reaches were known as English Lake, part of the Grand Kankakee Marsh. The name is derived from the Shawnee name We-thau-ka-mik, meaning "yellow waters," possibly due to the sand in the riverbed.

The Iroquois River

The ninety-four-mile Iroquois River rises northwest of Rensselaer and makes a near 360-degree loop—taking twenty miles to travel maybe three miles—passes through the city, and flows generally southwest across the Illinois state line. The Jasper County seat is the only Indiana town the Iroquois flows through. About fifteen miles into Illinois, the Iroquois turns north and merges into the Kankakee River about four miles southwest of Kankakee.

The Iroquois is a shallow, winding, slow-moving waterway that drops only inches per mile through what in presettlement times was a mix of swamps, sand ridges, and prairies. Consequently, the Iroquois Valley was among the last areas in Indiana to be settled and developed. Until 1853, the river drained the thirty-six-thousand-acre swamp known as Beaver Creek to the north, and the settlers considered it unproductive and unhealthy. In 1853, ditching redirected the water flow to the Kankakee, opening the region to agriculture.

The river was named for the Iroquois Indians, a confederation of six tribes—Mohawk, Seneca, Cayuga, Oneida, Onondaga, and Tuscarora—that lived in Upstate New York but dominated much of the Great Lakes when Europeans arrived in the seventeenth century.

The Wabash River

The 475-mile Wabash River is indeed "The Essence of Indiana," as Richard S. Simons dubbed it back in 1985 in *The Rivers of Indiana*. "To Hoosiers the number one river is the Wabash," the vice president of the Indiana Historical Society wrote in the opening lines of the book's first chapter. "And to non-Hoosiers the Wabash is Indiana." Since 1996, it has been Indiana's official state river.

Wabash River, Hanging Rock National Natural Landmark

The Wabash drains 90 percent of the state's landmass—thirty-three thousand of its thirty-six thousand total square miles—from its source a couple miles east of the Indiana-Ohio state line near Fort Recovery, Ohio, to its discharge into the Ohio River in Posey County, Indiana, at the tristate junction of Indiana, Illinois, and Kentucky. With nearly a dozen tributaries, the Wabash watershed drains four-fifths of the state's counties.

Simons described the Wabash as three rivers in one: from its rise at Fort Recovery just east of the Ohio state line to Huntington, a narrow "trench" winding through flat farmlands; from Huntington to Lafayette, a riverine occupier of a glacial valley that in places "widens into beautiful prairies bordered by distant hills" and is "steep and narrow" in others; and from Lafayette to the Ohio River, a more complex waterway that variously passes through prairie and partially filled glacial valley, eventually becoming a "mighty stream" that at times is "wild and barren."

The Wabash bears northwest from its Ohio beginnings, forms the south border of Ouabache State Park, and passes through Bluffton to Huntington, where it collects the flow from its first major tributary, the Little River. Just past Huntington, the flow turns west through Wabash, Peru, and Logansport on a path to Lafayette. Along that stretch the Wabash is joined by the Salamonie River at Wabash, the Mississinewa River at Peru, and the Eel River at Logansport. The Tippecanoe River converges with the Wabash at Lafayette. The course from Lafayette to the Ohio River below Mount Vernon is south and west, forming the Illinois-Indiana state line from a few miles south of Terre Haute. Sugar Creek is the last major feeder to reach the Wabash above Interstate 70, passing through Shades State Park and Turkey Run State Park before its Wabash confluence about ten miles northwest of Rockville in Parke County.

The White River West Fork is the second-largest waterway above the state's Interstate 70 divide and drains significant portions of Central and Southwest Indiana before feeding the Wabash fifty miles above the Ohio River. About thirty miles before the Wabash, the West Fork merges with the East Fork, which has cut a wandering path southwest from Columbus.

The name Wabash is derived from the Native American name for the river, Wah-Bah-Shik-Ki, which means "pure white." The French renamed it Ouabache, which the English restyled as Wabash. The Wabash River and the state of Indiana were Miami Indian country when the French missionaries and fur trappers followed La Salle's initial venture into Northern Indiana via the St. Joseph River in 1679. Other related tribes included Delaware, Potawatomi, Kickapoo, and Shawnee.

As the French expanded their influence, the most direct trade route from their capitals in Quebec and New Orleans followed the Maumee River from Lake Erie to Fort Wayne and, via a nine-mile portage, to the Wabash Watershed. The French built Fort Miamis at Fort Wayne, Fort Ouiatenon at Lafayette, and Fort Vincennes at Vincennes.

Throughout the eighteenth century, numerous battles for control of the New World were engaged along the Wabash. At Vincennes in 1779, General George Rogers Clark attacked and defeated the British in the Siege of Fort Sackville, securing the Northwest Territory for the Americans. In 1811, General William Henry Harrison's army defeated Shawnee Indian chief Tecumseh and a multitribe Indian confederation at the Battle of Tippecanoe near Lafayette, effectively breaking Native American resistance to the white man in Indiana.

The Wabash's historic role as a transportation link continued in prerailroad Indiana history. Because the river was untamable, construction on the Wabash and Erie Canal, the nation's longest, began in 1832 and largely followed the river, once again connecting Lake Erie with the Ohio. But the locomotive's arrival in 1865 marked the beginning of the end for the canal era in Indiana and for water transportation in general.

The Little River

The Little River runs twenty-two miles from the southwest side of Fort Wayne to the Wabash River at the Historic Forks of the Wabash park on the west side of Huntington. Sometimes referred to on maps as the "Little Wabash," the Little follows the Wabash and Erie Channel, a remnant of the Glacial Lake Maumee's drainage at the end of the Wisconsin glacial event some thirteen thousand years ago.

While the Little's name applies to the river's size, its role in history is anything but small. Before the Miami Indians showed La Salle the portage at Fort Wayne that linked the Little and the Wabash River Watershed with the Maumee River and Lake Erie, this Wabash tributary had been valuable, strategic real estate. The Miami's largest village, Kekionga, sat at the portage.

In La Salle's day, the Little began as an expansive, tangled swamp that opened into a short river whose flow ultimately reached the Mississippi River at modern-day Cairo, Illinois. From there it was on to New Orleans on one of the most important trade routes of the time. The French named it Le Petite Rivière.

None other than George Washington was among the first to recommend channelizing the Little, and by the 1830s work had begun. The Little River was transformed into a stretch of the Wabash and Erie Canal. The watershed was drained in the late 1800s for agriculture, which today still surrounds the Little River.

The Salamonie River

The Salamonie River is an eighty-four-mile Wabash River tributary that originates near the village of Salamonia in southeastern Jay County, a couple miles inside the Ohio state line. It flows generally northwest past and through Portland, Montpelier, and Warren, meeting the Wabash River at the town of Lagro four miles east of Wabash.

In 1966, the Salamonie was dammed a couple of miles upstream from the Wabash confluence to form the sprawling 2,655-acre Salamonie Lake, which the Indiana Department of Parks & Lakes now manages. The 13,336-acre natural complex includes four state recreation areas and the 850-acre Salamonie State Forest, the largest of only two state forests in Northern Indiana.

From its rise through Portland to Pennville, the Salamonie is a series of agricultural ditches. Past Montpelier, the flow assumes the character of a natural river, at times making near-360-degree loops, gradually building in its upper reaches into a twisty valley between bluffs that rise seventy-five feet above the reservoir.

The name Salamonie is derived from the Miami Indian word *on-za-la-mo-ni*, for bloodroot, which grew along the riverbanks and was used to make yellow paint. Historically, the river has been known as Salamanie River, Salamonia River, and Salamanic River.

The Mississinewa River

The Mississinewa River originates in Darke County, Ohio, between Fort Recovery and Union City, and follows a one-hundred-mile journey west and north to the Wabash River on Peru's east side. One of the swiftest streams in Indiana, its bed falls nearly three-and-a-half-feet per mile through a morainal valley left behind by retreating glaciers some thirteen thousand years ago.

Seven Pillars, Mississinewa River

The Mississinewa's route begins as a reengineered agricultural ditch in West Central Ohio near the Indiana-Ohio state line.
It reassumes a more natural course a few miles past the border
and passes by the university town of Muncie. As it approaches
the industrial city of Marion, the river becomes more scenic as
it cuts a deeper valley through limestone bedrock. About five
miles southeast of Peru, the Mississinewa is dammed to create
the 3,210-acre Mississinewa Lake, part of a 14,386-acre, state-
run reservoir that includes several state recreation areas and
the obscure Frances Slocum State Forest.

Eons of wind and water exposure have left some dramatic geological formations in the limestone bedrock along the
Mississenewa. A series of round pillars and alcoves known as
the Seven Pillars (a.k.a. The Cliffs) border the river about two
miles downriver from the lake.

The river was named by the Miami Indians, who called it
"falling water." The final battle between the Shawnee and the

Americans occurred in 1812 in the Battle of the Mississinewa near Marion. Among the Miami leaders was Chief Shepoconah, known as Deaf Man, whose village was located on the Mississinewa. His wife, Ma-con-a-quah, or Little Bear Woman, was an American settler named Frances Slocum, who had been captured as a child from her Pennsylvania Quaker family in 1778. Nearly six decades later, while living on the Mississinewa on the last Indian reservation in Indiana, she shared her tale with an Indian trader, who relayed it to her family. Little Bear Woman chose to remain with the Miami until her death in 1847.

The Eel River

The Eel River is a 110-mile tributary of the Wabash River that rises as a shallow ditch southeast of Huntertown and flows southwest through Columbia City, South Whitley, and North Manchester to its confluence with the Wabash at Logansport. The largest town on its sparsely populated path is Columbia City, with 8,750 residents. The smallest is called Mexico, population 836.

One of two Indiana rivers named Eel, the northernmost flow is a quiet, scenic waterway that passes through vast acres of rich farmland, its banks tree lined much of the way. Just south of Columbia City, the riverbed widens after collecting outflows from the Blue River and the Gangwer Ditch. From there it is a slow and meandering path to the Wabash. Below North Manchester, bluffs reach seventy-five feet in places.

During the last glacial period, more than thirteen thousand years ago, the Eel formed as a single stream with the upper Cedar Creek. Fed by glacial meltwater and blocked by outwash, the Eel's upper channel changed course, creating the Cedar Creek. The Eel's flow today skirts a moraine left by the retreating Wisconsin ice sheets.

The Eel was Miami country when the French traders and missionaries arrived in the late 1600s. The Indians called it *Ke-na-po-co-mo-co*, which meant "river of the snake fish." The French called it Rivière L'Anguille, or Eel River. The river served as a bloody, territorial line in the sand for the Miami both before and after European encroachment. In *Rivers of Indiana*, Simons calls the Eel Indiana's "ABC river—stream of ambush, battle, and conquest."

Before the French arrived, the Miami built a garrison on a swampy area of the Eel south of Columbia City known as "the island" to fend off the Potawatomi advance from their ancestral homelands in Michigan. The Eel became the tribal boundary between the Miami and Potawatomi. The island later served as an outpost through a century of struggles against European encroachment from the east. In the late eighteenth and early nineteenth centuries, the fearsome Miami chief Little Turtle waged war with the French, British, and Americans up and down the Eel River Valley.

The Tippecanoe River

The Tippecanoe River runs a gentle, winding 166 miles from its rise in a ditch below Big Lake near Columbia City to the Wabash River just above Lafayette. Sometimes called the river of lakes, it is fed by eighty-eight natural lakes, including some of Indiana's largest: Tippecanoe Lake, 851 acres, also the state's deepest; Lake Manitou, 775 acres; and Winona Lake, 562 acres. The Tippecanoe's water is described as the state's cleanest river water. Its ecosystem is so diverse and supports so many endangered species that The Nature Conservancy has named it one of the top ten rivers in the United States that should be preserved.

The Wabash River's second-longest tributary follows a torturous, up-and-down westerly route from its rise along a steep moraine near the Whitley-Noble county line, through Tippecanoe Lake, and past Warsaw and Rochester, where it escapes the moraine. For the next sixty miles the Tippecanoe winds through the flat bed of the preglacial Lake Kankakee to the Tippecanoe River State Park north of Winamac, where the flow takes a hard turn south. Between Winamac and the Wabash, two dams built in the 1920s contain the 1,291-acre Lake Shafer and 1,547-acre Lake Freeman. Draining many small tributaries that originate in swamps and lakes, the Tippecanoe's waters meander through and past scenic wetlands, fields and forests, tree-lined banks, bubbling cold springs from high bluffs and banks, and small green islands.

The name "Tippecanoe" is derived from the Potawatomi Ki-tap-i-kon-nong, for "place of the buffalo fish." The Potawatomi established the Chip-pe-wa-nung village just north of Rochester, where they entered into nine treaties with the United States before being forced west to Kansas in 1838 on the Trail of Death. In 1811, the decisive Battle of Tippecanoe—where General William Henry Harrison defeated Tecumseh and a confederation of tribes—was fought along the river at Prophetstown State Park.

The Sugar Creek

The ninety-three-mile Sugar Creek originates in a farm field about ten miles east and south of Frankfort and travels west-southwest past Thorntown and through Crawfordsville before meeting the Wabash River five miles north of Montezuma. In its upper reaches, Sugar Creek flows through a broad and open glacial valley. But as it runs west and approaches the Wabash, the valley deepens and slices through some of the state's most dramatic, picturesque sandstone canyons and cliffs.

The Sugar Creek's path begins in open fields but quickly becomes tree lined, with the bankside cover gradually growing wider. Downstream from Crawfordsville, the creek valley contains the largest block of contiguous forest in Central Indiana, as well as two spectacular state parks—Shades State Park and Turkey Run State Park—and some of the state's most rugged terrain.

Formed by glacial meltwaters that began more than thirteen thousand years ago as the Wisconsin glacial ice sheets receded from Indiana, the ancient Sugar Creek Valley supported vast northern forests of birch and spruce like those of modern-day Northern Canada. The valley today supports relict stands of state rare eastern white pine and state watch-listed eastern hemlock, which survive at the far southern limit of their territory

White River, Muncie

here. Legend holds that a large village of Piankeshaw Indians, a branch of the Miami, lived on land that is now Shades State Park and that a decisive Native American battle was fought there.

The White River

The White River feeds the Wabash River at Mount Carmel, Illinois, thirty miles west of the merger of its East Fork and West Fork where Knox, Daviess, and Pike Counties meet. The two branches originate near one another in Henry and Randolph Counties, east and a little north of Indianapolis, not far from the Ohio state line. Following divergent paths to the southwest and their junction in Indiana coal country, the twin forks drain runoff from five other rivers and their tributaries. Indiana's second-largest river, the White drains a third of the state. The East Fork of the White River is shorter than the West Fork in terms of river miles, 192 versus 312. But it drains a larger area: 5,700 square miles versus 5,300.

The East Fork, which is by far the more complex ecosystem of the two, officially begins at Columbus in Southern Indiana.

But its origins lie in the till plain above Interstate 70 northeast of New Castle, where the Big Blue and Flatrock Rivers rise just a few miles apart. Each flows some one hundred miles south to Columbus, where they converge and form the East Fork's official headwaters.

The West Fork, by contrast, flows exclusively through Central Indiana's glaciated terrain; its valley, with limited exceptions, is mostly broad and flat. It rises a few miles southwest of Winchester in Randolph County near the Ohio state line and flows north for about ten miles before turning west along a moraine. For thirty miles the West Fork follows this ridge of glacial debris before heading southwest through the flatlands. Before crossing the Wisconsin glacial boundary into unglaciated Southern Indiana hill country near Martinsville, the West Fork bisects the cities of Muncie, Anderson, and Indianapolis.

While the West Fork is fed by multiple ditches, streams, and creeks, the other Eel River—not the Eel of the north—is its only river tributary. The Eel, which originates at the juncture of Big Walnut Creek and Mill Creek in southwest Putnam County, meets the West Fork in Greene County near Worthington.

Evidence of human life on the White River dates to prehistoric times. Mounds State Park, located just outside Anderson, features ten earthworks built by the Adena-Hopewell people around 160 BCE. Archaeology suggests the mounds were used as gathering places for religious ceremonies.

When the Europeans first arrived in Indiana in the late seventeenth century, the White River and Central Indiana were unsettled, though the Miami tribes dominated the state. The historically northeastern Delaware, or Lenape, began moving to both White River forks in the late 1700s. After the Battle of Fallen Timbers in northeastern Ohio in 1794, when the Delaware, Shawnee, and other tribes fell to General "Mad Anthony" Wayne, more Delaware joined their predecessors in Indiana at the Miami's invitation. Four years after the Battle of Tippecanoe in 1811, the Delaware ceded their lands to the Americans.

Five years later, when ten men were appointed by the young Indiana General Assembly to find a central location for a new state capital, they chose the confluence of the White River West Fork with the Fall Creek and named the city Indianapolis, which meant "land of the Indian."

Northern Indiana Physiography

Over billions of years, the geologic forces of rock, ice, and water transformed the northern part of the state into three distinct physiographic regions that are set apart by the natural features that exist at the earth's surface. The Northern Moraine and Lake Region, Maumee Lake Plain Region, and Central Till Plain Region of today are slightly redefined from their first characterizations in the *Handbook of Indiana Geology* (Logan 1922) by Indiana University geology professor Clyde A. Mallott. The moraine and till plain regions are subdivided into seven and five units, respectively.

All of Indiana's contemporary landforms are remnants of untold numbers of glacial advances and retreats over the past couple hundred thousand years, each of which radically reformed the earth surface in their wakes. Combined with thousands of years of human reformation, today's Northern Indiana landforms are remnants of the Wisconsin glacial event, which covered all of Northern Indiana's six natural regions before retreating roughly 13,600 years ago.

NORTHERN MORAINE AND LAKE REGION

The Northern Lake and Moraine Region covers all or parts of twenty-two counties from the Michigan-Indiana state line south to a ragged line from Newton to Allen Counties. As the retreating glaciers leveled and ground the landscape, in some places they deposited ridges of earth and rock known as moraines. In between, they scraped out depressions that became drainageways and small lakes. These lowland areas feature sand dunes, bogs, marshes, and plains, some of which rank among the best of their kind in the world.

Moraine Nature Preserve

The Northern Lake and Moraine Complex is divided into seven units: Lake Michigan Border, Valparaiso Morainal Complex, St. Joseph Drainageways, Kankakee Drainageways, Plymouth Morainal Complex, Warsaw Moraines and Drainageways, and Auburn Morainal Complex.

MAUMEE LAKE PLAIN REGION

The Maumee Lake Plain Region is by far the smallest physiographic unit in Indiana, essentially occupying the Maumee River Valley east of Fort Wayne through Allen County and small slices of southeast Dekalb and northeast Adams Counties. This region's landscape was formed as the post–Wisconsin glacial Lake Maumee's western shore receded through the ages into Lake Erie today.

CENTRAL TILL PLAIN REGION

The Central Till Plain stretches from border to border across Central Indiana, spanning all or parts of four-dozen counties south of the northern lakes and moraines to an uneven line from Vigo to Wayne Counties. In this region, the receding glaciers deposited great amounts of earthen material, or till, up to several hundred feet deep. Most of the land is flat to gently rolling, though there are small hills and ridges with gentle slopes.

Reliefs occur along rivers and creeks where glacial meltwaters carved through underlying bedrock. Some of the state's most dramatic bluffs and canyons occur along the Wabash River Valley from Tippecanoe to Parke Counties. Unexpectedly, Indiana's highest elevation—1,257 feet—is situated on rolling countryside on the southeastern edge of the Central Till Plain in northern Wayne County. The region's height is the result of underlying Ordivician bedrock, which is the highest in the state, topped with more than a hundred feet of glacial sediments.

The Central Till Plain Region is divided into five units: Central Wabash Valley, Iroquois Till Plain, Tipton Till Plain, Bluffton Till Plain, and New Castle Plains and Drainageways.

The Natural Regions

Northern Indiana is ecologically divided into six natural regions, as defined in the *Proceedings of the Indiana Academy of Science* in 1985. A team of researchers, led by Michael A. Homoya, the Indiana Department of Natural Resources' chief botanist/plant ecologist since 1982, defined *natural region* as "a major, generalized unit of the landscape where a distinctive assemblage of natural features is present. It is part of a classification system that integrates several natural features, including climate, soils, glacial history, topography, exposed bedrock, presettlement vegetation, species composition, physiography, and flora and fauna distribution to identify a natural region."

Natural regions can be subdivided into sections if "sufficient differences are evident such that recognition is warranted," the Homoya paper said. Three of the Northern Indiana's six natural regions—Northwestern Morainal, Grand Prairie, and Central Till Plain—are subdivided with three sections each.

LAKE MICHIGAN NATURAL REGION

The Lake Michigan Natural Region includes Indiana's portion of the southernmost Great Lake, which was formed by meltwater from the retreating Wisconsin glacial ice some thirteen thousand years ago. Like the Ohio River on the state's far southern boundary, this region's aquatic natural features differ from the rest of Indiana to a degree that justifies its designation as a separate natural region. Among the fish species unique to the lake are three state species of special concern: lake whitefish, longnose sucker, and slimy sculpin. Others that appear rarely or only occasionally include brook trout and lake trout.

NORTHWESTERN MORAINAL
NATURAL REGION

The Northwestern Morainal Natural Region fans outward from the Lake Michigan shoreline for about thirty miles south and twenty miles east. Formed by glacial deposits from the last advances of the Wisconsin ice sheets, this relatively tiny region supports tremendous ecological diversity, as eastern deciduous forest, tallgrass prairie, and northern forest and wetland merge along the Lake Michigan shoreline. The diversity of its floral species is unmatched in any other Indiana natural region, at least on an acre-by-acre basis.

While this region is small, populous, and heavily industrialized, some high-quality natural areas still exist. In postglacial times, the land was occupied by vast wetlands and was agriculturally weak, and therefore it was never cultivated or developed.

The Northwestern Morainal Natural Region is subdivided into three sections: Lake Michigan Border Section, Chicago Lake Plain Section, and Valparaiso Moraine Section.

Lake Michigan Border Section

The Lake Michigan Border Section, a narrow strip along the lakeshore, is characterized by three major natural features: beach, high dunes, and pannes, which reflect natural communities that border much of Indiana's forty-five miles of Lake Michigan shoreline. The beach community is an area of shifting sands along narrow stretches between Lake Michigan and the first line of dunes and the high dunes complex. The high dunes are more stable than the beach due to the plants that thrive in their environs. Woodlands downwind from the high dunes are a mixture of moist forest and savanna. Pannes are depressions between dunes that are composed of wet, chalky sand that is usually downwind from the first or second lines of dunes. Their unique plant compositions resemble fens.

Animal and plant species of concern in the Lake Michigan Border Section include the federally endangered piping plover, as well as the sea rocket, which is on the state watch list. Species that still survive elsewhere but are gone from Indiana include Hooker's orchids.

Chicago Lake Plain Section

The Chicago Lake Plain Section encompasses the ridge-and-swale and lake plain ecosystems that have formed between the Valparaiso Moraine and the Lake Michigan Border Section. The ridges and marshy lowlands that lie in between are remnants of water-level fluctuations from the Glacial Lake Chicago more than ten thousand years ago. Almost all this section is sand, with muck soils scattered throughout.

Major natural communities of this section include marsh, lake, sand savanna, sand prairie, and swamp, along with various forest types. The sand savannas are primarily two types: black oak and black oak-pine. Stands of black oak characterize the savannas throughout most of this section. The black oak-pine are supported by the dune complexes in this section's north part. The Chicago Lake Plain Section was dominated by marsh as Glacial Lake Chicago receded, especially along the Little Calumet and Grand Calumet Rivers. Given the similarities between the Chicago Lake Plains' natural communities and those of the Kankakee Sand Section of the Grand Prairie Natural

Region, it is not surprising that many of the same animals live in both.

Valparaiso Moraine Section

The Valparaiso Moraine Section is the Northwest Morainal Natural Region's southernmost section. In its eastern portions, this section features the knob-and-kettle topography of the Valparaiso Moraine. In the west, the land is gently rolling till plain. In presettlement times, the eastern portion was mostly forested; the western portion was prairie.

Fen, bog, lake, marsh, savanna, seep spring, and swamp are other natural communities that are supported in this section. The Valparaiso Moraine features some excellent fens, which are unforested areas of mineral-rich seepage that support high species diversity. The bogs are similar to those of the Northern Lakes Natural Region. The moist forest communities in this section mark the western limit of the beech-maple forest in the lower Lake Michigan area. The drier sites are mostly oak-hickory. The natural prairies are mostly gone, except for a few small relicts.

GRAND PRAIRIE NATURAL REGION

Natural areas in the Grand Prairie Natural Region, which stretches northeast from the Illinois state line a hundred miles or so south from Lake County to Vigo County, are dominated by tallgrass prairie. Its southern and eastern borders are the Wabash River Valley and the Maxinkuckee Moraine, a glacial ridge that runs north from Logansport.

The name Grand Prairie is derived from the vast grasslands that spread from this part of Northwest Indiana across much of Northern Illinois when the Europeans arrived in the late 1670s. The landform is glaciated plain on loose deposits of Wisconsin-age glacial debris that includes dune sand, lake sediments, sand and gravel outwash plain sediments, and till. Percentagewise, the Grand Prairie is the most altered natural region in the state,

Jasper-Pulaski Fish & Wildlife Area

with less than a thousand acres of its original two-million-acre landscape known to still exist.

The Grand Prairie Natural Region is subdivided into three sections: Grand Prairie Section, Kankakee Sand Section, and Kankakee Marsh Section.

Grand Prairie Section

The Grand Prairie Section is the southernmost of this natural region's three sections and differs from the other two in its predominance of loamy soil, as opposed to their sandy and highly organic soils.

Outwash and lake deposits supported the best of the tallgrass prairies that spread west before European encroachment in the late seventeenth century. While this landscape's variety of natural community types must have been extensive, all that is known about the species composition comes from small remnants in railroad rights-of-way and abandoned pioneer cemeteries. Other community types in the Grand Prairie Section include savanna, marsh, pond, bog (rare), and forest, the latter mostly along stream courses and in oak groves.

Kankakee Sand Section

The Kankakee Sand Section is composed of two irregularly shaped blocks that are separated by the Kankakee Marsh Section. This section is predominantly prairie and savanna that are associated with sandy soils and consist mostly of dune sand and outwash plain sediments.

The sand prairies and savannas support species composition similar to the Grand Prairie Section, although a number of sand-dwelling species are also present. Savannas dominated by black oak and prairie species occur on the dune areas. Swales between the dunes include wet prairie, marsh, swamp, wet sand flat, and wet muck flat communities. An unusual assemblage of plants with coastal plain affinities are found in the wet sand/muck flat communities. Natural forest communities occur primarily in the eastern part of the section, where white oak and black oak dominate. Pin oak flatwoods are common in some of the swales. State endangered clustered sedge, sandplain yellow flax, and creeping St. John's-wort thrive there.

Kankakee Marsh Section

The Kankakee Marsh Section skirts the southern edge of the Northwestern Morainal Natural Region on the west, bending northeast toward the Indiana-Michigan state line. Its nature preserves are dominated by marsh, lake, and wet prairie communities that existed along the Kankakee River and surrounding Grand Kankakee Marsh in presettlement times. The marsh was several miles wide on both sides of the river, which had more than two thousand turns and flowed 250 miles to travel 85 miles from South Bend to the Illinois state line. Extensive ditching from the late 1800s on effectively eliminated this section's natural wetlands. Good examples of the original prairie and marsh are rare. The area was formerly a significant breeding habitat for waterfowl.

NORTHERN LAKES NATURAL REGION

The Northern Lakes Natural Region is an angular block of freshwater lake country that stretches some eighty-five miles along the Michigan state line from the Grand Prairie Natural Region east to the Ohio state line. Influenced by various Wisconsin glacial ice sheets, this natural region is covered with thick, complex deposits of glacial material that are more than 450 feet thick in places. The retreating ice sheets left in their wake small, round lakes known as kettles, hills or mounds known as kames, and flatlands called outwash plains and valley trains.

Natural communities include bog, fen, marsh, prairie, sedge meadow, swamp, seep spring, lake, and various deciduous forest types. In presettlement times dry and dry-moist upland forests covered approximately one-half of the region.

Bogs are more frequent in the Northern Lakes than in any other of the state's natural regions. They commonly consist of floating mats of sphagnum moss occupying glacial depressions. Marsh areas are common around lake communities. Wet sand flats and muck flats border some of the lakes and shallow basins.

Plant species of concern in this region include the state endangered Missouri rockcress and horsetail spike rush. Fauna of the region include the state endangered marsh wren and the sandhill crane, a state species of special concern.

CENTRAL TILL PLAIN NATURAL REGION

With the exception of the Entrenched Valley Section, which follows this region's major watersheds on the west, the vast majority of the Central Till Plain Natural Region is topographically homogenous. These Central Indiana flatlands have evolved from presettlement times, when they occupied a forested plain of Wisconsin glacial till. But occupying land formed at the southern edge of the last glacial advance some 13,600 years ago, they do feature some glacial attributes, moraines in particular.

The region, which also includes the Tipton Till Plain and Bluffton Till Plain Sections, marks the geographic boundary between species with northern and southern affinities. The Entrenched Valley Section adds eastern- and western-leaning species to the ecological mix. Areas of prairie, marsh, fen, seep spring, bog, swamp, and lake survive alongside the predominant forest types.

Entrenched Valley Section

The Entrenched Valley Section is characterized by deep valleys along Western Indiana's major waterways, particularly the Wabash River, Big Pine Creek, Sugar Creek, and Big Walnut Creek. Bedrock of sandstone, siltstone, shale, and limestone from the Pennsylvanian, Mississippian, Devonian, and Silurian Periods is exposed in many places. Massive cliffs are common.

Major natural communities in the Entrenched Valley include upland forests, bottomland forests, and flatwoods. Except in the cliff and ravine communities, the forests are mostly northern flatwoods of beech, maple, and oak. Other natural community types include prairie, gravel hill prairie, fen, marsh, savanna, cliff, seep spring, and pond.

The nearly neutral seep spring is perhaps more common in the Entrenched Valley than anywhere else in Indiana. This community is typically situated on the lower slopes of hills, especially along large waterways, like the Wabash. Water diffuses through a muck soil and creates environments where plants such as the skunk cabbage, marsh marigold, and jewelweed thrive.

The Entrenched Valley's cliff and ravine communities support an unusual grouping of species, many with northern affinities. The state endangered Canada yew, state rare eastern white pine, and state watch-listed eastern hemlock, for example, lend the landscape a boreal appearance.

Gravel hill prairies are unique to the Entrenched Valley. Along with the typical grassland species, the gravel hill prairies also support rare species, including many that have southern and western affinities—the state threatened sand-dune wallflower and western rock jasmine among them.

This section marks the northern limit of several reptile and amphibian species, including cave salamander, zigzag salamander, long-tailed salamander, earth snake, and copperhead. Other rare or unusual species in the Entrenched Valley include state endangered plains muhly, Forbe's saxifrage, Canada yew, and velvetleaf blueberry and state rare forked aster.

Tipton Till Plain Section

The Tipton Till Plain Section is a mostly undissected plain that in presettlement times was covered by an extensive northern flatwood forest of beech, maple, and oak, a forest type now confined to scattered woodlots. Common forest species in the Tipton Till include red maple, pin oak, bur oak, swamp white oak, Shumard's oak, American elm, and green ash. Slightly better-drained sites include American beech, sugar maple, black maple, white oak, red oak, shagbark hickory, tulip poplar, basswood, and white ash. Other community types include bog, prairie, marsh, seep spring, pond, and a few fens.

Bluffton Till Plain Section

The Bluffton Till Plain Section occupies a relatively level plain that was one of the last areas of the state to be covered by glacial ice. Indeed, the Union City Moraine in Indiana and Ohio marks the Wisconsin ice sheet's southernmost penetration. It features a distinct series of moraines.

Natural communities are mostly forested, with bog, prairie, fen, marsh, and lake communities. Forest species are similar to the Tipton Till Plain's, with the addition of swamp cottonwood, which formerly occurred regularly in swamps in the Bluffton Till Plain.

Northern wetland species—cotton grass and northern St. John's-wort, for example—are more common in the Bluffton Till than in the Tipton Till and Entrenched Valley Sections. The state watch-listed large marsh St. John's-wort and the state threatened log sedge—southern swamp species—survive in the Bluffton Till Plain.

BLACK SWAMP NATURAL REGION

The Black Swamp Natural Region, which forms a broad, sideways U shape from Fort Wayne east through Allen County to the Ohio state line, is the western lobe of a large lake plain occupying what was the Glacial Lake Maumee. Formed when Wisconsin glacial meltwater was dammed at the Fort Wayne Moraine, the lake shrank over thousands of years to modern Lake Erie, leaving behind a floodplain that settlers called the Great Black Swamp.

This natural region was predominantly swamp forest dominated by American elm, black ash, red maple, and silver maple when the Americans occupied the landscape in the early nineteenth century. Extensive agricultural draining has virtually eliminated the swamp forest ecosystem from this region of Indiana today.

Part 3

DESTINATIONS

Section 1

LAKE MICHIGAN NATURAL REGION

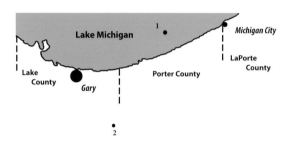

NORTHWESTERN MORAINAL NATURAL REGION

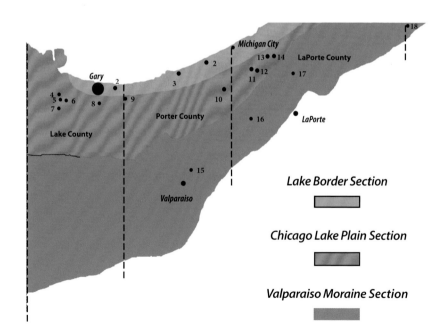

Section 1

LAKE MICHIGAN NATURAL REGION
1. J. D. Marshall Preserve

NORTHWESTERN MORAINAL NATURAL REGION

Lake Border Section
2. Indiana Dunes National Lakeshore / Cowles Bog / Pinhook Bog
3. Indiana Dunes State Park / Dunes Nature Preserve / Dunes Prairie Nature Preserve

Chicago Lake Plain Section
4. Gibson Woods Nature Preserve / Tolleston Strand Plain
5. Seidner Dune and Swale Nature Preserve
6. Ivanhoe Dune and Swale Nature Preserve / Ivanhoe South Nature Preserve
7. Hoosier Prairie Nature Preserve
8. Cressmoor Prairie Nature Preserve
9. John Merle Coulter Nature Preserve
10. Reynolds Creek Game Bird Area
11. Barker Woods Nature Preserve
12. Trail Creek Fen
13. Ambler Flatwoods Nature Preserve
14. Wintergreen Woods Nature Preserve

Valparaiso Moraine Section
15. Moraine Nature Preserve
16. Little Calumet Headwaters Nature Preserve
17. Springfield Fen Nature Preserve / Galena Marsh Wetland Conservation Area
18. Spicer Lake Nature Preserve

Lake Michigan

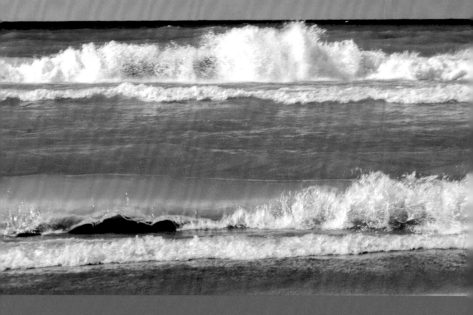

LAKE MICHIGAN
NATURAL REGION

LAKE MICHIGAN NATURAL REGION

1. J. D. Marshall Preserve

Owned by Indiana Department of Natural Resources,
Division of State Parks & Lakes

The one-hundred-acre J. D. Marshall Preserve is situated six hundred yards off the Indiana Dunes State Park shoreline *in* Lake Michigan. Indiana's first and only underwater dedicated state nature preserve, Marshall was established in 2013 to protect the cultural values embodied by the *J. D. Marshall* shipwreck and to preserve this portion of the Lake Michigan Natural Region. The preserve is accessible by canoe, kayak, and nonmotorized fishing boat with a draft less than eight feet. Anchoring is not permitted.

In addition to preserving unique natural characteristics on land and water, state nature preserves are also established to promote understanding and appreciation of cultural values— to protect them against threats. At the Marshall preserve, the goals are to keep the ship in an undisturbed condition and educate the public on the role shipwrecks play in history and culture.

The *J. D. Marshall* was a 154-foot steam-powered transport ship built in 1891 that capsized in a storm in 1911, reportedly carrying one thousand tons of sand. The captain and six crewmen survived; four crew members died. Archaeologists have documented fourteen shipwreck sites in Indiana's 241 square miles of Lake Michigan. More ships have sunk, but their wreckages have been covered or destroyed by sand, waves, and ice.

The Marshall preserve includes the shipwreck and associated debris field. The boundary lines are denoted by seasonally placed marker buoys along the northern edge and at the corners. They extend vertically from the lake bed into space. Mooring buoys for fishing or diving within the preserve boundary may be placed. Access to the J. D. Marshall Preserve, as well as information and artifacts, is available at the Indiana Dunes State Park Nature Center. The park offers educational programs on Marshall and other shipwrecks in Lake Michigan.

Activities

Boating (paddling only, boats with less than eight feet draw), diving, fishing, nature study, photography.

Directions to Dunes State Park

GPS coordinates: 41.657692, –87.063892

From I-65

- East on I-94 to State Road 49, 14.0 miles
- North on State 49 to State Park Road and park, 2.6 miles

From US 31

- West on I-80/I-90 (Toll Road) at South Bend to State Road 39, 23.0 miles
- North on State Road 39 to US 20, 1.5 miles
- West on US 20 to I-94, 3.5 miles
- West on I-94 to State Road 49, 13.6 miles
- North on State 49 to State Park Road and park, 2.6 miles

Indiana Dunes
National Lakeshore

NORTHWESTERN MORAINAL
NATURAL REGION

NORTHWESTERN MORAINAL NATURAL REGION

Lake Border Section

2a. Indiana Dunes National Lakeshore
Owned by National Park Service

The fifteen-thousand-acre Indiana Dunes National Lakeshore lines and protects fifteen miles of Indiana's Lake Michigan shoreline, from Gary to Michigan City. Its sandy landforms span Lake, Porter, and LaPorte Counties, encompass the Indiana Dunes State Park, and protect three National Natural Landmarks. At Miller Woods, the Lakeshore literally occupies the southernmost point of the entire Great Lakes.

This fraction of the world's largest freshwater lakes complex is the only natural area in Indiana that is part of the National Park System. With support from the entire Indiana congressional delegation, a bill that would elevate the National Lakeshore's status to National Park passed the US House of Representatives in November 2017 and awaits action in the US Senate..

In addition to supporting one of the most biodiverse natural areas in the world, the Indiana Dunes National Lakeshore also offers a diverse variety of recreational opportunities, including undeveloped beaches, hiking trails, boat launches, river walks, scenic overlooks, historic sites, a biking trail, and a campground.

Situated just east of Chicago in one of the planet's most heavily populated and industrialized regions, the Lakeshore's natural features include beaches, sand dunes, oak savannas, prairies, forests, swamps, bogs, marshes, fens, ponds, lakes, and a river. Inland from the beaches, sand dunes climb nearly two hundred feet through a series of ridges, blowouts, and valleys. Interdunal wetlands soak many of the depressions between the dune ridges.

The National Lakeshore is composed of two separate lakeshore blocks. The smaller, western section runs from Gary to Ogden Dunes; the larger stretches from Portage to Michigan

City and surrounds the state park. Both are further dissected by highways and local roads. In places, they surround small towns and industrial facilities—Dune Acres, Beverly Shores, and Burns Harbor, for example.

The park also includes two inland sites: Pinhook Bog, which is a National Natural Landmark (NNL), and Heron Rookery, which abuts the state's Reynolds Creek Game Bird Area, parallels the Little Calumet River's upper reaches, and is named for a great blue nesting colony on its heavily wooded northeastern section.

Supporting more than eleven hundred flowering plants and ferns, the Indiana Dunes National Lakeshore's biological diversity ranks among the highest in the nation, ranging from bog plants to native prairie grasses, from rare algae to towering eastern white pine trees, the latter of which are state rare.

The habitat range supports several hundred animals—more than three hundred and fifty bird species among them. The sandy landforms offer prime feeding and resting areas for migrating land and water birds, including several rare loons, bitterns, raptors, gulls, and terns.

The seventy-five-acre Miller Woods and the adjacent Gary Parks Department's Marquette Park have jointly been designated an Important Bird Area (IBA) by the National Audubon Society. Together they protect two miles of beach and dune habitat at Lake Michigan's southernmost point. "For migratory birds and their habitat, this is a critical position along the Great Lakes migration route," the Audubon Society says on its website, calling Miller Woods "one of the most critical sites for migrating waterfowl, shorebirds, and waterbirds in Indiana."

Its environs support parasitic jaeger, long-tailed jaeger, and pomarine jaeger, which are rare in the Great Lakes but frequent Miller Woods from August through November. The federally endangered piping plover, state endangered golden-winged warbler and black tern, and state species of special concern buff-breasted sandpiper have been recorded in the area, as have the Audubon WatchListed whimbrel, red knot, wood thrush, and

Canada warbler. Other species of note include common tern, Hudsonian godwit, and marbled godwit.

Miller's landscape, which occupies part the Lakeshore's western end, features high dunes, prime foredunes, and oak savannas, along with interdunal ponds, marshes, and lagoons. It's accessible from the Paul H. Douglas Center for Environmental Education. One of the Lakeshore's better-known natural features, the 126-foot-tall Mount Baldy just west of Michigan City, is closed to the public due to unstable conditions. Baldy is a living dune that is constantly reshaping and drifting inland, burying trees as it does. Over time, the decaying trees leave holes inside this ever-changing dune, which leads to periodic collapses. The Mount Baldy beach is safe and open.

The Indiana Dunes National Lakeshore—modeled after the Cape Cod National Seashore—was dedicated in 1972 after more than a half century of citizen pushback against Indiana politicians' plans to industrialize the state's entire lakeshore. Grassroots efforts launched in 1916 to establish the Indiana Dunes State Park succeeded in 1925. The Dorothy Buell Memorial Visitor Center is named for one of the most prominent of those preservationists; Buell founded the Save the Dunes Council in 1952. The Douglas Center is named for the Republican Illinois senator who led the political fight in Congress for the dunes' preservation.

In addition to the National Lakeshore, the National Park Service operates two other historic sites in Indiana: the George Rogers Clark National Historic Park at Vincennes and the Lincoln Boyhood Memorial at Lincoln City, just north of the Ohio River.

From Ice to Beach: The National Lakeshore's Evolution
The Indiana Dunes National Lakeshore occupies a small portion of the twenty-two-thousand-square-mile Lake Michigan ecosystem, a remnant of the Glacial Lake Chicago that covered the region as the last Ice Age glacier receded about thirteen thousand years ago. Lake Chicago's eastern cousin, Glacial Lake Maumee, extended to Fort Wayne and left Lake Erie in its place.

As these Wisconsin Era ice sheets slowly retreated north, they left behind ridgelines composed of glacial deposits of earth and rock called moraines that formed rims around the lake basins. The U-shaped Valparaiso Moraine, Lake Michigan's largest, shadows the lakeshore from the Illinois-Wisconsin state line, through Northwest Indiana, to a hundred miles north of the Indiana-Michigan state line. Between that ridgeline and the lake, glacial water levels fluctuated through the ages, creating as many as seven successive shorelines, reaching as far inland as Dyer in Lake County.

Four of these historic dune complexes are evident today in the Indiana Dunes National Lakeshore, from oldest to youngest they are the Glenwood, the Calumet, the Tolleston, and the present dune formations. Their landmasses support open beaches, blowouts, ridges covered with grasses and woody shrubs, pine-forested dunes, oak savannas, and prairies.

The older two dunes are stabilized by oak forest communities. The younger two are still being formed and reformed by the lake environment's constantly changing winds, waves, currents, ice, and storms. In summer, the beaches slope slightly; in winter, they are narrower and steeper. The younger dunes support plant life in all stages of succession.

Activities

Hiking Trails: Fourteen trail systems with 50 miles of trails, easy to rugged, 0.5 to 4.7 miles.

Multiuse Trails: Calumet Trail (9.2 miles)—biking, cross-country skiing (no ski rental), running.

Camping: Sixty-six campsites, fifty-four drive-ins, twelve walk-ins, four fully accessible; restrooms and showers; no electric or water hookups; accessible to visitors with mobility impairments. Some sites limit recreational vehicle length.

Other Activities: Biking, boating, fishing, horseback riding, nature study, photography, picnicking, wildlife watching, winter activities.

Directions to Dunes National Lakeshore Visitor Center
GPS coordinates: 41.633376, –87.053812
From I-65
- East on I-94 to State Road 49, 14.1 miles
- Northwest on State Road 49 to visitor center, 0.7 mile

From US 31
- West on I-80/I-90 (Toll Road) at South Bend to State Road 39, 23.0 miles
- North on State Road 39 to US 20, 1.5 miles
- West on US 20 to I-94, 3.5 miles
- West on I-94 to State Road 49, 13.6 miles
- Northwest on State Road 49 to visitor center, 0.7 mile

2b. Cowles Bog: National Natural Landmark

The 205-acre Cowles Bog has been called the birthplace of ecology because of studies conducted there by University of Chicago botany professor Henry Chandler Cowles more than a century ago. Before joining the faculty in 1901, this pioneer in the emerging field of ecology wrote a dissertation titled "An Ecological Study of the Sand Dune Flora of Northern Indiana." Throughout his tenure, Cowles continued working the Indiana site and using it as a learning lab for his students.

Today, this National Natural Landmark protects locally rare flora, along with marsh and bog wetlands that are in transition to swamp. More accurately defined as a fen due to its higher alkalinity, Cowles Bog features ponds, marshes, swamps, black oak savannas, beaches, and steep sand dunes on Lake Michigan. Heading inland from the dunes, surrounding the gated, lakeside town of Dune Acres, the main body is composed of muck created by the encroachment of marsh and woody plants. Wet depressions extend south through the marsh area.

Over the last half century, Cowles Bog has succeeded to more wetland woods than actual bog and is dominated by red maple and yellow birch. The noticeably open bog of the 1960s has effectively closed. The herb layer includes columbine, common boneset, jewelweed, mayapple, hispid green brier, narrow-leaved

Cowles Bog, Indiana Dunes National Lakeshore

cattail, and grape. The shrubs along the bog's edge include spicebush and poison sumac, whose predominance makes access difficult.

Through the Cowles Bog Wetlands Complex Restoration Project, the Park Service has reintroduced native plant species to the preserve, which in turn attract native insects and animals. The project's goal is to increase native plant and animal diversity, provide resting areas for migratory birds, protect rare plants, create high-quality plant and animal habitat, protect the beaches, improve lake water quality by reducing and controlling runoff, enhance educational opportunities for the public, and leave a natural resource legacy for future generations.

The once common, now state watch-listed, northern pitcher plant has disappeared due to poaching.

Activities
Hiking Trails: One (4.7 miles), strenuous.
Other Activities: Nature study, photography, wildlife watching.

GPS coordinates: 41.644996, –87.086643
From Dunes National Lakeshore Visitor Center
- Northwest on State Road 49 to US 12, 1.0 mile
- West on US 12 to Mineral Springs Road, 1.3 miles
- North on Mineral Springs Road to bog, 0.7 mile

2c. Pinhook Bog: National Natural Landmark

The 580-acre Pinhook Bog has been called Indiana's best and only "true bog," a type of wetland defined by a limited exchange of water. Pinhook's only water source is runoff from higher ground, so the only moisture loss is through evaporation from plants and surface water.

Located south of Michigan City about nine miles inland near the headwaters of the Little Calumet River, this National Natural Landmark is separate from the rest of the Indiana Dunes National Lakeshore. The Pinhook Trail System features two branches. The Upland Trail passes through a beech-maple forest on a glacial moraine; the Bog Trail, with its floating board-walk, leads to a bog in a depression in the moraine. Due to its fragile ecosystem, the Bog Trail is closed to the public and accessible only through regularly scheduled interpretive walks with park rangers.

Pinhook Bog offers a prime example of ecological succession from pond to woodland. The site lies within a kettle—a bowl-shaped depression created by retreating glaciers—that is surrounded by wooded hills. A sister bog, Volo Bog, is located nearby. Pinhook's kettle formed at the end of the Wisconsin glacial event when a large chunk of ice broke from its parent glacier and remained buried there as the ice receded north. As the environment warmed and the ice melted, clay soil sealed the basins.

This natural landmark's outstanding feature is the tree-covered mat of stringy, delicate, light-green sphagnum moss that floats atop the water and occupies a quarter of its surface. It is three to six feet deep, with pockets only a few inches thick in the middle. As the mat thickens, larger plants take root, and a peat bed develops underneath. In pioneer days, the moss was used as an antiseptic for wound care. The mat is separated from the uplands by a moat. Over time, the peat will fill the bog to the bottom. As the moisture becomes less acidic, land plants will take root, and the bog will disappear.

Pinhook Bog supports a range of plants that includes a variety of insect-eaters, state watch-listed tamarack trees, and stands of blueberry bushes. Although the tamarack is a conifer, its needles turn gold in the fall and drop in the winter. Poison sumac is prevalent in the bog area, particularly around the moat. Carnivorous plants at the preserve include the state endangered hidden-fruited bladderwort and state threatened horned bladderwort.

Activities
Hiking Trails: Two (0.5–1.7 miles), easy to moderate. (Bog Trail accessible only through regularly scheduled interpretive walks with park rangers.)
Other Activities: Nature study, photography, wildlife watching.

Directions
GPS coordinates 41.621068, –86.851011
From Dunes National Lakeshore Visitor Center
- South on State Road 49 to I-94, 0.7 mile
- East on I-94 to US 421, 8.5 miles
- South on US 421 to Snyder Road, 1.3 miles
- East on Snyder Road to North Wozniak Road, 2.3 miles
- South on North Wozniak Road to preserve, 1.0 mile

3a. Indiana Dunes State Park
Owned by Indiana Department of Natural Resources,
Division of State Parks & Lakes
The 2,182-acre Indiana Dunes State Park in Porter County is part of a more than seventeen-thousand-acre Lake Michigan dunescape that supports one of the most diverse plant and animal collections in the nation. Surrounded by the fifteen-thousand-acre

Indiana Dunes State Park

Indiana Dunes National Lakeshore, the state park's environs include a range of natural habitats: beach, sand dune, black oak forest, savanna, marsh, swamp, prairie, wooded wetland, and buttonbush swamp.

The preserve's eastern two-thirds are set aside as the 1,530-acre Dunes Nature Preserve, which is a National Natural Landmark and dedicated state nature preserve. (See the Dunes Nature Preserve below.) The Dunes Prairie Nature Preserve, also a dedicated state nature preserve, occupies fifty-eight acres of the southwest corner. (See the Dunes Prairie Nature Preserve below.)

Indiana Dunes State Park sprawls along three miles of Lake Michigan beach, hemmed in by dunes that rise in places nearly two hundred feet above the shoreline. More than sixteen miles of hiking trails traverse this ever-changing landscape, which, while it's been thirteen thousand years in the making, is still composed of "living" or "moving" dunes that are slowly blowing inland. As the dunes reconstitute, they bury the inland forests that have stabilized the dune formations through the ages. In places within the park, buried trees are being reexposed by wind erosion—a natural phenomenon known as a tree graveyard.

As part of the Indiana Dunes National Lakeshore complex, the Dunes State Park shares the national park's natural characteristics. (See the Indiana Dunes National Lakeshore above.) Dunes State Park was established in 1925—forty years before the National Lakeshore—under pressure from scientists, recreationists, and nature enthusiasts who were concerned about the rapid industrialization of Indiana's Lake Michigan shoreline.

Activities
Hiking Trails: Seven (0.75–5.5 miles), easy to rugged.
Multiuse Trails: Calumet Trail (9.2 miles), Indiana Dunes National Lakeshore, adjacent to Indiana Dunes State Park—Biking, cross country skiing (no ski rental), running.
Camping: 140 electric (fifty-amp) comfort stations heated year-round, flush toilets, hot water and showers; concession; youth tent area.
Other Activities: Fishing (smelt only), nature study, nature center and interpretive naturalist services, photography, picnicking, shelters, swimming beach, wildlife watching.

Directions
GPS coordinates: 41.657692, –87.063892
From I-65
- East on I-94 to State Road 49, 14.0 miles
- North on State Road 49 to State Park Road and park, 2.6 miles

From US 31
- West on I-80/I-90 (Toll Road) at South Bend to State Road 39, 23.0 miles
- North on State Road 39 to US 20, 1.5 miles
- West on US 20 to I-94, 3.5 miles
- West on I-94 to State Road 49, 13.6 miles
- North on State Road 49 to State Park Road and park, 2.6 miles

3b. Dunes Nature Preserve: National Natural Landmark

The 1,532-acre Dunes Nature Preserve occupies the eastern two-thirds of the Indiana Dunes State Park and represents the best surviving remnant of undeveloped and relatively unspoiled dunescape along Lake Michigan's southern shore. This National Natural Landmark and dedicated state nature preserve also contains the Ancient Pines Nature Area, a prehistoric tree graveyard that is exposed by dune blowouts. The bulk of the park's trails pass through the nature preserve.

From the lake through the foredunes, interdunes, and backdunes, the Dunes Nature Preserve's landscape features bearberry (also known as kinnikinnick), sumac, sand cherry, eastern cottonwood, prostrate juniper, and isolated stands of state rare jack pine. The sand hills, which peak at the 186-foot Mt. Tom, feature swales and blowouts. Nearly pure stands of black oak, mixed with a few white oaks and stunted sassafras, thrive in the protected environs, along with thick stands of blueberry and green brier in the understory.

Dunes Creek drains a wetland area in the preserve that supports marsh, shrub swamp, and swamp forest. A strip of sandy flats occupies the landscape between the dunes and the wetland, with one sheltered cove supporting native state rare white pines, along with oak, tulip, white ash, and basswood trees. Past the wetland, the preserve's southern boundary represents one of Glacial Lake Chicago's earlier shorelines.

Activities
Hiking, nature study, photography, wildlife watching.

Directions
North from park entrance at State Park Road to parking lots at either the pavilion, nature center, or Wilson's Shelter.

3c. Dunes Prairie Nature Preserve

The fifty-eight-acre Dunes Prairie Nature Preserve contains a significant prairie remnant and a tributary of Dunes Creek.

Natural features include black oak savanna, swamp forest, and grassy dune, as well as outstanding prairie and wildflowers. The state uses controlled burns on this dedicated state nature preserve to keep these natural communities healthy.

Activities
Hiking, nature study, photography, wildlife watching.

Directions
Preserve is accessible via trail from the parking lot by the gatehouse.

Chicago Lake Plain Section

4a. Gibson Woods Nature Preserve
Owned by Lake County Parks and Recreation
The 179-acre Gibson Woods Nature Preserve in Lake County is the largest of three nature preserves that The Nature Conservancy collectively calls the Tolleston Strand Plain. Together, Gibson, Ivanhoe Dune and Swale, and Seidner Dune and Swale protect rare relicts of the dune-and-swale natural community that has largely disappeared from the region over the past couple thousand years.

The Nature Conservancy's Guide to Indiana Preserves calls these sites "oases of natural beauty in a hostile landscape of highways, factories, and homes." Located within three miles of each other along the Interstate 90 corridor, their combined more than four hundred acres support a high concentration of biodiversity and a range of species of concern.

Gibson Woods protects a large remnant of globally rare dune-and-swale topography, as well as the Midwest's longest unbroken dune ridge outside of the Indiana Dunes National Lakeshore. Its natural communities include dry-moist sand savanna, moist sand prairie, and wet-moist forest. The parallel sand ridges support "one of the rarest ecosystems in the world, the black oak savanna, characterized by scattered black oak trees with prairie plants growing beneath them," according to the Gibson Woods trail map.

Gibson Woods Nature Preserve

Among the rare plants that survive at Gibson Woods are state endangered calamint; state rare golden sedge, fire cherry, and beach sumac; and state watch-listed speckled alder, paper birch, and butternut. Big bluestem grass and tall coreopsis dominate the prairie. The rare Franklin's ground squirrel is among the preserve's wide variety of wildlife.

Gibson Woods, which served as hunting grounds for the Potawatomi Indians in presettlement times, remained uninhabited by European Americans until the early 1850s, when the Michigan Central Railroad arrived. Named after what was called the Gibson Station to the west, the woods remained railroad property until it was purchased in 1980 by The Nature Conservancy. A year later the Lake County Parks and Recreation Department purchased the tract, and it was designated a dedicated state nature preserve.

The preserve is among the natural areas studied in the late nineteenth and early twentieth centuries by University of Chicago Professor Henry Chandler Cowles, also sometimes called the father of ecology. (See Cowles Bog in the Dune National Lakeshore section.)

4b. The Tolleston Strand Plain

The Tolleston Strand Plain's globally unique landscape features a series of roughly parallel sandy ridges and low, wet swales that were formed through the ages by glacial activity, wind, and weather. Lake Michigan's irregular cycles of low and high water have also contributed. Lake levels have dropped sixty feet from Glacial Lake Chicago levels more than ten thousand years ago to Lake Michigan's today. In the prehistoric past, the line of sandy ridges extended unbroken from Southwest Michigan, through Northwest Indiana, to Lake Calumet in Chicago.

Today the Tolleston dunes complex, which marks the lake's last major inland advance some five thousand years ago, includes high dune ridges that run from Michigan to the Miller area of Gary, where they fan out into the strand plain, a series of lower beach ridges.

The strand plain's remarkable biodiversity is a consequence of its unique geography—situated where the prairies from the west met the deciduous and boreal forests from the east and north. A number of species that prefer the lake's cool microclimates exist here at the southern ends of their ranges. Lake hydrology produces a variety of habitats—moisture levels range from dry sand savannas to open water ponds—that support a range of animal species.

Prairie wildflowers include hoary puccoon, Carolina rose, prairie phlox, and wild lupine. The swales are characterized by buttonbush swamp and sedge meadows, with wetlands forming when the swales dip into the groundwater table.

While habitat loss due to the lake region's industrialization has dramatically altered the Tolleston Strand Plain's species mix, these preserves collectively support more than 270 native plant and sixty butterfly species. Among the latter are nearly two dozen species that are rare, threatened, endangered, or of special concern in Indiana.

Activities

Hiking Trails: Three (0.5–1.6 miles), easy.

Other Activities: Nature center with naturalist services, nature study, photography, wildlife watching.

Directions

GPS coordinates: 41.599381, –87.451853

From I-65

- West on I-80/94 to Kennedy Avenue, 8.0 miles
- North on Kennedy Avenue to 165th Street, 1.3 miles
- East on 165th Street to Parrish Avenue, 0.5 mile
- North on Parrish Avenue to the preserve and nature center, 0.3 mile

5. Seidner Dune and Swale Nature Preserve

Owned by Shirley Heinze Land Trust

The forty-three-acre Seidner Dune and Swale Nature Preserve in the city of Hammond features globally rare dune-and-swale topography, with wetlands, black oak savanna, and floodplain marsh along the Grand Calumet River. Natural communities also include sand prairie, sedge meadow, cattail marsh, and buttonbush swamp, all of which support a diverse variety of plants and animals.

More than 250 plant species have been identified on this Lake County site, including wild lupine, harebell, fringed gentian, blue flag iris, white wild indigo, side-oats grama grass, and prairie lily. Egrets, herons, cormorants, and other birds are common along the river during the summer.

The triangular-shaped Seidner Dune and Swale preserve is bordered by an industrial plant, Interstate 90, and the Grand Calumet River. It is managed to maintain biological diversity and preserve the fire-dependent communities that occur here.

(See the Tolleston Strand Plain in the Gibson Woods section for more history and site details.)

Activities

Hiking Trails: Informal, frontage road and abandoned railroad beds, no maintained system.

Other Activities: Nature study, photography, wildlife watching.

Directions
GPS coordinates: 41.611176, −87.457336
From I-65
- West on I-80/94 to Kennedy Avenue, 8.0 miles
- North on Kennedy Avenue to first unnamed road past I-90, which leads to the back entrance of the RESCO Products plant and the preserve, 2.4 miles
- Park at bend in road and walk through the cable gate onto the dirt road leading east.

6. Ivanhoe Dune and Swale Nature Preserve / Ivanhoe South Nature Preserve
Owned by The Nature Conservancy and Shirley Heinze Land Trust
The 155-acre Ivanhoe Dune and Swale complex in Lake County is among the finest examples of globally rare dune-and-swale remnants in the state. The preserved area is made up of two separate preserves: the 105-acre Ivanhoe Dune and Swale Nature Preserve, a dedicated state nature preserve owned by The Nature Conservancy, and the fifty-acre Ivanhoe South Nature Preserve, which is owned by the Shirley Heinze Land Trust.

Both preserves feature dune ridges that transition through prairie patches and grade into swales. The ridges support scattered black oaks, with an understory of prairie grasses and wildflowers, such as puccoons, spiderworts, and phloxes. Buttonbush swamp and sedge meadow dominate the swales, which also support wet prairie and marsh.

(See the Tolleston Strand Plain section of the Gibson Woods section for more history and site details.)

Activities
Hiking Trails: Interpretive, minimal walking trails. (Please be careful not to disturb nesting birds.)
Other Activities: Nature study, photography, wildlife watching.

Directions to Ivanhoe Dune and Swale Nature Preserve
GPS coordinates: 41.607967, −87.416778

From I-65

- West on I-80/94 to Cline Avenue (State Road 912), 6.6 miles
- North on Cline Avenue (State Road 912) to US 20 (West 5th Avenue), 2.2 miles
- East on US 20 to Hobart Street, 0.8 mile
- North on Hobart Street to the preserve at the dead end, 0.4 mile
- Move the barrier, drive in, park, and move the barrier back. You may want to place a sign on your front dashboard indicating that you are there to visit the preserve.

Directions to Ivanhoe South Nature Preserve
GPS coordinates: 41.597957, –87.413195
From I-80/94

- North on Cline Avenue (State Road 912) to US 20 (5th Avenue), 2.0 miles
- East on US 20 to Colfax Street, 0.8 mile
- South on Colfax Street to the parking lot just before the railroad tracks, 0.3 mile

7. Hoosier Prairie Nature Preserve

Owned by Indiana Department of Natural Resources,
Division of Nature Preserves, comanaged by National Park Service
The 1,547-acre Hoosier Prairie Nature Preserve in Lake County protects the state's last large tract of tallgrass prairie, which once swept west from Northwest Indiana through Illinois to Western Iowa. This National Natural Landmark occupies the rolling sand plains north of the Valparaiso Moraine and supports sand prairie, wet prairie, marsh, sedge meadow, and savanna habitats. A dedicated state nature preserve inside the Hoosier Prairie preserve protects 430 acres of remnant prairie—the state's largest relict of native prairie habitat.

Black oak barrens thrive on the Hoosier Prairie's ridgetops. The sandy rises support black oak savannas. Moist sand prairie openings occupy the slopes between the rises and swales. Seasonally wet prairies, sedge meadows, and marshes lie in the depressions and flats.

Hoosier Prairie Nature Preserve

The preserve protects more than 350 native plant species. Roughly 12 percent are uncommon in Indiana. They include state watch-listed sweetfern, along with marsh blazing star, prairie sundrop, marsh phlox, Indian paintbrush, white wild indigo, rattlesnake master, leadplant, wild quinine, swamp milkweed, slender gerardia, blue flag iris, big bluestem, Indian grass, blue joint grass, and bracken fern.

State endangered sedge wrens inhabit the prairie and savanna. Other birds that frequent the preserve include red-headed woodpeckers, goldfinches, bobolinks, meadowlarks, yellowthroats, swamp sparrows, woodcocks, and red-tailed hawks. Mammals include white-tailed deer, minks, red foxes, and groundhogs. The wet prairie potholes support unusual plants, reptiles, and amphibians.

Prior to European settlement, fire played an integral role in prairie ecosystems, keeping trees to a minimum and producing prairie plants that adapted and survived fires caused by lightning strikes or Native American campfire sparks. Controlled

burns are used today to maintain the Hoosier Prairie's presettlement conditions.

The Hoosier Prairie Nature Preserve is located on Griffith's
East Main Street, where the city meets Schererville and
Highland. It is surrounded by homes, industry, busy streets,
and a railroad track. Main Street divides the preserve, though
no trails exist on the northern piece.

Activities
Hiking Trails: Self-guided (0.7 mile), accessible, easy.
Other Activities: Nature study, photography, wildlife watching.

Directions
GPS coordinates: 41.522918, −87.457556
From Dunes National Lakeshore Visitors Center
- Southeast on State Road 49 to I-94, 0.7 mile
- West on I-94 to Cline Avenue (State Road 912), 12.5 miles
- South on Cline Avenue (State Road 912) to Main Street in
  Griffith, 3.3 miles
- West on Main Street to preserve, 1.1 miles

8. Cressmoor Prairie Nature Preserve
Owned by Shirley Heinze Land Trust
The forty-one-acre Cressmoor Prairie Nature Preserve in
Lake County is the largest remnant of black-soil prairie left in
Indiana. This dedicated state nature preserve, located in the
city of Hobart and bordered by residential housing, a country
club, and a railroad track, supports one of the most biodiverse
ecosystems in the state.

Featuring tallgrass prairie, oak savanna, woodlands, and
wetlands, Cressmoor Prairie supports more than 250 species of
plants, including several that are threatened or endangered and
depend upon this ecosystem for survival. Typical prairie species
at the preserve include wild quinine, marsh blazing star, rattlesnake master, prairie dock, compass plant, and swamp milkweed. Others include black-eyed Susan, gray-headed coneflower,
Culver's root, whorled milkweed, tall coreopsis, wild bergamot,
and prairie dock. Cressmoor preserve's prairie grasses reach

Cressmoor Prairie Nature Preserve

eight feet tall in late summer and early fall, when its world-class wildflower display peaks. In turn, butterflies swarm to the wildflowers. In the fall, monarchs stop by on their way to Mexico.

Black-soil prairies were the most common grasslands in Indiana when the Europeans arrived in the late eighteenth century. But their rich soils were among the most fertile in the world, and the grasses were largely plowed under for agriculture and grazing.

Activities
Hiking Trails: One loop (0.5–0.75 miles), easy.
Other Activities: Nature study, photography, wildlife watching.

Directions
GPS coordinates: 41.544961, –87.259969
From I-65
- East on Ridge Road (Business US 6, East 37th Avenue) to Lake Park Avenue, 2.8 miles
- South on Lake Park Avenue to preserve on west side of road, 0.4 mile

From US 31

- Northwest on US 30 at Plymouth to County Road 600E at Hamlet, 16.1 miles
- North on County Road 600E to US 6, 6.0 miles
- West on US 6 to West 37th Avenue, 37.4 miles
- West on West 37th Avenue to Lake Park Avenue, 1.0 mile
- South on Lake Park Avenue to preserve on west side of road, 0.4 mile

9. John Merle Coulter Nature Preserve

Owned by Shirley Heinze Land Trust

The ninety-two-acre John Merle Coulter Nature Preserve in Porter County features a range of ecosystems—dune, interdunal wetland, sand prairie, black oak savanna, and sedge meadow—adjacent to the Indiana Dunes National Lakeshore, in the City of Portage. This natural area supports four hundred-plus plant species, more than three hundred of which are native. The site was sand mined in the 1930s and has been restored. More than two dozen of this dedicated state nature preserve's plants are rare in Indiana.

Coulter's botanic diversity produces spectacular wildflowers throughout the growing seasons. Bird's-foot violet, hairy puccoon, and wild lupine bloom in spring. Prairie plants like prairie blazing star and goldenrod color the landscape in late summer and fall. Prickly pear cactus and butterfly weed add to the deciduous oak, sassafras, and sumac trees' annual fall color display. The preserve's Yellow Birch Fen features a variety of ferns, along with skunk cabbage, marsh marigold, Canada mayflower, mayapple, wild columbine, wild geranium, starflower, and other wildflowers. Butterflies are attracted to the preserve's prairie wildflowers. Blue racers, hognose snakes, and six-lined racerunners are common.

The preserve is located on County Line Road across from Lake County, just south of an industrial plant that manufactures water-soluble polymer films, compounds, and solutions.

John Merle Coulter Nature Preserve

Activities

Hiking, nature study, photography, wildlife watching.

Directions

GPS coordinates: 41.601794, −87.222382

From I-65

- East on I-94 to Ripley Street, 3.1 miles
- North on Ripley Street to US 20 (Melton Road), 0.8 mile
- East on US 20 (Melton Road) to County Line Road on the north side of Lake Station, 0.9 mile
- North onto County Line Road to the preserve, 0.5 mile

From US 31

- West on I-80/I-90 (Toll Road) at South Bend to State Road 39, 23.0 miles
- North on State Road 39 to US 20, 1.5 miles
- West on US 20 to I-94, 3.9 miles
- West on I-94 to US 20, 18.5 miles
- West on US 20 (Melton Road) to County Line Road, 6.3 miles
- North onto County Line Road to the preserve, 0.5 mile

10. Reynolds Creek Game Bird Area

Owned by Indiana Department of Natural Resources,
Division of Fish & Wildlife

Established in 2011 as one of Indiana's youngest natural areas, the 1,250-acre Reynolds Creek Game Bird Area in Porter County adjoins an inland section of the Indiana Dunes National Lakeshore. It is managed to restore grassland habitat suitable for game birds like doves, pheasants, and quail.

Situated just southeast of the Dunes' Heron Rookery, the area is composed of agricultural fields, two small woodlots, and several restorable wetlands. Reynolds Creek, which contains one of the last naturally reproducing brown trout populations in the state, winds through the area's western portion on its way to the Little Calumet River.

Formerly owned by the Indiana Department of Corrections as a state prison farm, the Reynolds Creek area is managed by the Kingsbury Fish & Wildlife Area office. Its farmland is being converted to native prairies and its wetlands restored, with a particular emphasis on habitat for pheasant and quail, which have been absent from the area since the late 1990s. Due to its proximity to Lake Michigan, Reynolds Creek is also frequented by waterfowl. Much of the property is still farmed to produce revenue to offset the costs of wildlife plantings.

While there are no developed trails, Reynolds has several parking areas along County Roads 600E, 1500N, 1275N, and 1250N, Burdick Road, and County Line Road.

Activities

Hiking, hunting, nature study, photography, trapping, wildlife watching.

Directions

GPS coordinates: 41.617960, –86.951584
From I-65

- East on I-90/94 to US 421 at Michigan City, 22.5 miles
- South on US 421 County Road 300N, 0.4 mile

- West on County Road 300N, jogging to County Road 1500N, to County Road 600E, 3.0 miles
- South on County Road 600E to bird habitat area, 2.0 miles

From US 31

- West on I-90 at South Bend (Toll Road) to State Road 39, 22.6 miles
- North on State Road 39 to US 20 at Springville, 1.2 miles
- West on US 20 to I-94, 3.8 miles
- West on I-94 to US 421 at Michigan City, 5.7 miles
- South on US 421 County Road 300N, 0.4 mile
- West on County Road 300N, jogging to County Road 1500N, to County Road 600E, 3.0 miles
- South on County Road 600E to bird habitat area, 2.0 miles

11. Barker Woods Nature Preserve

Owned by Shirley Heinze Land Trust

The thirty-acre Barker Woods Nature Preserve in LaPorte County supports and protects a variety of trees, shrubs, and flowers whose habitats are common in more northern climes. This dedicated state nature preserve's low depression bordered by a sandy dune ridge supports a mixed-forest community that is a rare example of urban, old-growth forest. Several plants survive in Barker Woods that are state endangered, threatened, rare, or watch listed.

Pin oak and red maple dominate the forest, with white birch and yellow birch growing in the peaty soils. Natural stands of white oak, black oak, red oak, black gum, tulip poplar, American beech, and sugar maple thrive in the preserve's lower areas, with scotch pine, white pine, and red pine plantations occupying the higher ground.

The Barker Woods' low, wet depressions provide habitat for velvetleaf blueberry, lowbush blueberry, witch hazel, cinnamon fern, royal fern, Canada mayflower, Indian cucumber-root, Canada cinquefoil, and skunk cabbage. The drier areas support false Solomon's seal and wild lettuce.

Barker Woods Nature Preserve

The site was recommended for preservation in the landmark 1969 survey *Natural Areas in Indiana and Their Preservation* by Alton A. Lindsey, Damien Vincent Schmeltz, and Stanley A. Nichols. Originally owned by conservationist Marjorie Barker, the woods were among the state's first classified forests. Indiana's first state forester, Charles C. Deam, also a botanist who authored four books on Indiana plants, including *Flora of Indiana* in 1940, studied Barker Woods in the 1920s.

Development before the Lindsey survey had drained two natural ponds on the site. Continuing development is depriving the preserve of sufficient fresh water and altering the aquatic ecosystem. Nearby landscaping has introduced nonnative species like garlic mustard, lily-of-the-valley, periwinkle, and common privet.

Located on Michigan City's south side, the Barker Woods preserve is owned by the Shirley Heinze Land Trust, but it houses the Save the Dunes Council's headquarters in the Barker House. The trail is to the left of the outbuilding across from the house.

Activities
Hiking Trails: One, with two loops (0.24 and 0.54 mile), easy.
Other Activities: Nature study, photography, wildlife watching.

Directions
GPS coordinates: 41.687564, −86.883288
From I-65
- East on I-94 at Gary to US 421 (Franklin Street) at Michigan City, 22.5 miles
- North on US 421 (Franklin Street) to Barker Road, 2.0 miles
- East on Barker Road to preserve on north, 0.5 mile

From US 31
- West on I-80/I-90 (Toll Road) at South Bend to State Road 39, 23.0 miles
- North on State Road 39 to US 20, 1.5 miles
- West on US 20 to South Woodland Avenue in Michigan City, 7.8 miles
- North on South Woodland Avenue to Barker Avenue, 350 feet
- West on Barker Avenue to preserve on north, 0.5 mile

12. Trail Creek Fen
Owned by Save the Dunes
The thirty-eight-acre Trail Creek Fen in LaPorte County protects more than two hundred species of plants in rare natural communities that include raised grassy fen and sedge-covered wetland, along with riparian wetlands and woodlands, moist upland forest, and savanna. The preserve, which is in Michigan City, is bisected by the Trail Creek West Branch and features wetlands that exemplify a once-common ecosystem in Lake Michigan's southern region. Trail Creek Fen is home to the state rare Baltimore checkerspot butterfly.

Trail Creek Fen

The preserve's uplands consist of degraded remnant savanna, open field, dry-moist woodlands, and moist forests. Grasses such as Indian grass and fringed brome are the predominate plants, but they share the wetlands with swamp goldenrod, blazing star, and tall coreopsis. The forest is mostly tamarack and dwarf birch, with abundant carnivorous plants on the forest floor.

Restoration efforts by the Save the Dunes Foundation are ongoing to control invasive plants—such as Dame's rocket, privet, garlic mustard, autumn olive, tree-of-heaven, and reed canary grass—as well as to restore native vegetation and create a stewardship model for rare coastal wetlands and tributaries.

The Trail Creek's east and west forks merge about a half mile north of Trail Creek Fen and run another seven miles to Lake

Michigan at the Michigan City Harbor, adjacent to the city's lakefront Washington Park.

Trail Creek was part of the Potawatomi Trail that ran from Chicago to the French Fort St. Joseph on the St. Joseph River at Niles, Michigan, via the south shore of Lake Michigan, Trail Creek, and Hudson Lake. It was called *Myewes-zibiwe*, which in Potawatomi meant "trail creek."

The preserve has a small roadside parking lot and short, unmarked trail that quickly becomes impassable.

Activities
Nature study, photography, wildlife watching.

Directions
GPS coordinates: 41.682020, –86.848009
From I-65
- East on I-94 at Lake Station to US 421 at Michigan City, 22.3 miles
- North on US 421 to US 20, 1.3 miles
- East on US 20 to Johnson Road, 2.6 miles
- South on Johnson Road to preserve, 0.4 mile

From US 31
- West on I-80/I-90 (Toll Road) at South Bend to State Road 39, 23.0 miles
- North on State Road 39 to US 20, 1.5 miles
- West on US 20 to Johnson Road, 6.5 miles
- South on Johnson Road to preserve, 0.4 mile

13. Ambler Flatwoods Nature Preserve
Owned by Shirley Heinze Land Trust
The 390-acre Ambler Flatwoods Nature Preserve in LaPorte County protects a boreal flatwoods ecosystem that is rare in Indiana. Occupying relatively level, poorly drained soils on the eastern side of Michigan City, this site—310 acres designated as a dedicated state nature preserve—supports a couple dozen plants that are rare in Indiana and more that are considered rare in the Chicago region.

Ambler Flatwoods Nature Preserve

Much of the preserve's flora are rare to the state and typical of more northern species, including several types of clubmoss. Some are relics surviving at the far southern end of their distribution ranges. A few survive in Indiana only in the Ambler Flatwoods.

The preserve's densely wooded landscape supports red maple, northern pin oak, black gum, and tulip poplar. The forest floor, which is laced with pools, streams, and rivulets, provides habitat for a variety of animals and birds. Cinnamon fern and royal fern are common. Colorful fungi thrive in the forest floor's leaf litter.

Ambler Flatwoods' scattered seasonal woodland ponds provide important habitat for a wide range of salamanders and frogs. Migratory birds use the forest canopy for temporary shelter. Hooting owls are common.

Ambler Flatwoods is the largest Shirley Heinze Land Trust preserve. Restoration and management efforts are aimed at controlling invasive species, planting trees, and restoring native vegetation to improve wetland habitat, particularly for several species of reptiles and amphibians that depend on them. The preserve is separated into three sections by two county roads and has two parking lots.

Activities
Hiking Trails: Four miles; Louise H. Landau Trail (1.29 miles), includes boardwalks and interpretive signs.
Other Activities: Nature study, photography, wildlife watching.

Directions to Southern Trail Parking Lot
GPS coordinates: 41.728898, –86.816254
From I-65
- East on I-94 to US 20, 27.6 miles
- West on US 20 to Meer Road (County Road 600W), 0.3 mile
- North on Meer Road to preserve, southern trail, 2.3 miles

From US 31
- West on I-80/I-90 (Toll Road) at South Bend to State Road 39, 23.0 miles
- North on State Road 39 to US 20, 1.5 miles

- West on US 20 to Meer Road (County Road 600W), 4.2 miles
- North on Meer Road to preserve, southern trail, 2.3 miles

Directions to Northern Trail Parking Lot
from the Southern Trail
GPS coordinates: 41.738138, −86.809259
- North on Meer Road to Freyer Road (County Road 900N), 0.6 mile
- East on Freyer Road to lot on south side of road, 0.3

14. Wintergreen Woods Nature Preserve
Owned by LaPorte County Conservation Trust Inc.

The twenty-three-acre Wintergreen Woods Nature Preserve in LaPorte County is a remnant northern boreal flatwoods natural community, a lowland forest type that is restricted in Indiana to a narrow strip just south of the Lake Michigan dunes.

This dedicated state nature preserve harbors several species that are relatively rare in Indiana and more typical of the north. Among these state rare species are the preserve's namesake American wintergreen, white-edge sedge, tree clubmoss, and eastern white pine. Other notable species are state rare long sedge; state threatened branched bur-reed; state watch-listed paper birch, spotted wintergreen, dwarf ginseng, and gold-thread; as well as Canada mayflower, starflower, and a number of sedge species.

Flatwoods thrive on poorly drained sites, and during wet seasons, much of Wintergreen Woods has standing water. Numerous tip-ups—trees that topple over during windstorms—contribute to the soggy environs. Puncheons cross the wettest areas.

Interstate 94 passes by the preserve to the east, and freeway noise is constant.

Activities
Hiking (interpretive trail), nature study, photography, wildlife watching.

Directions

GPS coordinates: 41.740897, –86.768014

From I-65

- East on I-94 to US 20, 27.6 miles
- East on US 20 to State Road 39, 3.7 miles
- North on State Road 39 to County Road 925, 3.8 miles
- West on County Road 925 to preserve, 1.8 miles

From US 31

- West on I-80/I-90 (Toll Road) at South Bend to State Road 39, 23.0 miles
- North on State Road 39 to County Road 925, 3.8 miles
- West on County Road 925 to preserve, 1.8 miles

Valparaiso Moraine Section

15. Moraine Nature Preserve

Owned by Indiana Department of Natural Resources, Division of Nature Preserves

The 474-acre Moraine Nature Preserve in Porter County protects a rolling, rugged, and beautiful landscape with a diverse collection of landforms—steep hills, muck pockets, pothole wetlands, deep-wooded gorges, a natural kettle pond, and old farm fields that are reverting back to forest. This dedicated state nature preserve protects a diversity of natural communities, including pond, shrub swamp, moist upland forest, and dry-moist upland forest.

Part of a broader eight-hundred-acre natural complex, the Moraine preserve supports nearly two dozen plant species that are rare in Indiana, including state endangered gray birch, Montgomery hawthorn, and Vasey's pondweed, along with state threatened branched bur-reed. Species that are state rare include Michaux's stitchwort, chamomile grape-fern, eastern white pine, fire cherry, and catbird grape.

The Moraine preserve represents the various landforms associated with the Valparaiso Moraine, a U-shaped line of glacial ridges that runs from Southern Wisconsin through Northern

Moraine Nature Preserve

Illinois and Northwest Indiana into West Central Michigan—and divides the region's drainage patterns between Lake Michigan and the Kankakee River. The ridges are composed of earth and rock left behind when the Wisconsin ice sheets began melting some thirteen thousand years ago.

Among the ecosystems supported on the Moraine Nature Preserve are old-growth remnants of oak-hickory forest, moist beech-maple forest, and old farm fields that are reverting to nature. Mature beech-maple forests occupy some of the uplands and ravines, while buttonbush and black willow surround some of the potholes and ponds. Many of the upland areas are in various stages of succession.

One of the largest unfragmented blocks of forest in Northwest Indiana, the Moraine preserve supports nesting forest interior birds and migrating species. Many common and rare species frequent the ponds and wetlands. Wildflowers cover the forest floor, particularly in the spring.

Activities

Hiking Trails: Easy to moderate terrain, no established trails.
Other Activities: Nature study, photography, wildlife watching.

Directions

GPS coordinates: 41.542318, −87.017842
From I-90 toll road

- South on State Road 49 to Calumet Avenue, 3.7 miles
- Southeast on Calumet Avenue to Meska Road (Country Road 750N), 2.1 miles
- East on Meska Road to parking lot, 1.4 miles

16. Little Calumet Headwaters Nature Preserve

Owned by LaPorte County Parks Foundation

The 107-acre Little Calumet Headwaters Nature Preserve in LaPorte County protects the headwaters of the Little Calumet River south of Michigan City. The dedicated state nature preserve is located in the Red Mill County Park. The river now originates at Round Lake, which was previously dammed to provide water power to a former mill on the property. Along with the lake and surrounding wetlands, this preserve's landforms include seeps, spring runs, and upland forest.

The preserve, which is bordered by a railroad track, supports more than a dozen rare plants, including state endangered rough sedge and jointed rush; state threatened American golden-saxifrage and northeastern smartweed; and state rare narrow-leaved cotton grass, roundleaf dogwood, and eastern white pine.

The wet areas support a variety of sedges, along with marsh marigold, blue flag iris, swamp thistle, white water lily,

Little Calumet Headwaters Nature Preserve

sycamore, red maple, and several willows. The drier sites support roundleaf dogwood and white pine, harbinger-of-spring, partridgeberry, Canada mayflower, large-flowered trillium, pawpaw, white oak, and several different ferns.

Among the Little Calumet Headwaters' more colorful flora is beech drop, a parasite that lives on beech tree roots and cannot grow without them; spotted coralroot, an orchid that grows in black oak and white oak woods; and the uncommon swamp thistle, which is found in bogs, marshes, swamps, and fens.

The preserve is accessible from the park's south gate. The trailhead is located behind the Environmental Education Center. A trail leads to a bench on the water's edge.

Activities
Hiking, nature study, photography, wildlife watching.

Directions
GPS coordinates: 41.601603, –86.880480

From I-94

- South on US 421 to Holmesville Road, at the intersection with County Road 100N, 2.4 miles
- Southeast on Holmesville Road to Red Mill County Park, South Gate, 1.6 miles

17. Springfield Fen Nature Preserve / Galena Marsh Wetland Conservation Area

Owned by Indiana Department Of Natural Resources,
Divisions of Nature Preserves and Fish & Wildlife

The forty-five-acre Springfield Fen Nature Preserve in LaPorte County supports an example of a prairie fen, with several plant species that are rare, threatened, or endangered in Indiana. The wetland, which is part of the 165-acre Galena Marsh Wetland Conservation Area, lies at the base of high ridge and was formed by calcium-rich (calcareous) seepage from the hillside via year-round springs. Calcareous fens are among the rarest plant communities in North America.

Calcium in this dedicated state nature preserve's water creates habitat that harbors a variety of rare plant species, including state endangered calamint, hairy valerian, and marsh valerian, as well as state threatened Leiberg's witchgrass, and northeastern smartweed. Several species—white-edge sedge, tufted hairgrass, northern witchgrass, rough rattlesnake-root, false asphodel, and white camas—are state rare. Prairie plants dominate the preserve, including big bluestem, Indian grass, and numerous prairie forbs. Sedges are common. Mosses occur. Wildflowers are spectacular in season.

Two streams that originate in the marsh and preserve join about a mile to the north and form the Galena River, which flows north into Michigan, eventually feeding Lake Michigan at New Buffalo, via the Galien River.

The Galena Marsh Wetland Conservation Area is a cooperative project between the state Divisions of Nature Preserves and Fish & Wildlife. This natural complex has no trails but is accessible from the road. The parking lot at the intersection of US 20 is not part of the preserve.

Galena Marsh Wetland Conservation Area

Activities
Hiking, hunting, nature study, photography, wildlife watching.

Directions
GPS coordinates: 41.692262, –86.714504
From I-65
- East on I-94 (Toll Road) to US 20, 27.8 miles
- East on US 20 to Wilhelm Road, 5.9 miles
- North on Wilhelm Road to preserve, parking along west side of road, 0.8 mile

From US 31
- West on I-80/I-90 (Toll Road) at South Bend to State Road 39, 23.0 miles
- North on State Road 39 to US 20, 1.5 miles
- East on US 20 to Wilhelm Road, 5.9 miles
- North on Wilhelm Road to preserve, parking along west side of road, 0.8 mile

18. Spicer Lake Nature Preserve
Owned by St. Joseph County Parks Department

The 196-acre Spicer Lake Nature Preserve in St. Joseph County protects large expanses of swamp forest and marsh surrounding Spicer Lake and Lancaster Lake, both kettle lakes formed by melting ice blocks when the last glacier retreated from Indiana some thirteen thousand years ago. The dedicated state nature preserve is surrounded by 320 acres owned by St. Joseph County Parks.

The Spicer preserve supports seven rare plants in Indiana, including the state endangered northern wild-raisin; state threatened Atlantic sedge and Bebb's sedge; state rare false hop sedge, and weak stellate sedge; and state watch-listed goldthread.

Typical of the succession a site would follow from open water to swamp forest, Spicer Lake's five acres of open water—two hundred acres in postglacial times—are surrounded by a ring of yellow pond lily-swamp loosestrife marsh, which is encircled by a spicebush-winterberry-buttonbush shrub swamp that slowly rises to red maple swamp forest.

Spicer Lake Nature Preserve

Spicebush dominates the swamp forest's shrub layer. Skunk cabbage and rice cut-grass thrive in a small marsh in the southwest corner. Ferns—sensitive, cinnamon, and royal among them—are abundant. So are a diverse collection of sedges. Swamp rose dot the liquid green landscape in summer.

The park features a network of trails along wetlands, woods, and old-growth fields, with a boardwalk that leads through the wetland to Spicer Lake. Located on the LaPorte County line just south of the Michigan state line, Spicer Lake is known for its early-fall color display, which begins in mid-September.

Activities
Hiking Trails: Four (0.3–1.5 miles), one accessible boardwalk (0.25 mile).

Other Activities: Nature center, nature study, photography, wildlife watching.

Directions

GPS coordinates: 41.753283, –86.524297

From I-65

- East on I-94 at Gary to State Road 239 in Michigan northeast of Michigan City, 34.9 miles
- South on State Road 239 to County Road 1000N in Indiana, 1.6 miles
- East on County Road 1000N to County Line Road, 10.3 miles
- North on County Line Road to park, 225 feet

From US 31

- West on US 20 to Marvel Lane, 8.2 miles
- West on Marvel Lane to Timothy Road, 0.3 mile
- North on Timothy Road to Auten Road, 2.5 miles
- West on Auten Road to County Line Road, 1.0 mile
- North on County Line Road to park, 0.5 mile

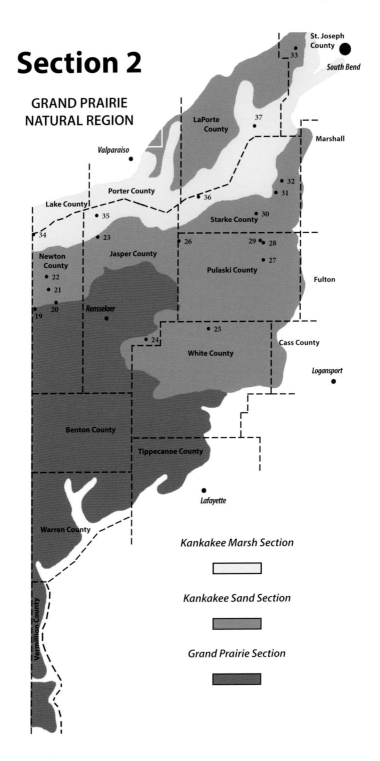

Section 2

GRAND PRAIRIE
NATURAL REGION

St. Joseph County

South Bend

33

LaPorte County

37

Marshall

Valparaiso

32

31

Porter County

36

30

Lake County

Starke County

35

26

29 28

34

23

27

Newton County

Jasper County

Pulaski County

22

Fulton

21

19 20

Rensselaer

25

24

Cass County

White County

Logansport

Benton County

Tippecanoe County

Lafayette

Warren County

Vermillion County

Kankakee Marsh Section

Kankakee Sand Section

Grand Prairie Section

Section 2

GRAND PRAIRIE NATURAL REGION

Grand Prairie Section

19. Willow Slough Fish & Wildlife Area /
    Barnes Nature Preserve

Kankakee Sand Section

20. Holley Savanna
21. Kankakee Sands
22. Conrad Savanna Nature Preserve / Conrad Station
    Nature Preserve
23. Ciurus Park Nature Preserve
24. Fisher Oak Savanna Nature Preserve
25. Spinn Prairie Nature Preserve
26. Jasper-Pulaski Fish & Wildlife Area / Tefft Savanna
    Complex / Tefft Savanna Nature Preserve /
    Coastal Plains Ponds Nature Preserve
27. Berns-Meyer Nature Preserve
28. Tippecanoe River State Park / Sandhill Nature
    Preserve / Tippecanoe River Nature Preserve
29. Winamac Fish & Wildlife Area
30. Round Lake Wetland Conservation Area &
    Nature Preserve
31. Ober Sand Savanna / Ober Savanna Nature Preserve
32. Koontz Lake Nature Preserve / Koontz Lake Wetland
    Conservation Area
33. Bendix Woods Nature Preserve / Bendix Woods
    County Park

Kankakee Marsh Section

34. LaSalle Fish & Wildlife Area
35. NIPSCO Savanna / Aukiki Wetland Conservation Area
36. Kankakee Fish & Wildlife Area
37. Kingsbury Fish & Wildlife Area

GRAND PRAIRIE
NATURAL REGION

GRAND PRAIRIE NATURAL REGION

Grand Prairie Section

19a. Willow Slough Fish & Wildlife Area

Owned by Indiana Department of Natural Resources, Division of Fish & Wildlife

The 9,956-acre Willow Slough Fish & Wildlife Area in Newton County is composed of sandy ridges, oak barrens, marshes, ponds, flooded croplands, sloughs, and a centerpiece 1,200-acre lake, all of which attract a wide variety of wildlife. Managed for hunting and fishing, this wildlife area bordered by the Indiana-Illinois state line also includes a dedicated state nature preserve and has been designated by National Audubon Society as an Important Bird Area.

When combined with two other IBAs—the adjacent Kankakee Sands to the north and Iroquois State Wildlife Area just west of the border—Willow Slough is part of a nearly twenty-thousand-acre natural area that is managed to produce critical habitat for nesting grassland, savanna, and marshland birds. According to the Audubon Society, Willow Slough's "mosaic of habitats . . . supports some of the most diverse nesting and migratory avian populations of any Indiana Important Bird Area."

In early spring, the 1,200-acre J. C. Murphey Lake and adjacent Pogue's Marsh support some of the state's most abundant waterfowl populations. At least five rare species may have bred there in recent years: least bittern, common moorhen, Virginia rail, and marsh wren, all state endangered; and sandhill crane, a state species of special concern.

While the wildlife area's natural state has been altered significantly, a remnant of the original Willow Slough lies in an eighteen-acre swamp wetland to the lake's south. Several hundred upland acres are maintained as early successional and shrubland habitat. State endangered sedge wrens nest in some brushy habitats, along with willow flycatcher and Bell's vireo.

J. C. Murphey Lake, Willow Slough Fish & Wildlife Area

A GUIDE TO NATURAL AREAS OF NORTHERN INDIANA

Willow Slough's southern portion supports oak savanna, pin oak flats, and small areas of sand prairie and sedge meadow, where conservation-priority species such as whippoorwill, redheaded woodpecker, and wood thrush are common. These areas also attract more southerly nesting species, including yellow-throated warbler, Kentucky warbler, and summer tanager. Fields of planted sunflowers attract doves, finches, and a variety of other birds.

The area, a portion of which was submerged under the thirty-thousand-acre, seven-mile-long, and five-mile-wide Beaver Lake, was drained for agriculture in the 1800s and early 1900s. The state purchased it in 1949. Remnants of a railroad station can be found at the Conrad Station Nature Preserve, which adjoins Willow Slough to the northeast. (See the Conrad Station Nature Preserve section below.)

Among the game animals at Willow Slough are white-tailed deer, quail, rabbit, squirrel, dove, woodcock, waterfowl, and turkey. Fish include bass, bluegill, channel catfish, redear sunfish, crappie, and northern pike.

The wildlife area has no trail system. Access is via service roads, levees, and unofficial user paths.

19b. Barnes Nature Preserve

The 249-acre Barnes Nature Preserve contains a mixture of black oak savanna, sand forest, pin oak flatwood, dry and dry-moist sand prairie, and a sedge meadow, which together are rare remnants of the region's original sand-country landscape. Periodic controlled burns maintain the prairie and savanna communities.

The Barnes preserve harbors rare and unusual plant species, including state endangered clustered sedge; state threatened northeastern smartweed; and state rare slim-spike three-awn grass, seabeach needlegrass, and western silvery aster.

The preserve, which has no trails, is composed of four separate tracts within Willow Slough. Tract 1 is accessible from parking lot No. 8. Tract 2 is accessible parking lot 12A via a 0.75-mile walk. Tracts 3 and 4 are accessible from parking lot 11.

Activities
Camping: Fifty primitive sites.
Other Activities: Berry, nut, and mushroom hunting; boating, two ramps, electric motors only; dog training area; fishing; hiking; hunting; nature study; photography; rifle range; trapping; wildlife watching.

Directions
GPS coordinates: 40.975660, –87.526041
From I-74
- North on US 41 at Veedersburg, through Attica, and Kentland to County Road 400S (at State Road 114 intersection) at Morocco, 61.4 miles
- West on County Road 400S to County Road 700W, 4.8 miles
- North on County Road 700W to area, 2.1 miles

From I-65
- West on State Road 14 (Division Road) to County Road 700W, 13.1 miles
- South on County Road 700W to wildlife area, 2.6 miles

Kankakee Sand Section

20. Holley Savanna
Owned by NICHES Land Trust
The seventy-nine-acre Holley Savanna in Newton County is a regenerating oak woodland–savanna mix that supports a variety of ecosystems, including wet areas dominated by silver maples and pin oaks, with various sedges and grasses; upland woods covered with white oaks; and a significant population of hazelnuts in the understory. Among the preserve's more unique landforms are ephemeral pools—depressions that fill with water in the spring and dry during the summer.

Because predators that require constant water, such as fish or crayfish, cannot survive in the Holly Savanna's ephemeral

Holley Savanna

pools—also known as vernal pools—unique species thrive in them. The upside-down-swimming freshwater fairy shrimp, for example, lives its entire life in vernal pools. Other inhabitants include tiger salamanders, spring peepers, leopard frogs, and gray tree frogs, among others.

Holly Savanna's diverse landscapes—roughly sixty-nine acres of wet woods and ten acres of high-diversity, low-stature prairie—support an array of plants and animals, including the state threatened primrose-leaf violet. More than one hundred herbaceous plants coexist at Holley Savanna. Mast from the oak trees attracts turkeys, squirrels, and woodpeckers.

The preserve is situated atop the Iroquois Moraine—a ridge of glacially deposited materials—and straddles two geographic regions: the former sand-and-muck soils of the Kankakee Marsh to the north and the rich, loamy soils of the Grand Prairie to the south. Rocks deposited by retreating glaciers more than ten thousand years ago are present.

In 1989, Carroll O. Holley donated the refuge to The Nature Conservancy on the condition that it be preserved as timberland and a wildlife preserve. In December 2005, ownership transferred to NICHES Land Trust.

The two nonprofits cooperate in the savanna restoration at Holley Savanna. They employ periodic controlled burns to replicate natural conditions and eliminate unwanted woody species.

Activities
Hiking Trails: One (1.1-mile loop), easy.
Other Activities: Nature study, photography, wildlife watching.

Directions
GPS coordinates: 40.984107, –87.327894
From I-74
- North on US 41 at Veedersburg to State Road 114 at Morocco, 61.2 miles
- East on State Road 114 to County Road 300E, 5.3 miles
- North on County Road 300E to County Road 150S (North State Road), 2.9 miles
- East on County Road 150S to preserve, 1.3 miles

From I-65
- West on State Road 114 to County Road 300E, 5.8 miles
- North on County Road 300E to County Road 150S (North State Road), 2.9 miles
- East on County Road 150S to preserve, 0.2 mile

21. Kankakee Sands
Owned by The Nature Conservancy
The 7,800-acre Kankakee Sands in Newton County is one of Indiana's largest prairie restoration projects, managing remnants and restorations of the marsh, sedge meadow, and sand prairie ecosystems that dominated the region in presettlement times. Known as the Efroymson Restoration at Kankakee

Sands, the site supports more than one hundred rare, threatened, or endangered plant and animal species.

Kankakee Sands forms the core of a larger natural complex that is similarly managed for natural characteristics. It is connected to the east by the 640-acre Beaver Lake Nature Preserve, to the north by the 795-acre Conrad Savanna natural complex, and on the southwest by the 9,965-acre Willow Slough Fish & Wildlife Area. The Sands preserve surrounds the state-owned Beaver Lake preserve, which was secured in 1945 by the Izaak Walton League and the state in an ill-fated effort to restore the prairie chicken, which was known to frequent Indiana as late as 1953. The restoration is in an area that was once the deepest part of Beaver Lake, a shallow, thirty-thousand-acre, seven-mile-long and five-mile-wide waterbody that covered the preserve and surrounding areas before it was drained in the 1920s.

The most unusual animal at Kankakee Sands is the American bison, twenty-three of which The Nature Conservancy relocated there from South Dakota in 2016. The herd, which had grown to fifty by 2017, has free access to roam the more than one thousand fenced-in acres of the preserve, which is bisected by US 41 and three county roads. Like the smaller herd at Ouabache State Park, the Kankakee Sands bison are part of a nationwide conservation effort designed to ensure a future for North America's largest mammal, which had been driven from Indiana by the 1830s. (The wood bison of Northern Canada and Alaska are larger than the plains bison in Indiana.)

Between 2001 and 2017, more than two hundred bird species were recorded at Kankakee Sands, which the National Audubon Society designates as an Important Bird Area. The adjacent Willow Slough is classified separately as its own IBA. "Few sites in the state of Indiana rival the Kankakee Sands Project in overall diversity and abundance of obligate and facultative grassland, savannah, and wetland birds," the Audubon Society says on its IBA website.

Grassland species of concern that nest at the preserve include state endangered upland sandpiper, sedge wren, and Henslow's

Kankakee Sands

sparrow, as well as grasshopper sparrow, dickcissel, bobolink, and eastern meadowlark. Migratory shorebirds seasonally frequent the area, including marbled godwit and state species of special concern American golden plover. The Kankakee restoration also provides breeding grounds for wetland birds that are rare or gone from the state, including state species of special concern Wilson's phalarope.

Kankakee Sands provides habitat to a wide range of grassland birds, which have experienced the greatest declines of any American bird group, primarily due to habitat loss. According to The Nature Conservancy, four of the twenty-five fastest-declining bird species in North America breed at Kankakee Sands: Henslow's sparrow, grasshopper sparrow, field sparrow, and northern bobwhite. Three more declining species stop during migration: lesser yellowlegs and the state endangered short-eared owl. The field sparrow flies to Indiana and Kankakee Sands from the southern United States to breed; the bobolink flies from as far away as Argentina.

Another thirteen of the preserve's bird species—including state endangered northern harrier, American bittern, and black tern—are threatened in Indiana. Other rare and threatened species supported at the preserve include the state species of special concern plains pocket gopher, along with the blue racer and the western harvest mouse.

Frogs, toads, and salamanders thrive in the prairie, as does the grass lizard, a legless reptile that looks like a snake with earholes and eyelids.

More than six hundred native plant species have been planted in the Efroymson Restoration, including blazing star, common milkweed, cardinal flower, and blue flag iris. The state endangered Drummond hemicarpha is among the notable plant species.

Activities
Hiking Trails: Two (0.6–2.0 miles).
Other Activities: Fishing, hiking, hunting, nature study, photography, wildlife watching.

Directions
GPS coordinates: 41.046816, −87.449545
From I-74
- North on US 41 at Veedersburg to preserve, 69.1 miles
From I-65
- West on State Road 14 to US 41 at Enos, 9.1 miles
- North on US 41 to preserve, 2.3 miles

22. Conrad Savanna Nature Preserve / Conrad Station Nature Preserve

Owned by The Nature Conservancy and Indiana Department of Natural Resources, Division of Nature Preserves

The 795-acre Conrad Savanna natural complex in Newton County protects remnant examples of the oak savanna–sand prairie ecosystem that dominated the region south of the Kankakee River in presettlement times. US 41 divides its two dedicated state nature preserves—453-acre Conrad Savanna Nature Preserve and 342-acre Conrad Station Nature Preserve. The Division of Nature Preserves owns Conrad Savanna; The Nature Conservancy owns Conrad Station.

The Conrad preserves' landscape alternates between rolling hills and broad sand flats, both composed of fine quartz sand and dominated by widely spaced black oak and white oak trees, grasses, and sedges. The understory is sparse. In pioneer days, the savannas were called oak openings or barrens.

Rare and unusual plants at Conrad Savanna include the state endangered small bristleberry, state threatened pale corydalis, state rare slim-spike and three-awn grass, and state watch-listed wild sensitive plant.

Due to the open-canopy nature of sand savannas, the Conrad preserves support typical prairie plants that thrive in dry conditions with abundant light, such as hairy puccoon, cleft phlox, goat's rue, blunt-leaved milkweed, leadplant, and New Jersey tea. Grasses and sedges include Pennsylvania sedge, Indian grass, big bluestem, little bluestem, June grass, and porcupine grass. Prickly pear cactus, the state's only native cactus, also grows on the Conrad Savanna.

The Conrad Station preserve is named after the abandoned town, which was platted in 1904 and constructed after the nearby thirty-thousand-acre Beaver Lake was drained in the 1920s. The site features remnant foundations of its blacksmith shop, church, and school.

Management at both Conrad preserves is designed to simulate presettlement conditions and maintain a premier example of black oak savanna in Indiana. Both sites are periodically

Conrad Savanna Nature Preserve

burned to re-create the natural conditions created by wild-fires and accidents. Woody plant species inconsistent with the sand savanna—sassafras and black cherry, for example—are removed.

Birds that frequent the Conrad Savanna include the redheaded woodpecker, wild turkey, and quail. Glass lizards, which live underground, are common but rarely seen.

The Conrad preserves are part of a larger natural area that includes the 640-acre Beaver Lake Nature Preserve, 7,800-acre Kankakee Sands prairie restoration, and the 9,965-acre Willow Slough Fish & Wildlife Area. Both Kankakee Sands and Willow Slough are designated as National Audubon Society Important Bird Areas. (See the Willow Slough Fish & Wildlife Area and Kankakee Sands sections above for details.)

Activities

Hiking Trails: One at Conrad Station (2.0 miles), interpretive.
Other Activities: Hunting, nature study, photography, wildlife watching.

Directions to Conrad Savanna
GPS coordinates: 41.101236, –87.468078
From I-74
- North on US 41 at Veedersburg to County Road 700N south of Lake Village, 73 miles
- West on County Road 700N to preserve, 0.3 mile

From I-65
- West on State Road 10 at Roselawn to US 41 at Lake Village, 9.6 miles
- South on US 41 to County Road 700N, 3.0 miles
- West on County Road 700N to preserve, 0.3 mile

Directions to Conrad Station
GPS coordinates: 41.104808, –87.439451
From I-74
- North on US 41 to County Road 725N south of Lake Village, 73.1 miles
- East on County Road 725N to preserve, 0.5 mile

From I-65
- West on State Road 10 at Roselawn to US 41 at Lake Village, 9.6 miles
- South on US 41 to County Road 725N, 2.9 miles
- East on County Road 725N to preserve, 0.5 mile

23. Ciurus Park Nature Preserve
Owned by Town of DeMotte
The forty-acre Ciurus Park Nature Preserve in Jasper County protects a remnant of the rare black oak savanna ecosystem and a handful of rare and unusual plants, including the state watch-listed cream wild indigo, thicket sedge, short-point flatsedge, and butternut. Other plants in this dedicated state nature

Ciurus Park Nature Preserve

preserve more typical of the Kankakee River Valley's sandy hills include bracken fern, cleft phlox, rough blazing star, New Jersey tea, bird's-foot violet, and butterfly weed.

Located two miles southeast of DeMotte at the end of a cul-de-sac across from a golf course, this square block of forest was donated by Thomas Ciurus in 1969 and became the Town of DeMotte's first park. The donation carried with it the condition that the site become a park or a nature preserve in perpetuity—or revert back to the Ciurus family.

Activities
Hiking Trails: One (0.7-mile loop), easy.
Other Activities: Nature study, photography, wildlife watching.

Directions
GPS coordinates: 41.167843, –87.163458
From I-65
- East on State Road 10 at Roselawn to County Road 1000N, 4.3 miles

- East on County Road 1000N County Road 600W, 2.0 miles
- North on County Road 600W to Owen Court, 0.6 mile
- West on Owen Court to preserve, 0.2 mile

From US 31

- West on State Road 14 at Rochester, and Winamac, to US 231, 49.4 miles
- North on US 231 to County Road 1000N, 9.0 miles
- West on County Road to 1000N to County Road 600W, 0.5 mile
- North on County Road 600W to Owen Court, 0.6 mile
- West on Owen Court to preserve, 0.2 mile

24. Fisher Oak Savanna Nature Preserve

Owned by NICHES Land Trust

The 220-acre Fisher Oak Savanna Nature Preserve in Jasper County protects three natural habitats: pin oak flatwood, sand-prairie savanna, and wet black-soil prairie. Black oak savanna dune ridges mixed with pin oak flatwoods comprise the preserve's bulk. The Fisher Oak Savanna Nature Preserve is a 133-acre dedicated state nature preserve within the larger protected area.

These rare pin oak flatwoods support black oak and white oak as well as pin oak. They hold water in the spring and dry out as the season progresses—unique features that support rare plants and amphibians that require access to such wet-and-dry cycles. The flatwoods and sedge meadows that occupy Fisher Oak's wet sections have less than 40 percent tree cover.

The entire black-soil prairie and a portion of the sand prairie-savanna are undergoing restoration to more approximate natural conditions. The Fisher Oak Savanna's natural balance is maintained by removing brush and thinning trees to promote the oak species. Controlled burns are employed to return nutrients to the soil and kill invasive species that cannot survive the heat. Blueberry bushes, lupines, and puccoons are native species that benefit from the management. An adjacent agricultural field is being restored to high-quality prairie and wetland. A

Fisher Oak Savanna Nature Preserve

notable flower that grows in late summer is the orange-fringed orchid.

Fisher Oak Savanna Nature Preserve, which is dedicated to the memory of Evelyn Fisher Cotton, is open to the public December 1 through October 31.

Activities
Hiking Trails: Loop trail (2 miles), easy.
Other Activities: Nature study, photography, wildlife watching.

Directions
GPS coordinates: 40.846559, –87.042639
From I-65
- North on US 231 north of Remington to County Road 1300S, 0.8 mile
- East on County Road 1300S, becoming County Road 500N, to County Road 900W, 5.8 miles
- North on County Road 900W to preserve, 1.6 miles

From US 31

- West on US 24 to US 421 at Reynolds, 41.5 miles
- North on US 421 to County Road 500N, 5.1 miles
- West on County Road 500N to County Road 900W, 8.7 miles
- North on County Road 900W to preserve, 1.6 miles

25. Spinn Prairie Nature Preserve

Owned by The Nature Conservancy

The twenty-nine-acre Spinn Prairie Nature Preserve in White County protects a rare remnant of the tallgrass prairie that in presettlement times occupied two million acres of Indiana west of the Illinois state line, from the Valparaiso Moraine south a hundred miles to Terre Haute.

This long and narrow dedicated state nature preserve is surrounded by farmland and light industry, wedged in between a highway-railroad corridor and a county road. The preserve's nearly flat surface features scattered wet swales that are dominated by cordgrasses.

The landforms on this tiny but critical site are oak savanna, moist prairie, wet prairie, willow shrub thicket, and pin oak flatwood. The higher areas are moist prairie that are dominated by big bluestem grass, Indian grass, and oak savanna, which, while degraded, is dominated by black and white oaks. The lower, moist prairie supports blazing star, white wild indigo, prairie dock, rattlesnake master, and downy sunflower.

Spinn Prairie's grasses reach eight feet and thrive alongside other colorful prairie plants that include state watch-listed green-fringed orchids, along with woodland sunflowers, sweet coneflowers, purple coneflowers, nodding ladies' tresses, compass plants, common milkweeds, and morning glories. Among the butterflies that thrive in the prairie environment are black dash, black swallowtail, Acadian hairstreak, eastern-tailed blue, viceroy, and monarch. Bird species include soras, summer tanagers, little blue herons, and redheaded woodpeckers.

While the Spinn Prairie is tiny when compared with other nature preserves, its mere existence is noteworthy. Fewer than

Jasper-Pulaski Fish & Wildlife Area

a thousand of Indiana's original two million acres of prairie still exist, most of them along railroad tracks and around cemeteries. Periodic controlled burns are employed at Spinn Prairie Nature Preserve to re-create the natural conditions such grasslands need to survive, to nourish the soil, and to discourage nonnative plants that cannot survive fire.

The Spinn family owned the site from 1865 until 1987 and never plowed it.

Activities
Hiking (no trail), nature study, photography, wildlife watching.

Directions
GPS coordinates: 40.780335, −86.872195
From I-65
- West on US 24, through Wolcott, to US 421 at Reynolds, 13.6 miles
- North on US 421 to County Road 200N, 2.1 miles
- East on County Road 200N to North Meridian Road and the preserve, 0.1 mile
- Park along North Meridian road.

From US 31

- West on US 24 to US 421 at Reynolds, 41.7 miles
- North on US 421 to County Road 200N, 8.3 miles
- East on County Road 200N to North Meridian Road and the preserve, 0.1 mile
- Park along North Meridian road.

26a. Jasper-Pulaski Fish & Wildlife Area

Owned by Indiana Department of Natural Resources,
Division of Fish & Wildlife

The 8,142-acre Jasper-Pulaski Fish & Wildlife Area's wetland, upland, and woodland habitats are managed for hunting and fishing. But the area includes two dedicated state nature preserves within its boundaries, borders two others owned by The Nature Conservancy, and is a world-famous stopover site for sandhill cranes and other migratory birds.

The wildlife area, which spans portions of Jasper, Pulaski, and Starke Counties, forms the core of a thirty-thousand-acre Important Bird Area designated by the National Audubon Society. Of the cranes, the Audubon Society says on its website: "Virtually the entire eastern population of this subspecies stages at this site during fall migration." Daily counts can equal twenty thousand; the record set in 2002 is 34,969.

Sandhill cranes, a state species of special concern, stop in the area in late fall as they fly south from nesting grounds in Wisconsin and Michigan to winter as far south as Florida. Their numbers peak around November. The cranes are best seen in the early morning and late evenings. An accessible public viewing deck overlooking Goose Pasture, with an accessible parking lot, provides the best observation. The cranes pass through Jasper-Pulaski on their flights back north during early spring, but in smaller numbers.

Since the Federally Endangered whooping cranes were reintroduced in the Eastern United States in 2000, Jasper-Pulaski has also become an important migratory stop for them, as well. The largest number was five, recorded in 2005.

Because of its diversity of habitats, Jasper-Pulaski supports a wide range of other bird species, including the redheaded woodpecker in the oak flats, with large gatherings of migratory waterfowl in the marshes. The state endangered northern harrier, rough-legged hawk, and other raptors stop at Jasper-Pulaski during the winter months. Other animals that inhabit the wildlife area include deer, quails, rabbits, squirrels, snipes, doves, rails, woodcocks, waterfowl, and turkeys.

Jasper-Pulaski—the oldest managed fish and wildlife area in Indiana—was designated as a game farm and preserve in 1929, with most of the marginal farmland acquired in the 1930s and 1940s. Hunting began in 1958.

26b. Tefft Savanna Complex

The Tefft Savanna Complex is composed of 1,600-plus acres of protected natural areas—Tefft Savanna Nature Preserve, two Prairie Border Nature Preserves, and Coastal Plains Nature Preserve—that are within or adjacent to the Jasper-Pulaski Fish & Wildlife Area. Hunting is allowed throughout the complex.

More than thirty rare, threatened, or endangered plants in Indiana are among the more than 260 species identified at Tefft Savanna. Unique plants include species more likely found on the Atlantic Coastal Plain, including state endangered sandplain yellow flax and black-fruited spike rush, warty panic-grass, and primrose-leaf violet, all state threatened.

In addition to the black oak and pin oak, sassafras, aspen, and a few black cherry trees survive. State threatened Carey's smartweed coexists with the blueberry and huckleberry on the forest floor, along with mild water pepper, Pennsylvania sedge, June grass, and big bluestem.

More than 135 bird species—including the sandhill crane, eastern towhee, barred owl, and redheaded woodpecker—inhabit the complex. The dry, sandy soils support plains pocket gopher, a state species of special concern, along with the bull snake, glass lizard, and six-lined racerunner. Insects like butterflies, skippers, moths, and grasshoppers also thrive in this natural complex's unique environment.

26c. Tefft Savanna Nature Preserve

The 480-acre Tefft Savanna Nature Preserve, which has two separate sections, supports a complex of rare community types in Indiana: sand dunes with black oak savannas and prairie openings surrounding acid flats and depressions. The acid flats feature a black oak and pin oak canopy and an understory of blueberry and huckleberry. The depressions are composed of sedge meadows, wet prairies, and marshes.

A road with multiple parking lots bisects this dedicated state nature preserve's main section on County Road 400E.

The 360-acre Prairie Border and 137-acre Prairie Border South preserves, both owned by The Nature Conservancy, flank Tefft Savanna to the west and north.

26d. Coastal Plain Ponds Nature Preserve

The 628-acre Coastal Plain Ponds Nature Preserve, which also has two sections, protects ephemerally wet, shallow basins that have global ecological significance. It supports nearly two dozen unusual plants, many of whose primary distribution is along the Atlantic Coastal Plain and Gulf Coastal Plain. One portion borders the Tefft Savanna's main unit on its southwest corner; the other sits due east.

Several coastal ponds and marshes are located within this dedicated state nature preserve's boundaries.

Among the rare plants at Coastal Plain Ponds are state endangered creeping St. John's-wort, brown-fruited rush, globe-fruited false-loosestrife, sessile-leaved bugleweed, Torrey's bulrush, Muehlenberg's nutrush, and hidden-fruited bladderwort; and state threatened black-fruited spike rush, warty panic-grass, reticulated nutrush, primrose-leaf violet, Virginia chainfern, and Carolina yellow-eyed grass. Another six plant species are state rare, and two more are state watch listed.

Coastal Plain Ponds is a dedicated state nature preserve, and although it has no trails, it has two parking lots on County Road 1100N.

Activities

Archery range; berry, mushroom, and nut hunting; boat ramps at gravel pits, maximum twelve-volt electric motor; dog training; fishing, Ryan Ditch, gravel pits, ponds; hiking; hunting; nature study; photography; shooting range; wildlife watching; wetland trapping.

Directions to Jasper-Pulaski Office
GPS coordinates: 41.136542, −86.917420
From I-65
- East on State Road 10 at Roselawn to County Road 900N, 5.9 miles
- East on County Road 900N to County Road 300E, 8.5 miles
- South on County Road 300E to County Road 850N, 0.5 mile
- East on County Road 850N to State Road 143 and wildlife area, 3.8 miles

From US 31
- West on State Road 14 at Rochester to US 421, 33.4 miles
- North on US 421 to State Road 143, 5.5 miles
- West on State Road 143 to wildlife area, 1.3 miles

Directions to Tefft Savanna Nature Preserve from Jasper-Pulaski Office
GPS coordinates: 41.157592, −86.968888
- West on State Road 143 to County Road 400E, 2.7 miles
- North on County Road 400E to preserve, which is marked, 1.0 mile

Directions to Coastal Plain Nature Preserve from Jasper-Pulaski Office
GPS coordinates: 41.172206, −86.968285
- West on State Road 143 to County Road 400E, 2.6 miles
- North on County Road 400E to the preserve at County Road 1100N, 2.5 miles
- The preserve lies south of County Road 1100N and has two parking lots on east and west ends; neither is marked

Directions to Prairie Border North Nature Preserve from Jasper-Pulaski Office
GPS coordinates: 41.172352, –86.958921
- West on State Road 143 to County Road 400E, 2.7 miles
- North on County Road 400E to County Road 1100N, 2.5 miles
- East on County Road 1100N to preserve, which is marked, 0.5 mile

Directions to Prairie Border South from Jasper-Pulaski Office
GPS coordinates: 41.146992, –86.988330
- West on State Road 143 to County Road 300E, 3.7 miles
- North on County Road 300E to preserve, 0.8 mile
- The preserve is marked only with Nature Conservancy boundary signs.

27. Berns-Meyer Nature Preserve
Owned by Indiana Department of Natural Resources, Division of Nature Preserves

The twenty-acre Berns-Meyer Nature Preserve in Pulaski County is mostly mixed, moderately moist woodland that supports mature red oak, white oak, tulip tree, sugar maple, basswood, and shagbark hickory, with poorly drained areas that sustain black ash, red maple, pin oak, and swamp white oak.

This dedicated state nature preserve harbors state endangered thinleaf sedge. The Berns-Meyer preserve is rich in wildflowers, including marsh marigold, green dragon, prairie trillium, drooping trillium, mayapple, jack-in-the-pulpit, wild ginger, false Solomon's seal, and jewelweed.

The rectangular preserve, which the Berns and Meyer families donated, features a self-guided trail with forty-four identifications and discussions of trees, wildflowers, shrubs, ferns, and wildlife, along with various natural characteristics, including den trees, wet depressions, and annual growth rings.

Berns-Meyer Nature Preserve

Activities

Hiking Trails: Marked system.

Other Activities: Nature study, photography, wildlife watching.

Directions

GPS coordinates: 40.984359, –86.622774

From I-65

- East on State Road 14 to State Road 39, 26.5 miles
- South on State Road 39 to County Road 550S, 5.4 miles
- East on County Road 550S to State Road 119 at Pulaski, 6.3 miles
- Northeast on State Road 119 to County Road 100W, 2.2 miles
- South on County Road 100W to preserve, 0.5 mile

From US 31

- West on State Road 14 at Rochester to Old State Road 14 at Winamac, 17.9 miles
- Southwest on Old State Road 14 to State Road 119 (Franklin Street), 1.2 miles
- South on State Road 119 to County Road 100W, 4.7 miles
- South on County Road 100W to preserve, 0.5 miles

28a. Tippecanoe River State Park

Owned by Indiana Department of Natural Resources, Division of State Parks & Lakes

The 2,785-acre Tippecanoe River State Park in Pulaski County borders seven miles of the Tippecanoe River and protects a variety of habitats, including oak forests, pine plantations, abandoned fields, prairies, river bluffs, marshes, small sand dunes, and the river. The park is largely undeveloped—no inn or swimming pool—and is committed to outdoor recreation.

Within the state park's boundaries are two dedicated state nature preserves—Sandhill Nature Preserve and Tippecanoe River Nature Preserve—that harbor nearly a dozen rare plants. A fire tower, restored wetland with observation platform, and riverside deck by the nature center are among the scenic gems.

The park's namesake river is not called Tippecanoe until the flow reaches Warsaw some fifty miles to the east at the

Tippecanoe River State Park

confluence of the Walnut Creek and Lones Ditch. But it is known as the river of lakes because along a twisted, more than fifty-mile course from its source at the Crooked Lake in Whitley County northwest of Fort Wayne its flow is fed by eighty-eight natural lakes, with names like Smalley, Johnson, Webster, and Tippecanoe.

The Tippecanoe River State Park's sand hills—which reach forty feet—formed during the Wisconsin glacial event. As the ice sheets receded from Indiana some thirteen thousand years ago, outwash streams left behind large amounts of fine sand and created the northern moraine and lake region of Indiana. As the centuries passed, winds reworked the sands into today's flat sand plains and rolling dunes.

In presettlement times, the parkland was Potawatomi Indian country, and the river became a major trade route among Native Americans, French, British, and Americans in the late seventeenth and early eighteenth centuries. The Tippecanoe was always known for its scenic qualities, even after a half century of clearing, draining, and farming. As Richard S. Simons wrote in *The Rivers of Indiana* (Indiana University Press, 1985), an assistant state geologist in 1888 described the waterway as "a 'beautiful' stream"—in quotes because no term could "properly characterize its exceeding loveliness."

During the Great Depression, the National Park Service acquired 7,353 acres of this sandy, marginal farmland to promote outdoor recreation. Called the Winamac Recreation Demonstration Area, a Roosevelt-era Works Progress Administration project, it provided work for unemployed locals developing the site's recreational opportunities. Most of the facilities that serve today's visitors—shelters, ramps, trails—were built at that time.

In 1943, the land transferred to the Indiana Department of Conservation for the Tippecanoe State Park. Sixteen years later, 4,592 acres were transferred to the DNR Division of Fish & Game and renamed the Winamac Fish & Wildlife Area.

28b. Sandhill Nature Preserve

The 120-acre Sandhill Nature Preserve sits on the state park's far northern section and features upland and lowland sand hills that support a half-dozen rare species. Black oaks dominate the well-drained uplands; pin oaks, black gums, and red maples dominate the lowlands.

Prairie vegetation has moved into areas that previous disturbances have opened. Controlled burns and other techniques for brush control are employed to encourage and maintain these rare prairie areas. Among the rare species protected at Sandhill Nature Preserve are state threatened Carey's smartweed and state rare Hickey's clubmoss and tree clubmoss.

The preserve trail can become impassable during wet periods.

28c. Tippecanoe River Nature Preserve

The 180-acre Tippecanoe River Nature Preserve occupies extensive floodplain and bottomland along a mile and a half of the twisting river border in the park's southeast section. The lowlands support old oxbow sloughs and, in areas with frequent flooding, are dominated by silver maples, cottonwoods, and black willows. Red oak and black walnut dominate the drier areas.

The Tippecanoe River preserve supports state rare ostrich fern. Great blue herons, which have a nesting colony nearby, and other waterfowl are drawn to the park's oxbows. Other birds frequenting this area include wood ducks, green herons, belted kingfishers, redheaded woodpeckers, and prothonotary warblers. Mammals include white-tailed deer, muskrat, beaver, and mink.

The preserve trail can become impassable during wet seasons.

Activities
Hiking Trails: Ten (0.8–3.5 miles), easy to moderate.

Camping: Electric, 112 sites; horsemen's camp, 56 primitive sites; canoe camp, 10 sites; rent-a-camp cabins; group camp; youth tent areas; dumping station.

Other Activities: Boat launch ramp; bridle trails; cross-country skiing; fire tower; fishing; interpretive naturalist service; nature study; photography; picnicking, with shelters; wildlife watching.

Directions
GPS coordinates: 41.117301, –86.602731
From I-65
- East on State Road 14 to US 35 at Winamac, 37.5 miles
- North on US 35 to park, 4.1 miles

From US 31
- West on State Road 14 at Rochester, to US 35 at Winamac, 18.8 miles
- North on US 35 to park, 4.1 miles

29. Winamac Fish & Wildlife Area
Owned by Indiana Department of Natural Resources,
Division of Fish & Wildlife
The 4,880-acre Winamac Fish & Wildlife Area features second-growth oak forests, crop and fallow fields, small pine plantations,

brushy edges, and shallow wetlands. Located across US 35 from the Tippecanoe River State Park in Pulaski County, Winamac's acreage is managed for fishing and hunting and is part of a larger natural complex along the river.

Winamac's primary fish species are bluegill, channel catfish, and largemouth bass. Game animals include deer, rabbits, squirrels, pheasants, quails, turkeys, woodcocks, doves, and furbearers. Waterfowl are limited due to the small wetland areas.

Winamac's history as public land dates to the 1930s, when the US Department of Interior purchased 6,454 acres of marginal farm ground to provide jobs as part of the Roosevelt-era Works Progress Administration. Initially, the land was developed as a recreational demonstration area and furnished with picnic shelters, cabins, and campgrounds, mostly on the river.

In 1943, the federal government transferred the property to the state for the Tippecanoe River State Park. In 1959, 3,710 acres of land west of the highway were transferred to the Division of Fish & Game, later renamed Fish & Wildlife, as a fish and wildlife area.

The Winamac Fish & Wildlife Area has no trail system, though a series of service roads, fire breaks, and grassy strips lead to the site's ponds, dunes, forests, and fields.

Activities
Archery range; berry, nut, and mushroom hunting; fishing, two 2-acre ponds; hiking; hunting; nature study; photography; shooting; shotgun ranges; trapping, wetland only; wildlife watching.

Directions
GPS coordinates: 41.127878, −86.631351
From I-65
- East on State Road 10 at Roselawn to State Road 39 at North Judson, 30.4 miles
- South on State Road 39 to County Road 500N, 5.6 miles
- East on County Road 500N to wildlife area, 7.5 miles

From US 31

- West on State Road 14 at Rochester to US 35 at Winamac, 18.8 miles
- North on US 35 to County Road 500N, 4.8 miles
- West on County Road 500N to wildlife area, 1.5 miles

30. Round Lake Wetland Conservation Area & Nature Preserve

Owned by Indiana Department of Natural Resources,
Divisions of Nature Preserves and Fish & Wildlife

The 140-acre Round Lake Wetland Conservation Area & Nature Preserve protects the muck-bottomed, aptly named Round Lake, which occupies a shallow depression in a sandy plain in Starke County. The lake is surrounded by an emergent marsh, with a floating sedge marsh, cattails, and rare plants. It is managed as both a wetland conservation area and a dedicated state nature preserve.

Notable plants at Round Lake include state endangered cyperus-like sedge and Smith's bulrush; state threatened yellow sedge, northeastern smartweed, long-beaked baldrush, and lesser bladderwort; state rare slim-spike three-awn grass; and state watch-listed bristly-stalk sedge.

The lake is frequented by a wide variety of waterfowl.

Round Lake's wet woods rise into an upland oak environment with interspersed maples and cottonwoods. The southwest uplands are regenerating farmland, with plans for prairie restoration.

Two unmarked trails lead from the parking lot. The north path is mucky. The service road to the south and east leads through a wildflower-rich open area to the lake's southern edge.

Activities

Hiking, hunting, nature study, photography, wildlife watching.

Directions

GPS coordinates: 41.235392, –86.669414

Round Lake Wetland Conservation Area & Nature Preserve

From I-65
- East on State Road 10 at Roselawn, through DeMotte and North Judson, to County Road 100E, 35.4 miles
- North on County Road 100E to County Road 500S, 1.0 mile
- East on County Road 500S to County Road 150E, 0.5 mile
- North on County Road 150E to preserve, 0.4 mile

From US 31
- West on US 30 to US 35, 16.1 miles
- South on US 35 to County Road 400S, 9.9 miles
- West on County Road 400S to County Road 150E, 2.5 miles
- South on County Road 150E to preserve, 0.6 mile

31. Ober Sand Savanna / Ober Savanna Nature Preserve

Owned by The Nature Conservancy

The ninety-acre Ober Sand Savanna in Starke County preserves a high-quality example of black-oak sand savanna, which is a

Ober Sand Savanna

globally endangered ecosystem that once covered thirty million acres of the Midwest. Its rolling sand hills and ridges, which include a fifty-nine-acre dedicated state nature preserve, support large black oak trees and a diverse carpet of wildflowers and grasses, which attract an equally varied collection of fauna.

Prickly pear cactus—Indiana's only native cactus—survives at Ober Savanna, along with several unusual and rare plant species.

Characteristic plants at Ober Savanna include wild lupine, marsh bellflower, dwarf dandelion, Carolina rose, sand cherry, bird's-foot violet, June grass, porcupine grass, and Indian grass.

The savanna attracts numerous butterflies, such as the dusted skipper, mottled duskywing, cobweb skipper, and rare Persius duskywing butterfly. Clumps of prairie grass grow in an old, previously farmed field that is reverting to more native vegetation.

Invasive species control and controlled burns are used to enhance the savanna's regeneration.

A high-speed train track bisects the preserve.

Activities
Hiking (informal trails), nature study, photography, wildlife watching.

Directions
GPS coordinates: 41.273438, −86.535225
From I-65
- East on State Road 2 to State Road 8 at Hebron, 7.1 miles
- East on State Road 8 to County Road 700E, 34.9 miles
- South on County Road 700E to County Road 200S, 1.0 mile
- East on County Road 200S to preserve, 1.4 miles

From US 31
- West on State Road 8 south of Plymouth to State Road 23, 13.2 miles
- South on State Road 23 to County Road 200S, 1.0 miles
- West on County Road 200S to preserve, 0.6 mile

32. Koontz Lake Nature Preserve / Koontz Lake Wetland Conservation Area

Owned by Indiana Department of Natural Resources,
Division of Nature Preserves

The 148-acre Koontz Lake Nature Preserve in Starke County is composed of unique upland and lowland communities that lie in the northern portion of the Koontz Lake Wetland Conservation Area. The preserve's uplands consist of open areas with little bluestem and savannas that support black oaks, blueberries, and Pennsylvania sedge. The lowland communities include small open pockets of water, marsh, shrub bogs, and remnant tamaracks.

The dedicated state nature preserve supports some rare and unusual plant species, including several that are near the southern end of their range. Notable species at Koontz Lake include state endangered little prickly sedge; state threatened Atlantic sedge; state rare chamomile grape-fern; and state watch-listed cuckoo flower, three-seed sedge, goldthread, and tamarack, as well as leatherleaf and highbush blueberry. The fifty-eight-acre Koontz Lake Wetland Conservation Area, located adjacent to the preserve to the south, is managed by the Division of Fish & Wildlife.

The preserve parking lot lies at the end of a dirt road, which begins at the end of a residential street. The trails form a loop that pass near a private property gate. An unmarked spur angles to the right just inside the woods from the field path and leads to the property boundary.

Activities
Hiking (unmarked trails), nature study, photography, wildlife watching.

Directions
GPS coordinates: 41.425219, –86.475919
From I-65
- East on State Road 2 south of Merrillville to State Road 8 at Hebron, 7.2 miles

Koontz Lake Nature Preserve

- East on State Road 8 to State Road 39, 23.9 miles
- North on State Road 39 to US 30, 6.1 miles
- East on US 30 to State Road 23, 12.1 miles
- North on State Road 23 to County Road 825N, 4.8 miles
- East on County Road 875N to County Road 1150E, 0.7 mile
- South on County Road 1150E to preserve, 0.2 mile

From US 31

- West on US 30 at Plymouth to Plymouth-LaPorte Trail, 5.6 miles
- Northwest on Plymouth-LaPorte Trail to 4B Road, 4.7 miles
- West on 4B Road to Lake Drive, 1.2 miles
- North on Lake Drive to Pine Ridge, 0.5 mile
- North on Pine Ridge to County Road 900N, 1.2 miles
- West on County Road 900N to County Road 1150E, 0.5 mile
- South on County Road 1150E to preserve, 0.2 mile

33. Bendix Woods Nature Preserve / Bendix Woods County Park

Owned by St. Joseph County Parks Department

The twenty-seven-acre acre Bendix Woods Nature Preserve protects an old-growth forest in the St. Joseph County Bendix

Bendix Woods Nature Preserve

Woods County Park. The woods are dominated by majestic American beech and sugar maple, along with slippery elm, basswood, and black maple. Spicebush and pawpaw dominate the shrub layer.

The dedicated state nature preserve supports four rare plants in Indiana: state threatened herb-Robert and state watch-listed two-leaf toothwort, butternut, and dwarf ginseng. Heavy growths of jewelweed and nettle thrive in the preserve's wetter areas, while wild ginger, running euonymus, blue cohosh, sanicles, and a variety of ferns populate the drier sections.

A tornado in 1980 left several large openings in the canopy where the forest's recovery is being studied.

The 195-acre Bendix Woods park—St. Joseph County's first—supports woods, ponds, and fields; includes the second-highest point in St. Joseph County; and features a historic tree sign—eight thousand pine trees planted in 1938 to spell Studebaker—that is listed on the National Register of Historic Places and in the *Guinness World Records*.

The park and preserve are named after the Bendix Corporation, which donated the land to the county for a park in 1966. The company bought the property in 1963 from Studebaker Corporation, which used it as part of an 840-acre test facility, the first for an American automobile company. For roughly four decades, the company landscaped the park to keep its natural features.

In addition to the tree sign, the 1926 Studebaker Clubhouse that now houses the park's office and nature center is also listed on the National Register of Historic Places. The tree sign, reputed to be one of the world's largest advertisements, was damaged by an ice storm in 2004.

Activities
Hiking Trails: 5 miles.
Mountain Bike Trails: 6.5 miles.
Other Activities: Fishing ponds; nature center/interpretive services; nature study, photography; picnicking; playground equipment; sledding hill; sugar camp; wildlife watching.

Directions

GPS coordinates: 41.665425, –86.506826

From I-65

- East on I-94 at Gary to US 20 at Michigan City, 27.6 miles
- East on US 20 to State Road 2, 11.4 miles
- East on State Road 2 to Timothy Road, 4.2 miles
- South on Timothy Road to park and preserve, 0.4 mile

From US 231

- West on State Road 2 at South Bend to Timothy Road, 8.0 miles
- South on Timothy Road to park and preserve, 0.4 mile

Kankakee Marsh Section

34. LaSalle Fish & Wildlife Area

Owned by Indiana Department of Natural Resources, Division of Fish & Wildlife

The 3,797-acre LaSalle Fish & Wildlife Area in Newton County supports a diverse mix of habitats along five miles of the Kankakee River on the Illinois border, including hardwood forests, savannas, croplands, marshes, bayous, ditches, and ponds. Bisected by the river and protecting a remnant of the once-dominant Grand Kankakee Marsh, the property's natural characteristics provide breeding grounds, food, and cover for migrating waterfowl and shorebirds in winter and spring.

LaSalle's plant life includes wildflowers, such as the compass plant, along with prairie grass, sedge grass, and cattails. The croplands are planted with sunflower, sorghum, and other plants that attract wildlife.

The preserve's Black Oak Bayou Waterfowl Resting Area is fed by the Beaver Lake Ditch and is designated as a nature preserve on the LaSalle property map. Driving to it is seasonally limited. The resting area doubled in size in 2013 to attract more birds in greater varieties as well as to provide nesting and breeding habitat for other wetland creatures. Water levels are managed to create a variety of depths for diving birds that need deep water, puddle ducks that need shallow water, teal that need

LaSalle Fish & Wildlife Area

mud flats, and yellowlegs that need exposed mud flats with long edges. Hunting is prohibited in the Black Oak Bayou.

Managed for hunting and fishing, LaSalle's fish species include bluegill, crappie, smallmouth bass, largemouth bass, northern pike, walleye, and rock bass. Game animals include ducks, geese, turkeys, deer, quails, pheasants, rabbits, doves, squirrels, snipes, rails, and woodcocks.

When its namesake, René-Robert Cavelier, Sieur de La Salle, became the first European in the region in the late 1670s, today's LaSalle Fish & Wildlife Area was part of the Grand Kankakee Marsh, the world's largest wetland. After the Potawatomi Indians were expelled from the region in the early 1830s and the white settlers moved in, a burgeoning hunting and trapping industry developed around the wetlands. By the early 1900s, the Kankakee River had been straightened, and the entire marsh had been drained for agriculture. (See the Kankakee Fish &

Wildlife section below for more details.) The wildlife area's development began in 1952, when 1,800 acres were dedicated as the Kankakee River State Park. State officials acquired more land, and in 1963 they determined it was better suited for use as a fish and wildlife area.

Service roads serve as trails along the river's south bank and around the Black Oak Bayou Waterfowl Resting Area and another section to the west.

Activities

Berry, nut, and mushroom collecting; boat ramps; fishing; hiking (paths and service roads serve as trails); hunting; nature study; photography; wildlife watching.

Directions

GPS coordinates: 41.155235, −87.482829

From I-74

- North on US 41 to State Road 10 at Lake Village, 75.9 miles
- West on State Road 10 to County Road 475W, 1.4 miles
- North on County Road 475W to County Road 1050N and the preserve, 0.5 mile

From I-65

- West on State Road 10 at Roselawn to County Road 475W, 11.1 miles
- North on County Road 475W to County Road 1050N and the preserve, 0.5 mile

35. NIPSCO Savanna / Aukiki Wetland Conservation Area

Owned by The Nature Conservancy; Indiana Department of Natural Resources, Division of Fish & Wildlife; NiSource

The 221-acre NIPSCO Savanna in Jasper County is part of an 812-acre natural complex that is composed of sand ridges, flats, and damp depressions that are managed cooperatively between nonprofit, government, and private organizations. The savanna supports a diverse mix of black oak barren, sand prairie, and wetland communities.

NIPSCO Savanna

The long-term preservation goal is to restore and enhance native plants and animals that once covered vast expanses of this natural region, including blazing stars and prickly pear cacti, along with state species of special concern plains pocket gophers and sandhill cranes, as well as grassland-dependent skippers.

Black oak dominates the savanna's covered areas, with Pennsylvania sedge and wild lupine growing on the shaded floor. Little bluestem grass dominates the dry sand prairie sections, which also support rough dropseed grass, dwarf dandelion, and flowering spurge.

The savanna was part of a 650-acre donation from the Northwest Indiana utility NIPSCO and is located across the road from the company's Schahfer Generating Station electric power plant. The Nature Conservancy kept the savanna and transferred 429 acres of former farmland to the Indiana Division of Fish & Wildlife. That acreage is now managed as the Aukiki Wetland Conservation Area. These lands surround another 162 acres that are still owned by NIPSCO's parent, NiSource, but managed consistent with conservation goals.

Land management at the NIPSCO Savanna includes removing wooden understory to reduce canopy cover and controlled burns to enhance the barrens and prairie. The Aukiki farm field was planted with warm-season grasses to provide wildlife habitat. The wetland areas provide breeding and migration habitat for waterfowl along the Kankakee River.

The parking lot sign says Aukiki Hunting Information. A Nature Conservancy sign is located just east of the parking lot on the north side of the road.

Activities
Hiking (no trails, plant cover, easy), nature study, photography, wildlife watching.

Directions
GPS coordinates: 41.230570, –87.038467
From I-65
- East on State Road 10 at Roselawn to State Road 49, 14.3 miles
- North on State Road 49 to County Road 1500N, 3.0 miles
- East on County Road 1500N to preserve, 0.3 mile
From US 31
- West on US 30 at Plymouth to State Road 39, 24.2 miles
- South on State Road 39 to State Road 8, 6.1 miles
- West on State Road 8 to State Road 49 at Kouts, 14.9 miles
- South on State Road 49 to County Road 1500N, 6.3 miles
- East on County Road 1500N to preserve, 0.3 mile

36. Kankakee Fish & Wildlife Area
Owned by Indiana Department of Natural Resources, Division of Fish & Wildlife
The 4,095-acre Kankakee Fish & Wildlife Area's habitats include eleven miles of Kankakee River shoreline, open water, marshes, riverine forest, and periodically flooded crop fields. Managed for hunting and fishing in Starke County, this floodplain wildlife

Kankakee Fish & Wildlife Area

area stretches in a narrow five-mile swath northeast from the confluence of the Yellow River and Kankakee River and includes a total of forty-five miles of rivers and ditches.

State endangered osprey and state species of special concern bald eagle and sandhill crane are among the unusual bird species that inhabit the Kankakee River's lowland areas. They share the sloughs and marshy bottomlands with beavers, muskrats, hawks, owls, and a diverse variety of waterfowl.

Game animals at the Kankakee wildlife area include deer, quails, rabbits, doves, woodcocks, waterfowl, and wild turkeys. Fish include smallmouth bass, largemouth bass, bluegills, crappies, northern pikes, redear sunfish, walleyed pikes, and various panfishes and catfishes.

The wildlife area is situated in what was known in pre- and early settlement times as the Grand Kankakee Marsh—world-famous for waterfowl and game—which extended along Lake Michigan from the Illinois state line to Michigan City and covered nearly a million acres of Indiana and Illinois.

The marsh, also known as the "Everglades of the North" or the Grand Marsh, was Potawatomi Indian territory when La

Salle and other French explorers arrived in the late 1600s. After the Native Americans were exiled to western reservations in the early 1830s, the Kankakee River Basin became the province of fur trappers, who sold muskrat, beaver, and other fur-bearing pelts. Sportsmen's clubs, centered around fur trapping, hunting, and fishing, became prevalent and are still evident today.

In its natural state, the Kankakee River had more than two thousand bends. Drainage projects to convert it for agriculture continued throughout the 1800s; in 1911, a dredging and channelizing program for the Kankakee River began. Six years later, the main Kankakee channel had been straightened, with its original 250 miles reduced to eighty-five.

The state bought 2,312 acres of what marshland was left in 1927 to house Roosevelt-era Civilian Conservation Corps (CCC) workers, who restored public lands for parks and other public uses. The wildlife area was established as a game preserve in the post-CCC era, and waterfowl management was implemented in the 1950s.

Today, the Kankakee remains one of Indiana's most extensive water drainage systems, encompassing roughly three thousand square miles of river basin. The land is flat to moderately rolling, a consequence of extensive glaciation.

A ten-mile scenic drive follows levy roads along the Kankakee's southern bank and the Yellow's northern bank.

Activities
Berry picking; boating, twenty-four-volt electric motors only, outboard motors on rivers only; boat ramps, two; canoeing; fishing (accessible); hiking; hunting (accessible); mushroom hunting; nature study; photography; scenic drive; wildlife watching.

Directions
GPS coordinates: 41.259126, –86.782041
From I-65
- East on State Road 2 south of Merrillville to State Road 8 at Hebron, 7.2 miles
- East on State Road 8 to State Road 39, 24.0 miles

- South on State Road 39 to Toto Road, 4.0 miles
- West on Toto Road to office, 2.3 miles

From US 31
- West on US 30 at Plymouth to US 35, 18.2 miles
- South on US 35 to State Road 8, 5.2 miles
- West on State Road 8 to State Road 39, 6.0 miles
- South on State Road 39 to Toto Road, 4.0 miles
- West on Toto Road to office, 2.3 miles

37. Kingsbury Fish & Wildlife Area

*Owned by Indiana Department of Natural Resources,
Division of Fish & Wildlife*

The 7,280-acre Kingsbury Fish & Wildlife Area in LaPorte County is a complex of landforms that are managed for hunting and fishing. Its grasslands, crop fields, thick brush, marshes, conifer and hardwood stands, thirty-acre lake, and Kankakee River shoreline support a diverse collection of wildlife, especially birds.

The Kingsbury wildlife area includes two scenic, adjacent wetlands just north of the Kankakee River: Grande Marsh and Tamarack Marsh. In addition to game species, Kingsbury's environs attract hawks, owls, eagles, shorebirds, wading birds, and songbirds, both resident and migrating. Among the fish species that inhabit the wildlife area's two creeks are channel catfish, bluegill, crappie, largemouth bass, and northern pike.

The former munitions plant has been managed for wildlife since it was deeded to the state by the federal government in 1965. The facility produced shells, cartridges, and mortar rounds for World War II and the Korean War. Kingsbury includes contaminated areas that are off limits to the public.

Activities

Archery range; berry picking; boat ramps on Kankakee River and Tamarack Lake, maximum twelve-volt electric motor for lakes, gas motors allowed on the river; dog training area; fishing; hiking; hunting; mushroom hunting; nature study;

Kingsbury Fish & Wildlife Area

photography; shooting range, ADA compliant; wetland trapping; wildlife watching.

Directions

GPS coordinates: 41.518982, –86.624314

From I-65

- East on US 30 at Merrillville to State Road 2 at Valparaiso, 13.3 miles
- East on State Road 2 to County Road 600N, 8.9 miles
- East on County Road 600N to US 6, 3.0 miles
- East on US 6, to US 35, 10.2 miles
- North on US 35 to Hupp Road, 400 feet
- East on Hupp Road to wildlife area, 3.7 miles

From US 31

- West on US 6 at LaPaz to State Road 104 at Walkerton, 76.6 miles
- Northeast on State Road 104 to County Road 675E, 6.5 miles
- South on County Road 675E to Hupp Road, 1.4 miles
- West on Hupp Road to wildlife area, 2.6 miles

Section 3

NORTHERN LAKES
NATURAL REGION

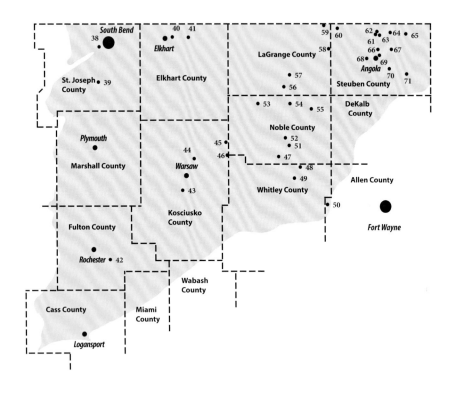

A GUIDE TO NATURAL AREAS OF NORTHERN INDIANA

Section 3

NORTHERN LAKES NATURAL REGION

60. Ropchan Memorial Nature Preserve
61. Pokagon State Park / Potawatomi Nature Preserve
62. Beechwood Nature Preserve / Foster Nature Preserve / Majneri Nature Preserve
63. Trine State Recreation Area
64. Marsh Lake / Marsh Lake Nature Preserve / Marsh Lake Wetland Conservation Area
65. Ropchan Wildlife Refuge / Ropchan Wetland Conservation Area
66. Wing Haven Nature Preserve
67. Charles McClue Reserve
68. Loon Lake Nature Preserve
69. Marion's Woods Nature Preserve
70. Robb Hidden Canyon
71. Douglas Woods Nature Preserve

NORTHERN LAKES
NATURAL REGION

NORTHERN LAKES NATURAL REGION

38. Potato Creek State Park

Owned by Indiana Department of Natural Resources,
Division of State Parks & Lakes

The 3,840-acre Potato Creek State Park in St. Joseph County features a variety of natural features, including creek, pond, lake, old farm field, sedge meadow, mature woodland, restored prairie, and diverse wetlands, including marshes and fens. These natural areas are largely the result of restoration efforts begun in the early 1990s.

Before Potato Creek became a state park in 1969, most of its landscape had been altered by farming and other land uses. The restorations are designed to re-create conditions resembling those that existed before Europeans began settling the area in the 1830s and to provide habitats—especially wetlands—for a variety of plant and animal species.

More than a square mile of Potato Creek is covered by the 327-acre Worster Lake and associated wetlands, which include saturated sedge meadows, shallow marshes, swamps, and beaver ponds, all of which support abundant wildlife, especially during spring and fall bird migrations. The Swamp Rose Nature Preserve protects a scenic stream that, over hundreds of years, has evolved into a wetland that flows into the lake. Native prairie plantings are restoring old fields, which are maintained by controlled burns to deter unwanted woody species that eventually would crowd out the grasslands.

Potato Creek State Park has been designated an Important Bird Area by the National Audubon Society because the "diversity of its habitats, combined with its relative isolation from other natural landscapes, helps make Potato Creek State Park one of the most significant areas in North Central Indiana for congregations of migratory birds, as well as breeding populations of species listed as those of conservation priority."

Since the restorations began, the parkland's open areas have attracted grassland species such as grasshopper sparrow, bobolink, and state endangered Henslow's sparrow, all of which had disappeared by the 1980s. The state endangered sedge wren nests at Potato Creek during the summer.

Potato Creek is home to two of the state's nine known nesting sites for osprey. In addition to the state endangered Virginia rail, the sandhill crane, a state species of special concern, has nested there in the past. So too has the alder flycatcher, which usually nests to the north of Indiana. State species of special concern red-shouldered hawks nest in the Swamp Rose preserve.

Audubon says on its Potato Creek Important Bird Area webpage that during migratory periods, the park supports "arguably the largest concentrations of neotropical migrants in the north-central section of Indiana." Among the Audubon WatchList species that pass through are the state endangered golden-winged warbler and cerulean warbler, along with the blue-winged warbler, American woodcock, and willow flycatcher.

Other areas of the park are succeeding to hardwood forest, which features spring wildflower displays and a variety of wildlife, including songbirds, raccoons, foxes, coyotes, and turkeys.

Native Americans used today's Potato Creek parkland as hunting and fishing grounds before the Europeans began settling there in the 1830s. They collected plants with potato-like roots from the creek banks, which the settlers' English translated as "wild potato"—hence the creek and park's name.

While their efforts were stymied by World War II, conservationists, led by self-taught naturalist Darcey Worster, proposed a man-made reservoir on Potato Creek as early as the late 1930s. Worster kept pressure on state officials by sending them handcrafted insects to "bug" them about the park. The park was finally created in 1969.

Activities
Hiking Trails: Eight (0.5–2.5 miles), easy to rugged.
Bridle Trails: Three (1.5–3.35 miles).
Bicycle Trail: One (3.3 miles).
Mountain Bike Trails: Three (0.9–3.3 miles), easy.

Camping: 287 electric, seventy horsemen sites, youth tent area; camp store, dumping station.

Other Activities: Bicycle rentals; boat launch ramps, electric trolling motors only; seventeen cabins; canoe, paddleboat, rowboat, kayak rentals; cross-country skiing, no ski rental; fishing, ice fishing, fishing pier; nature center/interpretive services; nature study; photography; picnicking, shelters; playground equipment; recreation building; swimming beach; tubing hill; wildlife watching, wetland observation deck.

Directions
GPS coordinates: 41.534970, –86.361985
From I-65
- East on I-80/90 (Toll Road) at Gary to US 421 at Michigan City, 26.5 miles
- South on US 421 to State Road 2, 1.9 miles
- East on State Road 2 to 18th Street on South Bend's east side, 8.2 miles
- East on 18th Street, becoming Crescent Drive, to US 35, 10.7 miles
- South on US 35 to Boyd Boulevard, 0.4 mile
- East on Boyd Boulevard to State Road 4 (Monroe Street), 1.9 miles
- East on State Road 4, through North Liberty to park, 18.6 miles

From US 31
- West on State Road 4 south of South Bend 4 to park, 5.7 miles

39. Chamberlain Lake Nature Preserve
Owned by Indiana Department of Natural Resources, Division of Nature Preserves
The 82.5-acre Chamberlain Lake Nature Preserve in St. Joseph County protects the western half of Chamberlain Lake, a shallow basin that has little open water during much of the year. The preserve harbors a dozen and a half sensitive plants—four of which that are endangered and seven that are threatened in Indiana.

Chamberlain Lake Nature Preserve

As the lake's water levels recede, wetland communities, such as muck flats and floating vegetation mats, develop in their places. Several plants that grow in the Chamberlain environs are more common to the Atlantic Coastal Plain and are out of their range there.

In the fall of 2001, a tornado leveled almost every canopy tree in the surrounding oak woods but did not damage the wetland.

Activities
Hiking Trails: 1.5 miles
Other Activities: Nature study; photography; wildlife watching, observation platform.

Directions
GPS coordinates: 41.647067, –86.369327
From I-65
- East on I-80/94 (Toll Road) to US 20 at Michigan City, 27.5 miles
- East on US 20 to State Road 2, 11.5 miles
- East on State Road 2 to Pear Road west of South Bend, 10.6 miles

- South on Pear Road to Crumstown Highway, 2.0 miles
- East on Crumstown Highway to preserve, 0.9 mile

From US 31

- West on US 2 on South Bend's west to Pine Road, 0.3 mile
- South on Pine Road to Crumstown Highway, 1.0 mile
- West on Crumstown Highway to preserve, 1.3 miles

40. Boot Lake Nature Preserve

Owned by City of Elkhart

The 201-acre Boot Lake Nature Preserve in Elkhart County is a wetland complex surrounding glacially formed kettle lakes that are naturally filling in and evolving into peaty muck flats and sand flats. These rare-in-Indiana ecosystems support several plants that are more common on the Atlantic Coastal Plain. The dedicated state nature preserve also features buttonbush swamp, upland woods and fields, savanna, tallgrass prairie, and a City of Elkhart tree nursery.

Boot Lake, which served as a dumping ground for Elkhart's Wastewater Treatment Plant from the 1970s until the 1990s, supports roughly 180 bird species and has been designated an Important Bird Area by the National Audubon Society. "Boot Lake Nature Preserve supports a diversity of nesting wetland and grassland species that typically are only paralleled at larger landscapes," Audubon says on its website. "This, combined with the paucity of similar habitat within North Central Indiana, makes Boot Lake a significant refuge for many bird species that are declining throughout the state."

Boot Lake's wet areas support nesting sandhill cranes, which are state species of special concern and were once considered gone as a breeding species in Indiana. Other rare wetland birds that may breed at Boot Lake are the American woodcock and state endangered Virginia rail. Both are listed on Audubon's WatchList.

As the prairie evolves, grassland birds, such as the state endangered sedge wren and Henslow's sparrow, are nesting at Boot Lake, as are the grasshopper sparrow and dickcissel.

Boot Lake Nature Preserve

Henslow's sparrow and dickcissel are on Audubon's WatchList. The grasshopper sparrow is one of the fastest-declining land-birds on the continent.

Boot Lake likewise supports rare plants, including state threatened umbrella-sedge and state rare weakstalk bulrush (also known as Smith's bullrush). The preserve is one of only four in Indiana with dwarf umbrella-sedge. Other plants include wildflowers, such as meadow beauty; rushes, sedges, and grasses, including big bluestem grass, Indian grass, blue joint grass; and hardwood tress such as sugar maple, American beech, and red oak. At its tree nursery, Elkhart's Forestry Division maintains about fifty tree varieties, which are planted around the city.

Boot Lake's public history dates to the early 1970s, when Elkhart began using the site as a sludge dump. In the early 1990s, the city removed some seventy thousand pounds of trash and built walking trails and a 108-foot plastic lumber board-walk. The nature preserve opened in July 1995. Roughly half of its four miles of trails are accessible. A viewing platform extends from the forest edge into the wetland.

Activities

Hiking Trails: Twelve (0.2–1.2 miles; 2 miles accessible), one with a photography blind).

Other Activities: Nature study, photography, picnic pavilion, wildlife watching.

Directions

GPS coordinates: 41.747194, –86.018915

From US 31

- East on I-90 (Toll Road) through South Bend to State Road 331, 10.6 miles
- North on State Road 331 to State Road 23, 0.3 mile
- Northeast on State Road 23, becoming Adams Road to County Road 2, 7.0 miles
- South on County Road 2 to Williams Lane, 0.4 mile
- East on Williams Lane to preserve, 0.2 mile

From I-69

- West on I-80/90 (Toll Road) near Fremont to County Road 4 via Elkhart East exit, 47.3 miles
- West on County Road 4 to Edwardsburg Road 5, 7.4 miles
- North on Edwardsburg Road to County Road 3, 0.2 mile
- North on County Road 3 to Williams Lane, 0.4 mile
- East on Williams Lane to preserve, 0.2 mile

41. Pipewort Pond Nature Preserve

Owned by Indiana Department of Natural Resources,
Division of Nature Preserves

The 135-acre Pipewort Pond Nature Preserve in Elkhart County occupies a shallow basin with wide seasonal fluctuations in water levels, which attracts a diversity of herons, ducks, and shorebirds. Also known as the William L. Lieber Memorial Preserve, this site protects a dozen rare plant species in Indiana.

Among the unusual plants at this dedicated state nature preserve are the state endangered pipewort, which is more common on the Atlantic Coastal Plain, the state threatened dwarf umbrella-sedge, and the state rare Robbins spike rush and green-keeled cotton grass, which are likewise out of their

Pipewort Pond Nature Preserve

geographical ranges. Other notable plants include the state threatened long-beaked baldrush and Carolina yellow-eyed grass, as well as state rare narrow-leaved cotton grass, tall beaked-rush, weakstalk bulrush, and purple bladderwort.

Pipewort may look like a pond, but it is actually a glacial basin that today features peaty muck flats and sand flats in late summer on areas that are submerged underwater in spring and early summer. During wet periods, the water supports yellow pond lilies and other wetland plants, including pipewort, which appears as a tiny white flower clusters on the water's surface.

The open, more shallow areas support carnivorous plants, including purple bladderwort. The boggier spots protect large cranberry, winterberry, and poison sumac.

Sandhill cranes are among the birds that frequent the preserve, along with Canada geese, wood ducks, mallards, great blue herons, downy woodpeckers, black-capped chickadees, tufted titmice, golden-crowned kinglets, red-winged blackbirds, and others.

Activities
Hiking Trails: Boardwalk, easy.
Other Activities: Nature study, photography, wildlife watching.

Directions
GPS coordinates: 41.744696, –85.822924
From US 31
- East on I-80–90 (Toll Road), through South Bend, to County Road 17 northeast of Elkhart, 23.7 miles
- North on County Road 17 to State Line Road on the Indiana-Michigan border, 1.7 miles
- East on State Line Road to County Road 19, 0.3 mile
- South on County Road 19 to County Road 2, 0.4 mile
- East on County Road 2 to County Road 23, 2.4 miles
- South on County Road 23 to preserve, 0.5 mile

From I-69
- West on I-80/90 (Toll Road) near Fremont to State Road 15 at Bristol, 42.5 miles
- Southwest on State Road 15 to Vistula Road in Bristol, 1.5 miles
- West on Vistula Road to County Road 23 (Division Street), 0.2 mile
- North on County Road 23 (Division Street) to preserve, 1.7 miles

42. Manitou Wetlands Complex / Manitou Islands Nature Preserve / Judy Burton Nature Preserve / Bob Kern Nature Preserve

Owned by Indiana Department of Natural Resources, Divisions of Fish & Wildlife and Nature Preserves

The 740-acre Manitou Wetlands Complex in Fulton County protects wetland communities on Lake Manitou that include high-quality marshland covered with cattails, lily pads, bulrushes, grasses, sedges, and aquatic flowers. In places, forested islands protrude from the marsh, supporting oak and hickory trees on the higher sites and tamarack trees on the lower sites.

Judy Burton Nature Preserve

Old fields have been converted to wildflower-rich savanna and prairie conditions.

Manitou Wetlands is composed of three adjacent dedicated state nature preserves on the south end of the spring-fed lake: 308-acre Manitou Islands Nature Preserve, 130-acre Judy Burton Nature Preserve, and 302-acre Bob Kern Nature Preserve. Altogether, the acreage totals more than a square mile and represents one of the largest landmasses in the state nature preserve system.

The preserves support almost two hundred plant species, including pickerel weed, yellow water lily, and white water lily. Wetland birds that live in or pass through Manitou Wetlands include the state endangered marsh wren, sedge wren, and Virginia rail, as well as red-winged blackbirds, swamp sparrows, mallards, wood ducks, Wilson's snipes, blue-winged teals, shovelers, canvasbacks, lesser scaups, ringnecks, and Canada geese. Muskrats, minks, white-tailed deer, raccoons, skunks, and opossums are among the animals that thrive in the preserves' soggy environs.

The Manitou Islands Nature Preserve is accessible by boat only and has no trails. The 775-acre Lake Manitou has two boat ramps that may be closed occasionally due to hydrilla infestations.

The Judy Burton Nature Preserve features a network of trails through the prairie and woods that are connected to the Nickel Plate Trail, a more than forty-mile rail trail that runs from Rochester south to Kokomo. Cyclists may use the Burton parking lot to connect to the Nickel Plate, but bicycles are not allowed on Burton trails.

The Kern Nature Preserve has two parking lots but no trails. The North lot has a launch for hand-carried boats, such as canoes and rowboats. It too may be closed occasionally due to hydrilla infestations.

Activities
Hiking, nature study, photography, wildlife watching.

Directions to Burton Nature Preserve
GPS coordinates: 41.041749, −86.187975
From US 31
- North on Wabash Avenue to Westside Road, 0.5 mile
- North on Westside Road to preserve, 300 feet

43. Wildwood Nature Preserve
Owned by ACRES Land Trust

The 235.5-acre Wildwood Nature Preserve in Kosciusko County protects a diverse, rolling landscape with upland and lowland forests, prairie plantings, pine plantings, restored wetlands, vernal pools, and a small pond. A ninety-four-acre dedicated state nature preserve within the larger area is composed of well-drained uplands and poorly drained swamp forest in low-lying areas.

The nature preserve supports a stand of mature oak-hickory forest, with particularly large white oak, chinquapin oak, swamp white oak, shagbark hickory, and black walnut trees. A variety of birds live in or pass through Wildwood, including wood ducks and woodpeckers—redheaded and pileated. Wet areas support

Wildwood Nature Preserve

turtles, frogs, birds, and snakes. Large-flowered trillium and other spring wildflowers blanket the forest floor in spring.

Wildwood has a caretaker's house with a kiosk and information. The house and property was originally owned by Robert and Alice Frantz, who had opened it to the public.

Activities
Hiking Trails: Network (4.5 miles), moderate.
Other Activities: Fishing, hiking, hunting, nature study, photography, wildlife watching.

Directions
GPS coordinates: 41.072619, –85.827217
From US 31
- East on State Road 14 at Rochester, past Silver Lake to preserve, 24.9 miles

From I-69
- West on State Road 14 on Fort Wayne's southeast side, through South Whitley, to preserve, 31.7 miles

Oppenheim Woods Nature Preserve

44. Oppenheim Woods Nature Preserve

Owned by The Nature Conservancy

The sixty-three-acre Oppenheim Woods Nature Preserve in Kosciusko County protects rolling, mixed-hardwood forest with dozens of tree species, including sugar maple, black cherry, and white oak, along with groves of pawpaw. Also called the Indiana banana, the pawpaw produces the largest edible fruit of any native North American tree.

Oppenheim, situated across a county road from Tippecanoe Lake, is reputed to have one of the most spectacular wildflower displays in the Midwest, with a diverse assemblage of spring flowers that include large-flowered trillium, wood (celandine) poppy, blue phlox, and others. In summer, lush ferns dominate the forest floor.

The woodland is managed for invasive species, such as burning bush, purple creeper, periwinkle, spindle tree, and other common landscaping plants that spread beyond their owners' yards.

Activities

Hiking Trails: One (1.2 miles).

Other Activities: Nature study, photography, wildlife watching.

Directions

GPS coordinates: 41.337105, –85.763903

From US 31

- East on US 30 at Plymouth to State Road 331, 8.6 miles
- North on State Road 331 to State Road 19 (Eighth Road), 3.0 miles
- East on State Road 19 to County Road 300E at Dewart Lake, 17.1 miles
- South on County Road 300E to County Road 750N, 1.4 miles
- East on County Road 750N to County Road 400E, 1.0 mile
- South on County Road 400E, becoming Kalorama Road, to preserve, 0.5 mile

From I-69

- West on US 30 at Fort Wayne to Lincoln Highway/Old US 30 at Columbia City, 17.1 miles
- Northwest on Lincoln Highway to State Road 13, 22.8 miles
- North on State Road 13 to County Road 500N before North Webster, 5.2 miles
- West on County Road 500N to County Road 675E, 1.2 miles
- North on County Road 675E to County Road 650N, 1.5 miles
- West on County Road 650N to Kalorama Road, 2.0 miles
- Northwest on Kalorama Road to preserve, 0.7 mile

45a. Tri-County Fish & Wildlife Area

Owned by Indiana Department of Natural Resources, Division of Fish & Wildlife

The 3,546-acre Tri-County Fish & Wildlife Area in Kosciusko and Noble Counties features a rolling landscape that ranges from upland woods and fields to low-lying wetlands, with 650 acres of lakes and impoundments. The area surrounds the ten-acre Greider's Woods Nature Preserve, which protects seven plant species that are rare in Indiana.

Tri-County Fish & Wildlife Area

Tri-County, which is managed for hunting and fishing, includes steep slopes of oak and hickory that surround ten natural lakes—which reach depths of up to seventy-five feet—and thirty-two man-made impoundments with two hundred acres of restored open wetlands. Situated near the Whitley County Line due south of Lake Wawasee, Indiana's largest natural lake, Tri-County's largest waterbodies are Shock Lake and Spear Lake. The area is known locally as Hoss Hills.

Great blue herons and other waterfowl frequent the lakes and wetlands. Primary fish include bass, bluegill, redear sunfish, crappie, and trout. Trapping and hunting is allowed for woodland game, upland game, waterfowl, and furbearers.

Tri-County was established in 1951. A dam was constructed in 1963 that created the Flatbelly Marsh from six natural lakes. The wetland supports migratory waterfowl, furbearers, shorebirds, and fish.

45b. Greider's Woods Nature Preserve

The ten-acre Greider's Woods Nature Preserve protects a mature, second-growth oak-hickory forest that supports sugar maple, black walnut, white ash, black oak, chinquapin oak, red oak, and tulip trees, some of which exceed thirty inches in diameter.

The dedicated state nature preserve supports the state endangered thinleaf sedge, state rare rushlike aster and fire cherry, and state watch-listed thicket sedge, butternut, and orange coneflower.

Black haw, maple-leaved viburnum, pawpaw, and hazelnut thrive in the preserve's understory alongside grape, gooseberry, and raspberry. Spring wildflowers include spring beauty, mayapple, and large-flowered trillium. False Solomon's seal, sweet cicely, northern bedstraw, and appendaged waterleaf flourish later in the year. Just across from the preserve, Heron Pond features floating logs with snakes and turtles that bask in the sun.

Greider's Woods, which was part of the Flatbelly Indian Reservation, was formerly owned by the Jethro Greider family.

The Spear Lake Nature Trail is a short loop that traverses the preserve.

Activities

Hiking Trails: One at Greider's Woods, interpretive; user paths and service roads.

Other Activities: Boats, electric motors only on lakes and ponds, no gas motors; fishing, shoreline from Goldeneye Pond, Bass Pond, and the Wawasee Family Fishing Area; hiking, hunting, nature study, photography, wildlife watching.

Directions to Fish & Wildlife Office

GPS coordinates: 41.357224, –85.682070

From US 31

- East on US 30 at Plymouth, to County Road 200W on Warsaw's west side, 21.7 miles
- North on County Road 200W to County Road 400N, 1.5 miles
- East on County Road 400N to State Road 15, 0.8 mile
- North on State Road 15 to County Road 600N, 2.0 miles

- East on County Road 600N to Old State Road 15, 0.5 mile
- North on Old State Road 15 to County Road 700N at Leesburg, 0.7 mile
- East on County Road 700N to County Road 300E, 3.1 miles
- North on County Road 300E to County Road 750N, 0.5 mile
- East on County Road 750N to County Road 400E, 1.0 mile
- North on County Road 400E to County Road 800N, 0.3 mile
- East on County Road 800N to State Road 13, 3.4 miles
- North on State Road 13 to County Road 900N, 1.0 mile
- East on County Road 900N to County Road 850E, 1.0 mile
- South on County Road 850E to office, 0.5 mile

From I-69
- West on US 33 at Fort Wayne to State Road 5, 27.0 miles
- West on State Road 5 to County Road 1000E, 5.8 miles
- South on County Road 1000E to County Road 1000N, 0.2 mile
- West on County Road 1000N to Hatchery Road by Lake Wawasee, 0.8 mile
- South on Hatchery Road to County Road 850E, 0.8 mile
- South on County Road 850E to office, 0.7 mile

Directions to Greider Woods Nature Preserve
GPS coordinates: 41.354896, −85.653254
From Office
- North on County Road 850E to Koher Road, 1.0 mile
- East on Koher Road to County Road 1200W, 1.8 mile
- South on County Road 1200W to preserve (sign says Spear Lake Nature Trail), 0.7 mile

46. Pisgah Marsh Fish & Wildlife Area / Pisgah Marsh Nature Preserve / Durham Lake Wildlife Conservation Area

Owned by Indiana Department of Natural Resources, Division of Fish & Wildlife

The 947-acre Pisgah Marsh / Durham Lake natural complex supports grassland, wetland, upland forest, and two lakes in adjoining units that provide habitat for nearly three hundred

Pisgah Marsh Fish & Wildlife Area

bird species. The 445-acre Pisgah Marsh Fish & Wildlife Area includes one of the state's newest dedicated state nature preserves and surrounds the 6.67-acre Pisgah Lake. The adjoining 502-acre Durham Lake Wildlife Conservation Area encompasses the thirteen-acre Durham Lake. The Tri-County Fish & Wildlife Area office manages both properties, which straddle the Kosciusko, Noble, and Whitley County lines.

Approved in 2017, the 118-acre Pisgah Marsh Nature Preserve protects a variety of ecosystems, including high-quality fen, sedge meadow, marsh, and oak woodland. Among its rare animals are Virginia rail, sedge wren, and least bittern, all of which are state endangered. The preserve also supports sandhill cranes, a state species of special concern, along with migratory waterfowl, beavers, rails, squirrels, raccoons, and deer.

The preserve's only access is via the 0.3-mile Pisgah Marsh Boardwalk and Golden Eagle Viewing Deck, which is ADA accessible. Access to the rest of the Pisgah Fish & Wildlife Area is limited.

The Durham Lake area is managed for fishing and hunting, though special rules and regulations exist. Primary fish species include largemouth bass and bluegill. Primary game species include furbearers, waterfowl, woodland game, and upland game.

Information about accessing both areas can be obtained from Tri-County Fish & Wildlife office.

Activities

Hiking Trails: Boardwalk and observation deck at Pisgah Lake (0.3 mile), easy, ADA accessible.

Other Activities: Boating, small boats only, no gas motors; fishing, Durham Lake; hiking, no trails; hunting; nature study; photography; wildlife watching.

Directions

GPS coordinates: 41.287641, –85.652138

From US 31

- East on US 30 at Plymouth to Old State Road 30 on Warsaw's east side, 82.6 miles
- East on Old State Road 30 to Old Trail Road, 34.4 miles
- East on Old Trail Road to County Line Road, 0.2 mile
- North on County Line Road to County Road 650N, 1.4 miles
- East on County Road 650N to State Road 5, 0.4 mile
- North on State Road 5 to County Road 350N, 2.3 miles
- West on County Road 350N to wildlife area, 0.5 mile

From I-69

- West on US 30 at Fort Wayne, through Columbia City, to State Road 5, 25.4 miles
- North on State Road 5 to County Road 350N (850:N92), 5.6 miles
- West on County Road 350N to wildlife area, 0.5 mile

47. Merry Lea Nature Preserve

Owned by Goshen College

The 1,150-acre Merry Lea Nature Preserve in Noble County protects a moraine lake and its associated meltwater wetlands and forested esker uplands, along with a range of natural communities that represent most habitats that exist in Northeast Indiana. Among them are wetlands, shallow marshes, tamarack bogs, natural lakeshores, swamp forests, upland forests, savannas, prairies, wet meadows, and seasonal flooded basins. The site also supports some unique geological features, such as peat bogs, a marl pit, and glacial gravel formations.

The sanctuary, which occupies the south shore of the developed 136-acre Bear Lake, provides habitat for 170 species of birds, thirty-two fish, twenty-eight mammals, and seventeen amphibians. Goshen College's Merry Lea Environmental Learning Center manages it and uses it for environmental and ecological education.

Within Merry Lea's boundaries is a 353-acre dedicated state nature preserve that protects a dozen rare state plant species, including state endangered Montgomery hawthorn, Nuttall pondweed, and northern wild-raisin; state threatened small cranberry; state rare bog rosemary, rushlike aster, and grove meadow grass; and state watch-listed thicket sedge. A notable animal species is the state species of special concern northern leopard frog. Merry Lea's bird species include pileated woodpecker, great horned owl, scarlet tanager, and indigo bunting. Mammals include mink, muskrat, squirrel, bat, and fox. Amphibians include western chorus frogs and pickerel frogs.

The Onion Bottom Wetland is a former onion field that has been restored. The meadows support native and nonnative grasses. The black oak savanna supports black oak trees and grasses and forbs that include little bluestem, butterfly weed, and round-headed bush clover. The tallgrass prairie supports native grasses—Indian grass, big bluestem, little bluestem, and side-oats grama.

The Environmental Learning Center is guided by a Christian theology of earthkeeping. Its mission statement calls for the following:

- Providing a natural sanctuary for Northern Indiana's plants and animals

Merry Lea Nature Preserve

- Providing environmental education for people of all ages
- Providing a setting for re-creating opportunities that benefit the human body and spirit while not exploiting the land or excessively disturbing its ecosystems

The Merry Lea Sustainable Farm demonstrates sustainable agriculture practices for students and the public. Permission is required to visit the Nature Preserve.

Activities

Hiking Trails: Eight miles of marked trails; no trails in nature preserve.

Other Activities: Nature study, photography, wildlife watching.

Directions

GPS coordinates: 41.313090, –85.517111

From US 31

- East on US 30 at Plymouth to Old Road 30 on Warsaw's east side, 24.9 miles
- East on Old Road 30 to Old Trail Road, 7.9 miles
- East on Old Trail Road to County Line Road, 0.2 mile
- North on County Line Road to County Road 650N, 1.2 miles
- East on County Road 650N to State Road 5, 0.4 mile
- North on State Road 5 to County Road 750N, 1.3 miles
- East on County Road 750N to County Road 650W, 1.5 miles
- North on County Road 650W to County Road 350S, 3.6 miles
- East on County Road 350S to County Road 500W, 5.0 miles
- North on County Road 500W to preserve, 0.8 mile

From I-69

- West on County Road 11A south of Auburn to County Road 56, 0.4 mile
- West on County Road 56 to State Road 205, 1.9 miles
- Southwest on State Road 205 to County Road 60, 1.8 miles
- West on County Road 60, becoming County Road 300S, to State Road 9, 13.5 miles
- South on State Road 9 to County Road 400S, 0.9 mile
- West on County Road 400S to State Road 109, 3.9 miles

Crooked Lake Nature Preserve

- North on State Road 109 to County Road 350S, 0.5 mile
- West on County Road 350S to County Road 500W, 0.9 mile
- North on County Road 500W to preserve, 0.8 mile

48. Crooked Lake Nature Preserve

Owned by Indiana Department of Natural Resources,
Division of Nature Preserves

The 145-acre Crooked Lake Nature Preserve protects more than a half mile of scenic, undeveloped shoreline on the glacial Crooked Lake, one of several interconnected waterbodies in Whitley and Noble Counties. The spring-fed lake, one of the state's cleanest and deepest natural waterbodies, encircles an island on its western side.

The dedicated state nature preserve consists of separate portions on the north and south sides of the lake and the interconnected Little Crooked Lake. The preserve protects several rare plant species, including state threatened Fries' pondweed, white-stem pondweed, straight-leaf pondweed, and lesser bladderwort; and state rare flatleaf pondweed.

The lake environs feature marshes and calcium-rich seeps along the shore, forested slopes—dominated by American beech and sugar maple, along with green ash, shagbark hickory, red oak, sassafras, and white oak—an open field, and a pond that is covered with spatterdock plants in summer. Sugar maple, hop hornbeam, green ash, American beech, and flowering dogwood thrive in the understory.

The Crooked Lake Nature Preserve includes a one-acre memorial to former Indiana Governor Ralph F. Gates, which is owned by ACRES Land Trust.

The trails that traverse the woods and pass along the shore are prone to flooding. Downed trees and other signs of beaver activity are present. One particularly scenic ravine is nicknamed the Tall Trees Memorial Grove.

Private homes dot Crooked Lake's unprotected shorelines.

Activities

Hiking Trails: Three loops, two on north section, one on south section.

Other Activities: Nature study, photography, wildlife watching.

Directions

GPS coordinates: 41.265292, −85.471611

From US 31
- East on US 30 at Plymouth, through Warsaw, to State Road 9 at Columbia City, 44.2 miles
- North on State Road 9 to County Line Road, 7.1 miles
- West on County Line Road to preserve, 0.4 mile

From I-69
- West on US 33 at Fort Wayne, through Churubusco, to County Line Road, 15.5 miles
- West on County Line Road to preserve, 3.6 miles

49. Dygert Nature Preserve

Owned by ACRES Land Trust

The 133-acre Dygert Nature Preserve in Whitley County supports a high-quality stand of oak-hickory forest on a rolling landscape that is cut by deep ravines and surrounds a fifty-six-acre

Dygert Nature Preserve

dedicated state nature preserve. This natural area is partially divided by a deep, steep-sided ditch and also supports a field and a deep-woods pond.

Named for land donors Wendell and Evelyn Dygert, this preserve boasts one of the best wildflower displays in Northeast Indiana, featuring blue-eyed Mary, jack-in-the-pulpit, spring beauty, blue violet, white violet, firepink, Dutchman's breeches, and prairie fleabane. Other plant life includes red clover, wild black raspberries, and stiff dogwood.

Red-tailed hawk, great horned owl, blue jay, cardinal, red-eyed vireo, downy woodpecker, hairy woodpecker, and red-bellied woodpecker inhabit Dygert Nature Preserve, along with white-tailed deer, groundhogs and other mammals, and a variety of butterflies, such as the giant swallowtail and red admiral.

In addition to oak and hickory, trees include ash, beech, maple, and cherry.

Activities
Hiking Trails: One (2 miles), moderate.
Other Activities: Nature study, photography, wildlife watching.

Directions

GPS coordinates: 41.225096, −85.501598

From US 31

- East on US 30 at Plymouth to State Road 109 at State Road 109 at Columbia City, 44.0 miles
- North on State Road 109 to County Road 400N, 3.6 miles
- West on County Road 400N to County Road 50W, 0.5 mile
- North on County Road 50W to preserve, 0.3 mile

From I-69

- West on US 30 at Fort Wayne to State Road 109 at Columbia City, 16.7 miles
- North on State Road 109 to County Road 400N, 3.6 miles
- West on County Road 400N to County Road 50W, 0.5 mile
- North on County Road 50W to preserve, 0.3 mile

50. Spring Lake Woods and Bog Nature Preserve

Owned by ACRES Land Trust

The 107-acre Spring Lake Woods and Bog Nature Preserve protects moist upland woodlands, a two-acre bog, and a thousand feet of lakeshore along Lake Everett, Allen County's only natural lake. The preserve's significance owes to its sphagnum bog, orchids, and other northern muckland woods plant life. Spring Lake—ninety-eight acres of which is a dedicated state nature preserve—supports skunk cabbage and cinnamon fern.

This natural area was among the sites listed in the seminal 1969 work *Natural Areas of Indiana and their Preservation*. In the book, authors Alton A. Lindsey, Damian Vincent Schmeltz, and Stanley A. Nichols say Spring Lake has "herb flora distinctive of northern muckland woods . . . including cinnamon ferns five feet tall as it stands, the most profuse and tallest of this species we have seen."

The bog lies between the county road and the lake. Due to its sensitive ecology—the ground is too soggy to support foot traffic, for example—there is no trail to the wetland or the shoreline. The bog also smells like rotten eggs and is ringed by poison sumac.

Spring Lake Woods and Bog Nature Preserve

The more than forty-acre Lake Everett, most of which is privately owned, is accessible from a public access site east of Spring Lake Woods and Bog Nature Preserve. Follow Lake Everett Road and bear left to South Shore Drive.

Activities
Hiking Trails: One (0.7 mile), easy.
Other Activities: Nature study, photography, wildlife watching.

Directions
GPS coordinates: 41.153964, −85.310664
From I-65
- East on State Road 14 at Rochester, through South Whitley, to County Road 800E, 49.3 miles
- North on County Road 800E to Washington Center Road, 4.1 miles
- East on Washington Center Road to Butt Road, 1.2 miles
- North on Butt Road to Leesburg Road, 0.4 mile

- Northwest on Leesburg Road to Butt Road (Butt Road jogs), 0.2 mile
- North on Butt Road to Lake Everett Drive, 0.6 mile
- Northeast on Lake Everett Drive to preserve, 0.3 mile

From I-69

- West on US 30 at Fort Wayne to Feigler Road and Leesburg Roads, 5.0 miles
- West on Leesburg Road to Butt Road, 1.9 miles
- North on Butt Road to Lake Everett Drive, 0.6 mile
- Northeast on Lake Everett Drive to preserve, 0.3 mile

51a. Chain O' Lakes State Park

Owned by Indiana Department of Natural Resources, Division of State Parks & Lakes

The 2,718-acre Chain O' Lakes State Park in Noble County features nine connecting kettle lakes that together total 212 acres of surface water and seven miles of diverse shoreline habitats. Within its boundaries, the 732-acre Glacial Esker Nature Preserve protects what is considered the state's finest example of this particular Ice Age remnant.

The Chain O' Lakes landscape, which includes four smaller, unconnected lakes, is mostly freshwater bog atop deep peat deposits, with steeply rolling bluffs and soft morainal hills that rise two hundred feet. Forested areas support a mix of oak and hickory, alongside cherry, elm, birch, sumac, spruce, and scattered pine plantings.

The two-mile-wide, four-mile-long state park supports a diverse assortment of wildflowers in the spring, summer, and fall. A two-hundred-acre restored prairie provides habitat for grassland birds and plants.

Nearly two hundred birds have been identified at Chain O' Lakes. Other wildlife includes deer, rabbits, squirrels, chipmunks, minks, opossums, skunks, raccoons, gophers, foxes, badgers, beavers, coyotes, and groundhogs.

The park's history is rich and dates back some thirteen thousand years, when the retreating Wisconsin glacial ice sheets reformed the area's surface and geology. The kettle lakes formed

Chain O' Lakes State Park

when melting glacial rivers carved the channels between the park's nine lakes.

This part of Indiana was Miami Indian country when French explorers reached the state in the late 1600s. A village with roughly thirty bark wigwams occupied the shore of one lake. Bowen Lake was named after one of the first families to settle the area in the 1830s.

The restored one-room Stanley Schoolhouse was originally built in 1915 and housed four different schools until 1954. Six years after the Indiana Department of Conservation, the DNR's predecessor, recommended the area as a future state park site, the park was established in 1960.

51b. Glacial Esker Nature Preserve
The 732-acre Glacial Esker Nature Preserve protects the flat-bottom lowland channels, wetlands, creeks, and floodplain forests that surround the park's lakes. Eskers are long, winding ridges of sand and gravel that were deposited by retreating glaciers. Tunnels that carried meltwater out of the glaciers left the eskers in their wakes. The dedicated state nature preserve features several glacial erratics—rocks that the glaciers dropped erratically. The ridgetop and ravines are upland forest.

Glacial Esker's natural communities harbor plant and animal species that require unbroken wetland and interior forest ecosystems. Among the bird species identified at the preserve are the brown creeper, hooded warbler, cerulean warbler, and prothonotary warbler, as well as the state endangered least bittern and black-crowned night heron.

Activities

Hiking Trails: Eight (0.5–2.5 miles), easy to rugged.

Camping: 331 electric, forty-nine nonelectric, thirty-three primitive, four rally camp, canoe camp, youth tent areas, camp store, dumping station.

Other Activities: Bicycle rental; boat ramp, electric motor only; cabins; canoe, paddleboat, kayak, and rowboat rental; cross-country skiing; fishing/ice fishing; hunting; nature center/seasonal interpretive naturalist services; nature study; photography; shelters; swimming beach; wildlife watching.

Directions

GPS coordinates: 41.341348, –85.402076

From US 31

- East on US 6 at LaPaz to US 33 at Ligonier, 36.8 miles
- South on US 33 to State Road 9, 14.0 miles
- North on State Road 9 to park, 1.3 miles

From I-69

- West on State Road 8 at Auburn, through Garrett, to State Road 3, 7.2 miles
- South on State Road 3 to Baseline Road, 1.0 mile
- West on Baseline Road to State Road 9, 10.5 miles
- South on State Road 9 to park, 0.7 mile

52. Lloyd W. Bender Memorial Forest / Bender Nature Preserve

Owned by ACRES Land Trust

The 116-acre Lloyd W. Bender Memorial Forest in Noble County protects floodplain swamp forests, upland ridges, and old fields reverting to woody vegetation along the South Branch of Elkhart River. Sixty acres are designated as a dedicated state nature preserve.

The Bender Memorial Forest's combination of lowland and upland habitats harbors a wide diversity of flora and fauna. Red maple, green ash, and slippery elm dominate the swamp forest, with swamp rose, red osier dogwood, and poison ivy dominating the shrub layer. Second-growth oak-hickory stands command the upland morainal ridges. Other trees that thrive in the preserve include burr oaks, white oaks, swamp white oaks, silver maples, black willows, and cottonwoods. Royal and cinnamon ferns are among the site's notable plants.

A winding stretch of river bottomlands support old trees and an abundance of ferns. Spring wildflowers include trillium, jack-in-the-pulpit, and false Solomon's seal.

Chipmunks and groundhogs are common.

The Bender preserve lies about a third of the way upstream from the lake-fed South Branch's rise some five miles to the south near Marl Lake and its merger with the North Branch just past the Mallard Roost Wetland Conservation Area east of Ligonier.

The South Branch of the Elkhart River borders the nature preserve on the north and west sides. The river bisects the memorial woods' eastern section.

Activities
Hiking Trails: One (1.3 miles), moderate.
Other Activities: Nature study, photography, wildlife watching.

Directions
GPS coordinates: 41.380398, –85.456420
From US 31
- East on US 6 at LaPaz to US 33 at Ligonier, 36.8 miles
- South on US 33 to County Road 200N, 5.1 miles
- East on County Road 200N to Long Lake Road, 3.4 miles
- South on Long Lake Road to County Road 175N, 0.3 mile
- East on County Road 175N to River Road, 0.7 mile
- North on River Road to preserve, 0.3 mile

From I-69
- West on County Road 8 at Auburn to State Road 3 at Avila, 9.3 miles
- South on State Road 3 to Baseline Road, 0.9 mile

Edna W. Spurgeon Woodland Reserve

- West on Baseline Road to State Road 9, 10.5 miles
- North on State Road 9 to County Road 100N, 1.0 mile
- West on County Road 100N to River Road, 1.7 miles
- North on River Road to preserve, 0.9 mile

53. Edna W. Spurgeon Woodland Reserve

Owned by ACRES Land Trust

The sixty-five-acre Edna W. Spurgeon Woodland Reserve in Noble County protects rolling uplands with small kames—ridges, hills, or mounds of glacial deposits left by melting ice sheets more than ten thousand years ago. The site's past land use has created a landscape that runs from an old field through sizable forest stands.

Known as the Knobs, this dedicated state nature preserve was the first natural area purchased by ACRES Land Trust in

1961. Its climax forest of American beech, sugar maple, and tulip poplar shelters some of the largest trees in Indiana.

The Spurgeon woods is divided into two sections: the previously grazed west side, which contains some mature beeches but lacks a dense understory; and the east side, which features low ridges and moist troughs that support beech and maple, along with green ash, tulip poplar, red oak, basswood, hackberry, black cherry, and slippery elm. Sugar maple is the primary understory tree.

Wildflowers at the Spurgeon Nature Preserve include large-flowered trillium, sessile trillium, spring beauty, blue-eyed Mary, hepatica, wood (celandine) poppy, Dutchman's breeches, and squirrel corn.

Stones and rocks known as glacial erratics deposited by retreating Wisconsin glacial ice sheets are scattered throughout the preserve. The trail in places is lined with small erratics.

Activities
Hiking Trails: One (1.2 miles), difficult.
Other Activities: Nature study, photography, wildlife watching.

Directions
GPS coordinates: 41.488558, –85.538723
From US 31
- East on US 6 at LaPaz, through Ligonier, to County Road 600W, 39.5 miles
- North on County Road 600W to preserve, 2.3 miles

From I-69
- West on US 6 at Waterloo, through Kendallville, to County Road 600W, 25.6 miles
- North on County Road 600W to preserve, 2.3 miles

54. Art Hammer Wetlands / Art Hammer Wetlands Nature Preserve
Owned by ACRES Land Trust
The 356-acre Art Hammer Wetlands in Noble County borders the North Branch of the Elkhart River and supports several wetland

Art Hammer Wetlands

ecosystems, including cattail marsh, shrub marsh, open pond, yellow birch swamp, and floodplain forest. The largest of the ACRES Land Trust properties, Hammer includes a 332-acre dedicated state nature preserve.

Green ash, red maple, sycamore, and cottonwood are among the more common trees that thrive in the Hammer preserve's moist conditions. Oaks and hickories dominate the upland forest.

The preserve supports numerous wetland animal species and water birds, including wood ducks, mallards, coots, great blue herons, and green herons. Wildflowers include cardinal flowers, marsh marigolds, and blue flag irises.

The North Branch of the Elkhart River rises near Messick Lake—six or so twisting miles to the north—and merges with the South Branch about six miles to the southwest near Ligonier. Along the way the northern stretch passes through and drains Jones Lake, Waldron Lake, and others.

Access to the North Branch of the Elkhart River is available across the road from the preserve at the Division of Fish & Wildlife's William T. Malle Public Access Site.

Activities
Hiking Trails: One (0.8 mile), easy.
Other Activities: Nature study, photography, wildlife watching.

Directions
GPS coordinates: 41.493085, –85.447799
From US 31
- East on US 6 at LaPaz, through Ligonier, County Road 450W, 41.2 miles
- North on County Road 450W to County Road 900N, 1.6 miles
- East on County Road 900N to County Road 125W, 3.2 miles
- North on County Road 125W to preserve, 0.7 mile

From I-69
- West on US 6 at Waterloo, through Kendallville to Baseline Road, 19.5 miles

Lonidaw Nature Preserve

- North on Baseline Road to County Road 900N, 2.0 miles
- West on County Road 900N to County Road 125W, 1.3 miles
- North on County Road 125W to preserve, 0.7 mile

55. Lonidaw Nature Preserve

Owned by ACRES Land Trust

The thirty-acre Lonidaw Nature Preserve in Noble County protects three-quarters of a mile of shoreline on the five-acre Little Whitford Lake, a kettle hole lake formed by glacial activity more than ten thousand years ago. A glacial esker—a ridge of gravel and sand deposited by a stream in or beneath a glacier—runs through the preserve's southern part. Twenty-five acres at Lonidaw are designated as a dedicated state nature preserve.

Spicebush, dogwood, willow, and swamp rose thrive on the mucky ground near the lake, where skunk cabbage and marsh marigold are common. The lower slopes abound in spring wildflowers. Wild columbine and wood (celandine) poppy thrive on the higher ground.

Mature woods with sugar maple, hackberry, slippery elm, and walnut dominate the low ground near the lake, with spicebush common in the understory. The upland areas support mature to old-growth sugar maple-beechwoods, with prickly ash common in the understory.

Lonidaw is a Native American term for "Spirit Queen of the Woods" and was the name given to the wife of Potowatomi Chief Simon Pokagon, after whom the state park is named.

Access to the Little Whitford Lake's edge is limited. The north side is privately owned.

Activities
Hiking Trails: One (0.8 mile), moderate.
Other Activities: Fishing, hiking, hunting, nature study, photography, wildlife watching.

Directions
GPS coordinates: 41.456192, –85.231714
From US 31
- West on US 6 at LaPaz, through Nappanee to Allen Chapel Road at Kendallville, 55.9 mile
- North on Allen Chapel Road to preserve, 0.7 mile

From I-69
- West on US 6 at Waterloo to Allen Chapel Road in Kendalville, 9.3 miles
- North on Allen Chapel Road to preserve, 0.7 mile

56. Olin Lake Nature Preserve
Owned by Indiana Department of Natural Resources, Division of Nature Preserves
The 269-acre Olin Lake Nature Preserve in LaGrange County encompasses and protects the crystal-clear, one-hundred-acre-plus Olin Lake—the largest undeveloped lake in Indiana—and its low, marshy shoreline and floodplain. The dedicated state nature preserve harbors more than a dozen rare plants, including the state endangered foxtail sedge, thinleaf sedge, and sharp-scaled manna-grass.

Olin Lake Nature Preserve

Other rare plants include state threatened white-stem pond-weed and horned bladderwort; state rare red baneberry, rush-like aster, and whorled water-milfoil; and the state watch-listed bristly-stalk sedge and tamarack.

The eighty-five-foot-deep Olin Lake is connected to Martin Lake, Smith Hole, and Oliver Lake through narrow, glacially carved streams that support a small, native population of cisco, also known as lake herring. Olin is one of only a handful of Northeast Indiana lakes in which this member of the salmon family survives.

In addition to the tamarack, the shoreline swamp forest supports yellow birch, silver maple, red maple, and green ash, along with winterberry, poison sumac, buttonbush, dwarf birch, and other uncommon plants.

The preserve's low, mucky spots support skunk cabbage, which is the first of the preserve's substantial collection of wildflowers to appear in early spring. Others include trout lilies, Dutchman's breeches, wood (celandine) poppies, mayapples, false mermaids, and jack-in-the-pulpits.

The southeast shore's upland portion harbors the Browand Woods, where large tulip, oak, and walnut trees were harvested in the 1960s. Large remnant sugar maple, American beech, hackberry, and red oak still survive, some with diameters that exceed three feet.

Olin Lake's clarity is in part due to its marl-covered bottom. A white substance composed of calcium carbonate, clays, and sediments, marl inhibits aquatic plant growth. The lake features a swampy, hourglass-shaped island near the south shore, which is visible from a north-leading spur from the main trail.

Mammals at Olin Lake include white-tailed deer, raccoon, and chipmunk. Fish include rainbow trout, brown trout, and largemouth bass. Birds include barred owl, common loon, and Canada goose.

Olin Lake's pristine character wasn't always assured. In 1975, The Nature Conservancy and some local residents outbid real estate developers and acquired the lake and 360 surrounding acres for nearly $260,000 at auction. They sold some of the surround-ing land for farming on the condition it would not be developed.

Boats may not be launched on Olin Lake, though it is acces-sible via a public access site on nearby Oliver Lake and a con-necting channel.

Activities
Hiking Trails: One (1.5 miles), easy.
Other Activities: Fishing, hiking, hunting, nature study, pho-tography, wildlife watching.

Directions
GPS coordinates: 41.561950, –85.400626
From US 31
- East on US 20 at South Bend to State Road 9 at LaGrange, 44.5 miles
- South on State Road 9 to County Road 600S, 6.9 miles
- West on County Road 600S to County Road 125E, 1.8 miles
- North on County Road 125E to preserve, 0.5 mile

From I-69
- West on US 20 at Angola to State Road 9 at LaGrange, 19.2 miles
- South on State Road 9 to County Road 600S, 6.9 miles
- West on County Road 600S to County Road 125E, 1.8 miles
- North on County Road 125E to preserve, 0.5 mile

57. Maple Wood Nature Preserve / LaGrange County Nature Preserve
Owned by Lagrange County Department of Parks and Recreation and ACRES Land Trust

The combined 103-acre Maple Wood Nature Preserve and LaGrange County Nature Preserve protect a mature, second-growth, moist upland forest that is dominated by beech, maple, oak, and hickory, along with the state watch-listed butternut. Other habitats include wooded swamp and wet prairie.

The LaGrange County portion, a dedicated state nature pre-serve, occupies the seventy-three acres to the west. It is part of

Maple Wood Nature Preserve

the county's Maple Wood Nature Center, which features a visitor center, a maple syrup camp, and a small sugar bush—a forest stand used for the production of maple syrup.

The Maple Wood preserve occupies the thirty acres to the east and is bordered on its northeast side by the East Fly Creek, which feeds the heavily developed Fish Lake just across a county road from the preserve.

The two preserves share a trail system.

Activities
Hiking Trails: One (2.2 miles), easy.
Other Activities: Nature study, photography, picnicking, visitor/interpretive center, wildlife watching.

Directions
GPS coordinates: 41.627498, –85.337392
From US 31
- East US 20 at South Bend to County Road 400E east of LaGrange, 48.2 miles
- South on County Road 400E to County Road 100S, 1.0 mile
- East on County Road 100S to preserve, 0.6 mile

From I-69
- West on US 20 at Angola to County Road 525E at Plato, 14.8 miles
- South on County Road 525E to County Road 100S, 1.0 mile
- West on County Road 100S to preserve, 0.6 mile

58a. Pigeon River Fish & Wildlife Area
Owned by Indiana Department of Natural Resources,
Division of Fish & Wildlife
The 11,794-acre Pigeon River Fish & Wildlife Area in LaGrange and Steuben Counties—with its 529 acres of lakes and impoundments and seventeen miles of free-flowing river—is managed for hunting and fishing. Within its boundaries are 235 acres that have been set aside as two dedicated state nature preserves, one that is a National Natural Landmark.

Dozens of rare plant and animal species have been recorded on a variety of Pigeon River landforms, including restored

Mongoquinong Nature Preserve, Pigeon River Fish & Wildlife Area

prairie, swamp forest, marsh, fen, muck pockets, cold-water streams, upland oak forests, and cultivated fields.

The wildlife area, which spans both the town of Mongo and the Pigeon River, has been designated an Important Bird Area by the National Audubon Society. "Given the property's large size and the diverse amount of habitats within its borders, Pigeon River Fish & Wildlife Area supports several bird species of conservation concern during the breeding season, as well as congregations of wading birds (such as herons and cranes) and waterfowl during migratory periods," Audubon says on its website. "To date, an approximate 220 bird species have been recorded on the property."

Among the rare bird species that live in or pass through Pigeon River are state endangered osprey, least bittern, sedge wren, and Virginia rail; state species of special concern sandhill crane, hooded warbler, and red-shouldered hawk; along with common moorhen, willow flycatcher, marsh wren, and blue-winged warbler. (See the Tamarack Bog Nature Preserve and Mongoquinong Nature Preserve sections below for rare plant examples.)

Shoreline fishing is allowed on Beaver Dam Lake, Stayner Lake, Little Stayner Lake, Troxel Mill Pond, Mongo Mill Pond, Nasby Mill Pond, Ontario Mill Pond, Massasauga Marsh, East Pool, Rainbow Pit, and Catfish Pond. Primary fish include crappies, bluegills, pikes, bass, redear sunfishes, perches, catfish, and trout. Trapping and hunting is allowed for furbearers, deer, quail, rabbit, squirrel, waterfowl, dove, pheasant, and turkey.

The Pigeon River wildlife area was established in 1956 when the electric utility NIPSCO donated to the state three hydroelectric impoundments in the Pigeon River Valley: Mongo, Nasby, and Ontario. Additional land has since been acquired.

58b. Tamarack Bog Nature Preserve: National Natural Landmark

The 170-acre Tamarack Bog Nature Preserve's National Natural Landmark status is derived from its distinction as "the largest, well-developed tamarack swamp-bog forest in Indiana," according to the National Park Service. "The site supports six distinct vegetation types and more than thirty-four mammal species." The preserve's tamarack-dominated, boreal relict swamp forest is more typically found in the Upper Great Lake states and Canada.

So unique is the Tamarack Bog preserve's ecosystem that it harbors nearly five dozen plants that are rare in Indiana, including seven that are state endangered: running serviceberry, Missouri rockcress, mud sedge, Montgomery hawthorn, purple avens, marsh valerian, and highbush cranberry.

Other northern species that survive at the preserve are state watch-listed speckled alder, as well as dwarf birch, highbush blueberry, Canada mayflower, and starflower. Trees and wildflowers that are more typical of the region are red maple, black ash, spicebush, willow, dogwood, skunk cabbage, and marsh marigold.

A sandy upland oak woods with lowbush blueberry and wintergreen also thrives on the Tamarack Bog preserve. A marsh that borders part of the Pigeon River supports emergent and floating aquatic vegetation.

This boreal relict community survives on this nature preserve because of the swamp's cool microclimate, which is created by groundwater flowing to the river just below the surface. The water surfaces in places as seepage and small springs.

Tamarack Bog preserve has no trails.

58c. Mongoquinong Nature Preserve

The sixty-five-acre Mongoquinong Nature Preserve protects a fen—a wetland that is kept wet by flowing alkaline groundwater. The water at this preserve percolates through calcium-rich gravel, seeps out of the bluff, and flows through the peaty soil to the Pigeon River.

The Mongoquinong preserve supports a dozen and a half rare and unusual plant species, including state endangered highbush cranberry; state threatened yellow sedge and autumn willow; and state rare rushlike aster, tufted hairgrass, narrow-leaved cotton grass, and green-keeled cotton grass.

This preserve's dominant plant is Carex stricta sedge. Wildflowers include marsh marigolds in spring, blazing stars in late summer, and fringed gentians in fall. While plant life in fens is largely herbaceous, some woody plants, such as the shrubby cinquefoil, are normal. Dogwoods and other woody plants, which form dense clumps that shade the natural fen plants, are periodically burned to keep the ecosystem from becoming too shrubby.

The Mongoquinong preserve has no trails.

Activities

Berry, nut, and mushroom picking; boating, electric motors allowed on lakes and ponds; dog training; fishing; hiking, no trails; hunting; nature study; photography; target ranges, rifle and archery; wildlife watching.

Directions to Pigeon River Fish & Wildlife Office
GPS coordinates: 41.685581, –85.267868
From US 31
- East on US 20 south of South Bend to State Road 3, 51.1 miles

- North on State Road 3 to County Road 300N in Mongo, 3.1 miles
- East on County Road 300N to wildlife area, 0.7 mile

From I-69
- West on US 20 at Angola to State Road 3, 12.0 miles
- North on State Road 3 to County Road 300N in Mongo, 3.1 miles
- East on County Road 300N to wildlife area, 0.7 mile

Directions to Tamarack Bog Nature Preserve from Office
GPS coordinates: 41.677930, –85.253479
- East on County Road 300N to County Road 900E, 0.7 mile
- South on County Road 900E to preserve, 0.7 mile

Directions to Mongoquinong Nature Preserve from Office
GPS coordinates: 41.694839, –85.310576
- West on County Road 300N to County Road 600E, 2.3 miles
- North on County Road 600E to preserve, 0.3 mile

59. Fawn River Nature Preserve
Owned by ACRES Land Trust

The 135-acre Fawn River Nature Preserve in LaGrange County protects what may be Indiana's clearest, most natural river, a waterway that crisscrosses the Indiana-Michigan state line on its way to the St. Joseph River and Lake Michigan. The dedicated state nature preserve, which abuts the state line, features sandy soil that supports a floodplain forest type that is otherwise not protected in the state's nature preserve system.

The Fawn River preserve harbors five rare plant species: state threatened autumn willow; state rare Michaux's stitchwort; and state watch-listed cuckoo flower, bristly-stalk sedge, and buckbean.

The preserve's floodplain forest is dominated by second-growth swamp white oak and pin oak, along with other trees and plants that can endure occasional flooding. Small pockets of older trees that have not been cleared are interspersed with the younger ones. The lowlands also support marsh and shrub

Fawn River, Fawn River Nature Preserve

swamp. The river features cattail marsh and a grass/sedge fen, along with a healthy population of aquatic life.

The preserve parking lot lies in Michigan.

Activities
Hiking Trails: One (1.5 miles), easy.
Other Activities: Nature study, photography, wildlife watching.

Directions
GPS coordinates: 41.759837, –85.235360
From US 31
- East on I-80/90 (Toll Road) at South Bend to State Road 9, 48 miles
- South on State Road 9 to County Road 700N, 0.8 mile
- East on County Road 700N to County Road 375E, 3.7 miles
- North on County Road 375E to County Road 750N, 0.5 mile

- East on County Road 750N to County Road 1050E at Greenfield Mills, 6.9 miles
- North on County Road 1050E to County Road 800N, 0.6 mile
- West on County Road 800N to preserve, 0.5 mile

From I-69
- West on I-80/90 (Toll Road) to County Road 750N (at service exit), 18.0 miles
- North on County Road 750N (via County Road 500E), then east to County Road 1050E at Greenfield Mills, 5.9 miles
- North on County Road 1050E to County Road 800N, 0.6 mile
- West on County Road 800N to preserve, 0.5 mile

60. Ropchan Memorial Nature Preserve
Owned by ACRES Land Trust

The eighty-acre Ropchan Memorial Nature Preserve in Steuben County protects a diverse collection of geological features—morainal ridges, kettle holes, swamps, and bogs. Seventy-seven acres of this refuge are designated a dedicated state nature preserve.

Ropchan Memorial's landscape, which has a northwoods feel, features sandy loam ridges that surround pockets of muck and peat. Among the rare plant species are state threatened small cranberry; state watch-listed broadwing sedge, tamarack, running pine, and elliptical-leaf wintergreen; and state rare bog rosemary.

The preserve's higher, drier sections support shagbark hickory, white oak, red oak, black oak, black cherry, and sassafras, with occasional largetooth aspen. The lower, moister slopes support red maple. The deeper peat pockets and swamps support tamarack and yellow birch. Depending on the soil conditions, the understory features hazelnut, dogwood, poison ivy, blackberry, raspberry, prickly ash, highbush blueberry, winterberry, and mountain holly. Cinnamon fern thrives in places where shallow-rooted red maples have fallen. Glacial erratics—stones

Ropchan Memorial Nature Preserve

and rocks randomly dropped by the Wisconsin glacial ice as it receded—are scattered throughout the Ropchan Memorial preserve.

The preserve, like the Ropchan Wildlife Nature Preserve, was donated by Sam and Adeline Ropchan of Fort Wayne, who were early members of ACRES Land Trust. Sam also served as president of the Izaak Walton League.

Activities
Hiking Trails: One (1.3 miles), moderate.
Other Activities: Fishing, hiking, hunting, nature study, photography, wildlife watching.

Directions
GPS coordinates: 41.741560, −85.132490
From US 31
- East on I-80/90, through South Bend, to State Road 9, 47.2 miles
- South on State Road 9 to State Road 120 at Howe, 2.2 miles

- East on State Road 120 to County Road 750W west of Orland, 15.6 miles
- North on County Road 750W to preserve, 0.1 mile

From I-69
- South on Old US 27 west of Fremont to State Road 120, 0.1 mile
- West on State Road 120 County Road 750W, 7.5 miles
- North on County Road 750W to preserve, 0.1 mile

61a. Pokagon State Park / Potawatomi Nature Preserve

Owned by Indiana Department of Natural Resources, Division of State Parks & Lakes

The 1,260-acre Pokagon State Park in Steuben County sustains a diverse variety of ecosystems, including natural lakes, marshes, fens, swamps, deep hardwood forests, pine groves, old fields, grasslands, and sand hills. Located in the Indiana county with the most natural lakes, the park's western end is framed by Lake James and Snow Lake. The 256-acre Potawatomi Nature Preserve lies within the park's boundaries and protects more than two dozen rare plant species.

The park is the largest portion of a broader natural area complex that includes the Beechwood Nature Preserve to the north and, across I-69, the Trine State Recreation Area, the Seven Sisters chain of lakes, Wing Haven Nature Preserve, Charles McClue Reserve, and Marsh Lake natural complex.

The lakes and Pokagon's rolling terrain are the consequence of glacial activity that occurred more than ten thousand years ago. As the Wisconsin glacial ice sheets melted and retreated, they gouged the land and left sunken blocks of ice that broke away and left lakes known as kettles and hills or mounds called kames. Lake Londiaw is an example of a kettle lake; Hell's Point is a kame. The ice sheets also deposited large rocks in random patterns known as glacial erratics, which are evident at Pokagon.

Indiana's fifth state park was proposed as Lake James State Park before it opened in 1925; local residents had purchased 580

Lake James, Pokagon State Park

acres on the eastern shores of Lake James and Snow Lake and
donated them to the state as a Christmas gift. But Indiana's first
State Parks committee chairman Richard Lieber, also known
as the Father of Indiana State Parks, suggested the name be
changed to recognize the region's and state's Native American
heritage.

Northeast Indiana was Potawatomi Indian country when
European immigrants began flooding the region in the early
nineteenth century. The nature preserve and Potawatomi Inn,
which features a northern fishing lodge theme, are named after the tribe. The Potawatomi's last two leaders were Leopold
Pokagon and his son, Simon.

Many of Indiana's public lands were designed and built
by the Civilian Conservation Corps (CCC) under the Works
Progress Administration, a New Deal program that hired unemployed workers to produce public projects during the Great
Depression. A CCC group lived and worked at Pokagon from
1934 to 1942, building roads and trails and constructing many

structures that still dot the park landscape, including the gate house, spring shelter, and saddle barn. They also built the original toboggan run. The CCC shelter is listed on the National Register of Historic Places for its social history, entertainment/recreation, and architectural significance.

Pokagon is a popular winter recreation destination, offering cross-country ski rental, sledding, ice fishing, and the quarter-mile-long twin-track toboggan run that reaches speeds of thirty-five to forty miles per hour.

The Potawatomi Inn opened two years after the park opened in 1927 with forty guest rooms, a dining room, and the Lonidaw Lounge. A pool and outdoor deck were added in the 1980s, the conference center in the 1990s.

The Trine State Recreation Area, located directly across I-69 from the park, is managed as part of Pokagon. (See the Trine State Recreation Area section below.)

61b. Potawatomi Nature Preserve

The 256-acre Potawatomi Nature Preserve occupies most of Pokagon State Park's southeastern and eastern portions. It harbors Lonidaw Lake, as well as cattail marshes, sedge meadows, tamarack and yellow birch swamps, and uplands covered with hardwoods. The preserve represents the Northern Lakes Natural Region's original landscape. The lake is named after Simon Pokagon's wife, Lonidaw, which means "Spirit Queen of the Woods."

Lake Lonidaw, whose formation, plants, and wildlife are representative of the Northern Great Lakes, sits in a depression and is bordered by marsh vegetation and an adjoining tamarack-black ash swamp, while other wet places support yellow birch and red maple. The morainal ridges support red oak, white oak, black cherry, shagbark hickory, and sugar maple.

Notable plants protected at Potawatomi Nature Preserve include state endangered Montgomery hawthorn; state threatened great St. John's-wort, northeastern smartweed, and autumn willow; state rare red baneberry, Michaux's stitchwort,

Potawatomi Nature Preserve

longstalk sedge, green-keeled cotton grass, and grove meadow grass; and state watch-listed two-leaf toothwort, butternut, tamarack, bog bluegrass, and alderleaf buckthorn.

Activities
Hiking Trails: Nine (0.7–2.2 miles), easy to moderate.

Camping: Two hundred electric, seventy-three nonelectric; group camp; youth tent areas; dumping station; camp store.

Other Activities: Cross-country skiing; fishing, nature center/interpretive naturalist services; nature study; paddleboat, pontoon, and rowboat rentals; photography; picnicking/shelters; playground equipment; saddle barn with escorted rides; sand volleyball court; swimming beach; toboggan run; wildlife watching.

Directions
GPS coordinates: 41.707737, –85.022586
From I-69
- West on State Road 727 north of Angola to state park, 0.6 mile

62. Beechwood Nature Preserve / Foster Nature Preserve / Majneri Nature Preserve
Owned by ACRES Land Trust

The seventy-four-acre Beechwood Nature Preserve in Steuben County harbors a diverse collection of depressional habitats

Beechwood Nature Preserve

that are drained by a small creek that feeds the Little Otter Lake to the north. Adjacent to Pokagon State Park, this dedicated state nature preserve is contiguous with two other ACRES Land Trust properties—Foster Nature Preserve and Majneri Nature Preserve—altogether forming a protected area of ninety acres.

Beechwood supports a second-growth beech-maple forest, rolling meadows, thickets, and a fen. Notable plant species include the state rare rushlike aster and state watch-listed tamarack. A stand of yellow birch, red maple, slippery elm, and blue beech thrive in the preserve's muck soil, with red osier dogwood, pale dogwood, and gray dogwood sharing the more open areas with poison sumac, elderberry, and spicebush. A small pond features cattails, sedges, and willows.

The preserve includes a small memorial with a marked tree called Garnette Foster's Tree.

Activities

Hiking Trails: Marked system (1.7 miles), rugged.
Other Activities: Nature study, photography, wildlife watching.

Directions
GPS coordinates: 41.717432, –85.003716
From I-69

- West and then north on State Road 127 north of Angola to Little Otter Lake Road (Lane 150), 1.0 mile
- Northwest on Little Otter Lake Road to preserve, 50 feet

63. Trine State Recreation Area

Owned by Indiana Department of Natural Resources, Division of State Parks & Lakes

The 186-acre Trine State Recreation Area in Steuben County sustains wooded hills, open meadows, and unique fen-marsh wetlands on the north shore of the pristine Gentian Lake (pronounced *genchun*), the first of the Seven Sisters chain of kettle lakes. Managed as part of Pokagon State Park, Trine is a restored lakeside resort that includes a meeting and conference center.

Kettle lakes, like the Seven Sisters Lake and Pokagon's Lake James, were formed by glacial ice sheets that gouged the area's surface more than ten thousand years ago and, as large chunks of ice broke off, left pools in their wakes. Lying across I-69 from the state park and Beechwood Nature Preserve, Trine is part of a broader larger natural area that includes the adjacent Marsh Lake natural complex, Wing Haven Nature Preserve, and Charles McClue Reserve.

The Seven Sisters area's ecology is so unique that it supports plants and animals found nowhere else in Indiana. In 1969, the landmark book *Natural Areas of Indiana and Their Preservation* noted that the area merited a position "at the very top of the priority ratings for potential nature preserves in Indiana." More than two dozen rare and endangered plants have been identified in the Potawatomi Nature Preserve, just across I-69 on Pokagon State Park's eastern end.

The Trine site was part of the original Wing Haven Resort, which operated from 1948 through the early 1970s. The resort and nature sanctuary had been owned by Helen and Ben Swenson, former innkeepers at that park's Potawatomi Inn. An artist and bird lover who studied at the Chicago Art Institute,

Trine State Recreation Area

Helen named each of the cabins for birds. The couple also built trails and a small "nature cabin."

After selling the resort to a Fort Wayne church, Helen kept a log home on the south side of Little Gentian Lake, which is now on the Wing Haven Nature Preserve. The church operated a camp on the lake's north shore, which later became Oakhill Resort and Conference Center. The state, with help from Ralph and Sheri Trine of Angola and several nonprofits, including ACRES Land Trust, acquired Oakhill in 2007.

Some resort buildings and facilities—a go-kart track, for example—were torn down, and others were restored, as were the wetland and fen ecosystem.

Activities

Hiking Trails: Two (0.25–2.5 miles), easy to moderate.
Biking Trails: One, accessible (0.5 mile), easy.
Other Activities: Boating, paddleboats, boats with electric motors, and kayaks for rent, no private boats; cross-country skiing; family cabins, single and duplex; fishing pier, accessible; ice skating; interpretive naturalist services; nature study, photography; shelters; Swenson Lodge rental; wildlife watching; welcome center.

Directions

GPS coordinates: 41.713218, –84.993611
From I-69

- East on State Road 727 north of Angola to County Road 50W, 500 feet
- North on County Road 50W to Feather Valley Road, 0.6 mile
- East on Feather Valley Road to area, 0.5 mile

64. Marsh Lake / Marsh Lake Nature Preserve / Marsh Lake Wetland Conservation Area

Owned by Indiana Department of Natural Resources,
Division of Fish & Wildlife

The 849-acre Marsh Lake is the centerpiece of a nearly 1,300-acre natural complex of protected wetlands in Steuben County

Marsh Lake

that form the headwaters of the St. Joseph River. The area includes the 103-acre Marsh Lake Nature Preserve, Marsh Lake Wetland Conservation Area, Seven Sisters Lakes chain, Wing Haven Nature Preserve, and Trine State Recreation Area.

The dedicated state nature preserve, which protects the lake's north and northeast shorelines, supports cattail marsh, sedge marsh, calcareous (calcium-rich) fen, and shrub swamp, along with dry-moist upland forest and a relict stand of yellow birch and state watch-listed tamarack trees. Other rare plants include state rare narrow-leaved cotton grass.

Several northern forest species accompany the tamaracks and yellow birches, which are near the southern end of their range at Marsh Lake, including dwarf birch, Canada mayflower, and starflower. Other common species at the Marsh Lake preserve are skunk cabbage, marsh marigold, red maple, and red osier dogwood.

Marsh Lake features a public access site on its southern shore. The Crane Marsh Wetland Conservation Area on County

Road 100E, across a county road to the east, has a walking trail that leads to Crane Pond and a view of I-80/90. Highway noise is steady.

The nature preserve has a parking lot on County Road 100E north of the Crane Marsh lot but no marked trail.

Activities
Boating, canoeing, fishing, hiking (no trails), hunting, nature study, photography, wildlife watching.

Directions
GPS coordinates: 41.720201, –84.971010
From I-69
- East on State Road 727 north of Angola to County Road 50W, 500 feet
- North on County Road 50W to Feather Valley Road, 0.6 mile
- East on Feather Valley Road to County Road 100E, 1.9 miles
- North on County Road 100E to preserve, 0.6 mile

65. Ropchan Wildlife Refuge / Ropchan Wetland Conservation Area
Owned by ACRES Land Trust; Indiana Department of Natural Resources, Division of Fish & Wildlife

The 157-acre Ropchan Wildlife Refuge and ninety-acre Ropchan Wetland Conservation Area in Steuben County support a variety of plant communities, including upland oak-hickory, mixed mesophytic, and lowland swamp forests; grassy and old fields in successional stages; and pine plantations. The glacially carved landscape features rolling hills, gravel and sand kames, and a kettle lake, with accompanying wetlands.

The dedicated state nature preserve supports several rare and unusual plant species, including the state endangered highbush cranberry, Montgomery hawthorn, and foxtail sedge; state threatened heartleaf willow and Bebb's sedge; state rare American wintergreen and red baneberry; and state watch-listed tamarack and butternut. Other notable plants include yellow birch and two species of shinleaf. Significant

Ropchan Wildlife Refuge

animal species include the state species of special concern star-nosed mole.

The natural complex surrounds a cemetery and is divided by Cemetery Lake and Garn Ditch. The preserve lies north of the ditch, the Wetland Conservation Area to the south. Each has trailheads that connect and feature multiple loops within the preserve. An observation deck on the ditch offers sightings of ducks, great blue herons, muskrats, beavers, and other wildlife.

Ropchan is bordered by manufacturing industries to the north and I-80/90 to the south. Road noise is problematic in places.

The preserve, like the Ropchan Memorial Nature Preserve, was donated by Sam and Adeline Ropchan of Fort Wayne, who were early members of ACRES Land Trust. Sam also served as president of the Izaak Walton League.

Activities
Hiking Trails: One (3.4 miles), moderate.
Other Activities: Nature study, photography, wildlife watching.

Directions
GPS coordinates: 41.715982, –84.936768

From I-69

- East on State Road 127 north of Angola to County Road 50W, 500 feet
- North on County Road 50W to State Road 120, 1.7 miles
- East on State Road 120 to Feather Valley Road at Fremont, 2.2 miles
- South on Feather Valley Road to State Road 827, 1.7 miles
- South on State Road 827 to preserve, 0.8 mile

66. Wing Haven Nature Preserve

Owned by ACRES Land Trust

The 255-acre Wing Haven Nature Preserve in Steuben County protects a chain of small, glacially carved kettle lakes surrounded by marshes, wetland fens, kames, upland oak-hickory forests, and rolling meadows. The dedicated state nature preserve's three clear-blue, undeveloped lakes are part of a chain called the Seven Sisters.

Wing Haven and the Seven Sisters comprise nearly a quarter of a 1,300-acre natural complex that includes the 849-acre Marsh Lake Conservation Area and 186-acre Trine State Recreation Area. Directly across I-69 from Wing Haven lie Pokagon State Park and several dedicated state nature preserves, including Lonidaw Nature Preserve and Beechwood Nature Preserve.

Wing Haven's kettle lakes—Gentian (pronounced *genchun*), Little Gentian, and the Seven Sisters—were created when the Wisconsin glacial ice sheets melted more than ten thousand years ago and left water-filled craters in their wakes. The trails are embedded in places with rocks that the glacier likewise left behind, which are also called glacial erratics.

The preserve's three distinct sections support diverse habitats that attract a variety of birds, including the state endangered marsh wren and state species of special concern sandhill crane, along with the blue-winged warbler, red-tailed hawk, rose-breasted grosbeak, and wood thrush. The cranes have established nests in a secluded area; they migrate south for the

Wing Haven Nature Preserve

winter and return in the spring. Bobolinks and meadowlarks nest in the preserve's upland fields.

Wildflowers blanket the preserve landscape in spring, with white trillium prominent in the deep ravines. Gentian and Little Gentian Lakes are named for the fringed gentian, a brilliant-blue wildflower that grows on their shores and reaches heights of three feet.

Wing Haven features a century-old log cabin—called a "studio/visitor ctr." on trail markers—and other old structures, one of which is used by ACRES Land Trust for events and another for the caretaker's residence.

The preserve was a gift from Helen Swensen, who, along with husband, Ben, used the property as a summer resort and "sanctuary for birds, wildflowers, and people" they called Wing Haven. She was an artist who had studied at the Chicago Art Institute in the 1930s. The couple ran Pokagon State Park's Potawatomi Inn from 1936 to 1948, when they purchased the resort.

Activities
Hiking Trails: One (1.9 miles), moderate to rugged.
Other Activities: Nature study, photography, wildlife watching.

Directions
GPS coordinates: 41.701019, –84.993589
From I-69
- East on State Road 127 north of Angola to County Road 400N, 0.5 mile
- East on County Road 400N to preserve, 0.4 mile

67. Charles McClue Reserve
Owned by Steuben County

The eighty-acre Charles McClue Reserve protects thirty acres of some of the best old-growth forest in Northeast Indiana, including mature tulip poplars, red oaks, and white oaks, with flowering dogwood in the understory. The site, also known as the Charles McClue Nature Preserve, is managed by volunteers working for the Steuben County Commissioners and is located a mile east of the Wing Haven Nature Preserve on the same road.

The dedicated state nature preserve's rolling morainal landscape, rounded hills, and swampy-wet depressions harbor nine rare plant species, including state endangered brownish sedge; state threatened yellow sedge; state rare tufted hairgrass; and state watch-listed fewflower spike rush, butternut, and smooth gooseberry. Spring wildflowers include jack-in-the-pulpit, mayapple, and false Solomon's seal. A variety of notable birds nest at the McClue preserve, including the cerulean warbler, hooded warbler, American redstart, and ovenbird.

The trails and downed tree root systems clutch rocks that were deposited by the Wisconsin glaciers when they began retreating some thirteen thousand years ago.

The nature preserve is named for the father of local attorney Maurice McClue, who kept notes of his time there during his last forty years and ceded the land to Steuben County for use as a nature preserve upon his death in 1957. The preserve is

Charles McClue Reserve

dedicated to the education of Steuben County children in the conservation and appreciation of the natural world.

Activities
Hiking Trails: Three (0.75–2.3 miles), moderate.
Other Activities: Nature study, photography, wildlife watching.

Directions
GPS coordinates: 41.701060, –84.977275
From I-69
- East on State Road 727 north of Angola to County Road 400N, 0.5 mile
- East on County Road 400N to preserve, 1.2 miles

68. Loon Lake Nature Preserve
Owned by Indiana Department of Natural Resources,
Division of Nature Preserves
The ninety-nine-acre Loon Lake Nature Preserve in Steuben County protects the southern shore of Loon Lake and supports

Loon Lake Nature Preserve

a number of wetland communities that harbor more than a dozen rare plants. Landforms include tamarack bog, open marsh, sedge meadow, upland woods, and an area of marl prairie that is considered high quality. The lake's northwest shore is owned by the state Division of Fish & Wildlife, but it is not part of the preserve.

Among the rare and unusual plant species at the dedicated state nature preserve are state endangered Nuttall pondweed; state threatened lesser bladderwort and small cranberry; state rare bog rosemary, roundleaf dogwood, tufted hairgrass, Robbins spike rush, narrow-leaved cotton grass, green-keeled cotton grass, water bulrush, and purple bladderwort; and state watch-listed tamarack and large cranberry.

A service road serves as a trail, but access to Loon Lake and most of the wetland areas is difficult. The lake is accessible from a public access site on its north end on County Road 100N.

The preserve's eastern boundary abuts I-69.

Activities
Hiking, nature study, photography, wildlife watching.

Directions
GPS coordinates: 41.644117, –85.052773
From I-69

- West on US 20 at Angola to County Road 325W, 0.1 mile
- North on County Road 325W to Loon Lake Road and the preserve, 0.6 mile

69. Marion's Woods Nature Preserve

Owned by ACRES Land Trust

The 19.5-acre Marion's Woods Nature Preserve in Steuben County protects a mature, moist, upland oak-hickory forest with small wetland depressions and a relatively open under-story—inside the Angola city limits. The depressions provide breeding areas for woodland frogs and salamanders and support a variety of plants and other animals.

The dedicated state nature preserve is named for longtime local resident Marion Eberhardt, whose family worked with the City of Angola, the Indiana Heritage Trust, and ACRES Land Trust to acquire and protect the site.

Activities
Hiking Trails: One (0.5 mile), moderate.
Other Activities: Fishing, hiking, hunting, nature study, photography, wildlife watching.

Directions
GPS coordinates: 41.650115, –84.988335
From I-69

- East on US 20 to Williams Street in Angola, 2.7 miles
- North on Williams Street to Calvary Lane, 1.0 mile
- East on Calvary Lane to preserve, 0.2 mile

70. Robb Hidden Canyon

Owned by ACRES Land Trust

The 87.5-acre Robb Hidden Canyon in Steuben County protects a steep-sided, wooded ravine on Ball Lake with a clear, intermittent stream. Twenty-nine acres are designated as a dedicated

Marion's Woods Nature Preserve

Robb Hidden Canyon

state nature preserve of the same name. The Hiram Sweet Ditch, a Fish Creek tributary that drains Ball Lake, borders the preserve on the northeast.

The Robb Hidden Canyon preserve supports a moist upland forest whose old, second-growth trees grow straight and tall on the ravine's steep slopes and feature a variety of species, including American beech, sugar maple, black cherry, and red oak. Kentucky coffee trees survive on the ravine's west side.

The understory includes flowering dogwood and spicebush, along with bishop's cap, jewelweed, rue anemone, blue phlox, spring beauty, Virginia waterleaf, and large-flowered trillium on the forest floor. Scarlet tanagers, indigo buntings, wood thrushes, rose-breasted grosbeaks, and a variety of warblers are among the birds that frequent Robb Hidden Canyon. The trail passes through a successional meadow that brims in summer with red clover and other wildflowers.

Dr. Robert and Phyllis Robb donated the preserve. Boy Scouts built the trail.

Activities
Hiking Trails: One (1.7 miles), moderate.
Other Activities: Nature study, photography, wildlife watching.

Directions
GPS coordinates: 41.536380, –84.937441
From I-69
- East on Old State Road 4 (County Road 800S) at Ashley to Homestead Drive at Hamilton, 6.4 miles
- North on Homestead Drive to Bellefontaine Road, 0.7 mile
- West on Bellefontaine Road to Lane 101 (Ball Lake Road), 0.8 mile
- South on Lane 101 to preserve, 0.5 mile

71. Douglas Woods Nature Preserve
Owned by The Nature Conservancy

The 1,327-acre Douglas Woods in Steuben and DeKalb Counties protects nearly four hundred acres of old-growth forest with trees whose diameters reach four feet and heights exceed a hundred feet. Other preserve landforms include small ponds and wetlands dominated by buttonbush and sedge. A 130-acre dedicated state nature preserve within the larger tract supports four rare plants.

Fish Creek, more than a mile of whose lower stretch winds through the Douglas Woods preserve, historically has supported the white cat's paw pearly mussel, which the US Fish & Wildlife Service says is one of the *world's* "most critically endangered animals" and that its recovery "may be impossible."

One of thirty mussel species that historically thrived in Fish Creek's healthier days, the white cat's paw was widespread in the Ohio River Basin, from Indiana to Alabama, and in a dozen

Douglas Woods Nature Preserve

or so river systems from New York to Lake Erie and Indiana. This mollusk requires midsized freshwater streams and rivers with coarse sand or gravel bottoms, shallow water, and swift currents so they don't get buried in silt. Erosion from intense agriculture has smothered the creatures in their streambeds. Oil spills and pesticides and fertilizers in runoff have poisoned them. Fish Creek was one of the last places the white cat's paw was known to breed.

In addition to the state endangered hairy woodrush, other rare plants at Douglas Woods are state rare rushlike aster and state watch-listed dwarf ginseng.

The preserve's dry-moist and moist upland forests harbor oak, hickory, ash, basswood, beech, and maple. The upland woods have several swamps that are home to breeding frogs and salamanders. Fish Creek features old oxbows, swamps, and ponds.

Great blue herons have an active colony in the woods. Hawks, pheasants, and deer are common, as are many amphibians. Wood ducks breed there.

The rest of the acreage is young, regenerating forest, old fields, and tillable land. Much of the farmland is leased to a local farmer, who practices conservation tillage to show how to reduce soil loss and chemical runoff. The rest of the farmland has been reforested to enhance wildlife habitat.

The property was owned by the Douglas family from 1926 on and has been largely undisturbed since the 1950s.

Activities
Hiking (no marked trails), hunting, nature study, photography, wildlife watching.

Directions
GPS coordinates: 41.517807, –84.865269
From I-69
- East on Old State Road 4 (County Road 800S) at Ashley to Wayne Street in Hamilton, 7.1 miles
- North on Wayne Street to State Road 1 (Bellefontaine Road), 0.4 mile
- East on State Road 1 to County Road 4A, 2.4 miles
- East on County Road 4A to preserve, 0.4 mile

Section 4

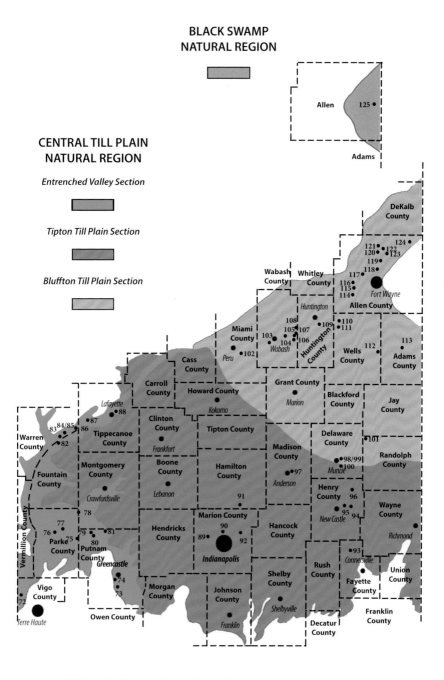

BLACK SWAMP NATURAL REGION

Allen   125

Adams

CENTRAL TILL PLAIN NATURAL REGION

Entrenched Valley Section

Tipton Till Plain Section

Bluffton Till Plain Section

DeKalb County

121 124
120 122
119 123
118
117
116
115 Fort Wayne
114
Allen County

Wabash County   Whitley County

Huntington

108
105 107 109 110
103 104 106 111
Peru 102   Wabash   Huntington County   Wells County   Adams County
Miami County   112   113

Cass County

Carroll County   Howard County   Grant County   Blackford County   Jay County

Kokomo   Marion

Lafayette
83 84/85 87 88
82 86   Tippecanoe County
Warren County

Clinton County   Tipton County   Delaware County   Randolph County
Frankfort   98/99
101
Madison County   Muncie 100
Montgomery County   Boone County   Hamilton County   Anderson 97   Henry County   Wayne County
Fountain County   Lebanon   91   96
Crawfordsville   95 94
78   New Castle   Richmond
77   Marion County   90
76 75   79 81   89   92   93
Parke County   80   Hendricks County   Hancock County   Connersville   Union County
Putnam County   Indianapolis   Rush County   Fayette County
Greencastle   74   Morgan County   Shelby County   Franklin County
Vigo County   73   Johnson County   Shelbyville   Decatur County
72
Terre Haute   Owen County   Franklin

Section 4

CENTRAL TILL PLAIN NATURAL REGION

Entrenched Valley Section

72. Jackson-Schnyder Nature Preserve
73. Deer Creek Fish & Wildlife Area
74. Fern Cliff Nature Preserve
75. Raccoon State Recreation Area / Cecil M. Harden Lake
76. Mossy Point Nature Preserve
77. Turkey Run State Park / Rocky Hollow-Falls Canyon Nature Preserve
78. Shades State Park / Pine Hills Nature Preserve
79. Big Walnut Preserve
80. Hall Woods Nature Preserve
81. Hemlock Ridge Nature Preserve
82. Portland Arch Nature Preserve
83. Fall Creek Gorge Nature Preserve
84. Weiler-Leopold Nature Preserve
85. Black Rock Barrens Nature Preserve
86. Black Rock Nature Preserve
87. Granville Sand Barrens Nature Preserve
88. Prophetstown State Park / Prophetstown Fen Nature Preserve

Tipton Till Plain Section

89. Eagle Creek Park / Spring Pond Nature Preserve / Eagle's Crest Nature Preserve
90. Marott Park Woods Nature Preserve
91. Ritchey Woods Nature Preserve
92. Fort Harrison State Park / Warbler Woods Nature Preserve / Lawrence Creek Nature Preserve
93. Shrader-Weaver Nature Preserve
94. Wilbur Wright Fish & Wildlife Area
95. Stout Woods Nature Preserve

96. Summit Lake State Park / Zeigler Woods Nature Preserve
97. Mounds State Park
98. Red-tail Nature Preserve

Bluffton Till Plain Section

99. Hughes Nature Preserve
100. John M. Craddock Wetland Nature Preserve
101. Davis-Purdue Agricultural Center Forest
102. Mississinewa Lake
103. Asherwood Nature Preserve
104. Hathaway Preserve at Ross Run
105. Salamonie River State Forest
106. Salamonie Lake
107. Kokiwanee Nature Preserve
108. Hanging Rock National Natural Landmark
109. J. E. Roush Fish & Wildlife Area
110. Anna Brand Hammer Reserve
111. Acres Along the Wabash Nature Preserve
112. Ouabache State Park
113. Baltzell-Lenhart Woods Nature Preserve
114. Fogwell Forest Nature Preserve
115. Fox Island Nature Preserve
116. Eagle Marsh
117. Lindenwood Nature Preserve
118. Mengerson Nature Reserve
119. Meno-aki Nature Preserve
120. Bicentennial Woods Nature Preserve
121. Little Cedar Creek Wildlife Sanctuary Nature Preserve
122. Tom and Jane Dustin, Robert C. and Rosella C. Johnson, and Whitehurst Nature Preserves
123. Vandolah Nature Preserve
124. McNabb-Walter Nature Preserve

BLACK SWAMP NATURAL REGION

125. Blue Cast Springs Nature Preserve

CENTRAL TILL PLAIN
NATURAL REGION

CENTRAL TILL PLAIN NATURAL REGION

Entrenched Valley Section

72. Jackson-Schnyder Nature Preserve

Owned by Ouabache Land Conservancy

The fifteen-acre Jackson-Schnyder Nature Preserve in Vigo County supports mature hardwood forest with two ravines that surround a former farm field that has been converted to prairie. Situated on the Little Sugar Creek just west of St. Mary of the Woods College, Jackson-Schnyder is a dedicated state nature preserve. It supports sturdy, towering old-growth hardwood trees and a wide selection of woodland and prairie plant and animal species.

A well-maintained trail circles the prairie, with side trails to the woods and the Little Sugar, which borders the preserve on the east. The grassland is subjected to periodic controlled burns to discourage woody growth and replicate conditions on natural prairielands.

Marion T. Jackson, an environmental science professor who taught at Indiana State University and St. Mary, donated the Jackson-Schnyder site to the Ouabache Land Conservancy in spring 2010. According to the Terre Haute *Tribune-Star*, Jackson used the landscape as a personal retreat and outdoor laboratory for students.

Conamed after Swiss immigrant Julius Schnyder, who purchased the land in 1921 and sold it to Jackson in 1969, the preserve is dedicated to Jackson's vision and still serves as a learning lab for students and nature lovers.

Activities

Hiking trail, nature study, photography, wildlife watching.

Directions

GPS coordinates: 39.509479, −87.474059
From I-70
- North on State Road 150 at Terre Haute to St. Mary's Road, 6.3 miles

- West on St. Mary's Road to Bloomtown Road, 1.3 miles
- West on Bloomtown Road to Concannon Avenue, 300 feet
- West on Concannon to preserve entrance on right, just past Little Sugar Creek, 500 feet

From I-74
- South on State Road 63 at Spring Creek to Pennington Road (not marked), 41.2 miles (7.5 miles south of State Road 163 at Clinton)
- West on Pennington Road to State Road 150, 0.6 mile
- South on State Road 150 to St. Mary's Road, 3.7 miles
- West on St. Mary's Road to Bloomtown Road, 1.3 miles
- West on Bloomtown Road to Concannon Avenue, 300 feet
- West on Concannon to preserve entrance on right, just past Little Sugar Creek, 500 feet

73. Deer Creek Fish & Wildlife Area

Owned by Indiana Department of Natural Resources,
Division of Fish & Wildlife

The 2,142-acre Deer Creek Fish & Wildlife Area in Putnam County is managed for hunting, fishing, trapping and wildlife watching. Its rolling agricultural and wooded landscape consists of two sections on either side of US 40 just west of Putnamville.

The scattered woodlands are mature oak-hickory forest. A four-acre pond provides fishing for bass, bluegill, and catfish on the area's northern section. Deer Creek, with a low-head dam, iron bridge, and concrete creek crossing, winds through the southern portion. Some accessible hunting and fishing areas are available.

The forests, shallow impoundments, and creek are managed for a variety of game and nongame wildlife, including songbirds, waterfowl, doves, quails, woodcocks, woodpeckers, hawks, squirrels, rabbits, turkeys, and deer.

The Deer Creek wildlife area surrounds the Putnamville Correctional Facility, which transferred 1,962 acres of the land to the Division of Fish & Wildlife in 2010.

Berry, mushroom, and nut gathering, fishing, hiking, hunting, nature study, photography, trapping, wildlife watching.

Directions

GPS coordinates: 39.573633, –86.886195

From I-70

- North on State Road 243 to US 40 at Putnamville, 3.9 miles
- West on US 40 to South County Road 200W, 1.2 miles
- North on South County Road 200W to wildlife area, 0.4 mile

From I-74

- South on US 231 at Crawfordsville, through Greencastle, to US 40 at Putnamville, 35.9 miles
- West on US 40 to South County Road 200W, 1.2 miles
- North on South County Road 200W to wildlife area, 0.4 mile

74. Fern Cliff Nature Preserve

Owned by The Nature Conservancy

The Nature Conservancy calls its 157-acre Fern Cliff Nature Preserve's unique vegetation "a botanists' floral paradise." Characterized by rugged sandstone topography, this dedicated state nature preserve in Putnam County also holds National Natural Landmark status for "outstanding biological and geological resources."

Multiple ravines and cliffs—carved from the sandstone by glacial meltwater—are spectacularly colored with leaching metals like iron and covered with ferns and, most notably, mosses and liverworts unique to this part of the planet. As lush are the moist upland and lowland forests, which support wildflowers, fungi, and other flora. The terrain is treacherously precipitous. Trailside signs warn of "dangerous cliffs."

Among Fern Cliffs' less-than-natural characteristics are a stark canyon and artifacts left behind by an early-twentieth-century quarry, which is now is filling with sphagnum moss. The Root Glass Company mined sandstone and crushed it onsite for shipping to its bottle manufacturing plant in Terre Haute. Fern Cliff is bordered by the Snake Creek, which feeds the Big

Fern Cliff Nature Preserve

Walnut Creek about a mile to the east, a few miles southwest of Greencastle.

A half-dozen unusual plant species survive at Fern Cliff, including state watch-listed spotted wintergreen. Oak, beech, hickory, maple, ash, cherry, and tulip trees thrive on the moist uplands, with an understory of dogwood, hydrangea, pawpaw, and other herbaceous plants, including mayapple, jack-in-the-pulpit, blue phlox, and wood (celandine) poppy.

Rock climbing and rappelling are prohibited at Fern Cliff.

Shawnee Indians encamped at Fern Cliff in pre-statehood days, using the canyon cliffs for shelter and ceremonial dances. The Shawnee, Miami, and other tribes were driven from the area in the 1830s, and the site evolved as an increasingly popular picnic and recreation destination until Root Glass closed it to visitors in 1910. The Owens Glass Company purchased the property, logged it through the 1930s, and gave 123 acres to the Greencastle Girl Scouts Council in 1944 for nature study.

Subsequently deeded to the Putnam Friends of Youth in 1962 and then The Nature Conservancy in 1987, Fern Cliff was declared a National Natural Landmark by the National Park Service in 1980 and a dedicated state nature preserve in 1988. A 1994 gift of 36 adjoining acres increased the preserve to 157 acres.

Activities
Hiking trail, nature study, photography, wildlife watching.

Directions
GPS coordinates: 39.607897, −86.968200
From I-70
- North on US 231 to Jackson Street on the square in Greencastle, 9.3 miles
- South on Jackson Street to Walnut Street, 1 block
- West on Walnut Street (becoming County Road 125S) to County Road 500W, 4.0 miles
- South on County Road 500W, bearing left at all intersections, to County Road 375S, 2.9 miles
- West on County Road 375S to preserve entrance, 0.8 mile

From I-74
- South on US 231 to Jackson Street on the square in Greencastle, 30.9 miles
- South on Jackson Street to Walnut Street, 1 block
- West on Walnut Street (becoming County Road 125W) to County Road 500W, 4.0 miles
- South on County Road 500W, bearing left at all intersections, to County Road 375S, 2.9 miles
- West on County Road 375S to preserve entrance, 0.8 mile

75. Raccoon State Recreation Area / Cecil M. Harden Lake

Owned by Indiana Department of Natural Resources, Division of State Parks & Lakes

The 4,065-acre Raccoon State Recreation Area in Putnam and Parke Counties is a long, narrow peninsula that juts into Cecil M. Harden Lake and features scenic lake overlooks, second-growth and mature forests, steep ravines, and rugged sandstone cliffs.

Raccoon State Recreation Area

As a state recreation area, Raccoon's emphasis is on outdoor activities, from skiing and swimming to hunting and hiking, with some three hundred campsites. Several trails offer scenic lake views and intimate interactions with the surrounding woods, its flora and fauna, and geologic features like sandstone cliffs.

The recreation area is so named because of its location on Big Raccoon Creek, which was dammed in 1960 to create the 2,060-acre lake, originally called Mansfield Lake after the nearby town of Mansfield. The lake was renamed in 1974 in honor of Congresswoman Cecil Murray Harden, who represented the area from 1949 to 1959 and led efforts to raise money for the lake project. The US Army Corps of Engineers constructed Harden Lake to control flooding in the Big Raccoon Creek and Lower Wabash River Watershed and to provide recreation and resource management.

Several Native American tribes, primarily the Delaware, Shawnee, and Miami, lived in East Central Indiana when the white settlers arrived in the early 1800s. They lost Parke County—and the land that is now Raccoon State Recreation Area—in the Ten O'clock Line Treaty of 1809 and Treaty of St. Mary's of 1818.

Activities
Hiking Trails: Five (1.3–2.1 miles), moderate to rugged.
Camping: 295, electric, nonelectric, primitive; occupancy limited to fourteen consecutive nights; camp store.
Other Activities: Boat ramps, five; boat rentals: fishing, pontoon, ski; fishing, hiking, Historic Mansfied Roller Mill; hunting, interpretative naturalist; nature study, photography, picnicking; shelters; swimming beach: modern bathhouse and concessions; wildlife watching; youth tent camping.

Directions
GPS coordinates: 39.758499, –87.074093
From I-70
- North on US 231, through Greencastle, to US 36, 17.9 miles
- West on US 36 to state recreation area, 10.1 miles

From I-74
- South on US 231 at Crawfordsville to US 36, 22.3 miles
- West on US 36 to state recreation area, 10.1 miles

76. Mossy Point Nature Preserve
Owned by Central Indiana Land Trust
The 191-acre Mossy Point Nature Preserve in Parke County lines nearly a mile of the Lower Sugar Creek Valley about four miles upstream from the Wabash River. The landscape at this preserve is characterized by high, dry ridges and wet ravines, with mature stands of the state watch-listed eastern hemlock on rocky points that drop to the creek.

The Nature Conservancy's *Guide to Indiana Preserves* says Mossy Point is perhaps "the most ecological[ly] varied land between the Wabash River and Turkey Run." Ninety-three acres of the preserve's nearly unbroken forest canopy have been designated as a dedicated state nature preserve.

Sugar Creek, Mossy Point Nature Preserve

Mossy Point's unique environs support a variety of breeding populations of vulnerable, forest interior birds, including the state species of special concern worm-eating warbler, along with wood thrush, cerulean warbler, Kentucky warbler, and Louisiana waterthrush. Spotted sandpipers and other waders are common on the flats.

White oak and shagbark hickory occupy the dry ridges, with a mix of American beech, white ash, sugar maple, tulip poplar, and red oak thriving in the ravines. Soft maples, black walnut, and green ash are common on the floodplain forest that occupies Mossy Point's northeast portion. Unusual plant species include partridgeberry and witch hazel.

The site lies at the end of a private driveway. A parking lot is located down the drive past the gate before a hunting lodge that is part of the property. The road ends in private property.

Two unmarked trails to the north lead along a ravine and drop to the floodplain. They get overgrown in summer and disappear in the winter.

Activities
Hiking (moderate to rugged terrain, no marked trails), nature study, photography, wildlife watching.

Directions
GPS coordinates: 39.853291, –87.285463
From I-70
- North on State Road 59 to State Road 236, 27.4 miles
- West on State Road 236, to US 41, 7.5 miles
- North on US 41 to Annapolis Road, 0.6 mile
- West on Annapolis Road, past Annapolis and through several turns, to driveway marked 2600, just after a sharp turn south, 2.8 miles
- West on driveway to property gate

From I-74
- South on US 41 at Veedersburg to Annapolis Road, 18.8 miles
- West on Annapolis Road, past Annapolis and through several turns, to driveway marked 2600, just after a sharp turn south, 2.8 miles
- West on driveway to property gate

77a. Turkey Run State Park
Owned by Indiana Department of Natural Resources, Division of State Parks & Lakes

The 2,382-acre Turkey Run State Park in Parke County is characterized by deeply dissected sandstone ravines, hemlock groves, stands of old-growth walnut and sycamore, and scenic views of the wild and flowing Sugar Creek, which bisects the park. Its stark gorges of Mansfield sandstone, carved by glacial meltwater a few miles west of Shades State Park, are unsurpassed in their distinct natural beauty.

In his 2016 book *A Place Called Turkey Run*, Purdue University geoenvironmental science and science education professor

Daniel P. Shepardson articulates the Turkey Run experience: "There's a feeling of awe standing next to a sandstone face that is hundreds of millions of years old. The trees that grow at the base of the bluff suggest a harmony between the living and non-living. The past and the present are seen in the rock and the tree, and in the green and yellow leaves of the trees."

The park's sheer sandstone cliffs reflect brilliant, multihued palettes that span the spectrum from deep red through shimmering green to metallic blue, in places illuminated by direct sun. Lush plant life, including lichens, mosses, and ferns, bedecks the park's canyon walls and regularly share the ecosystem with a variety of animal species, including white-tailed deer, beavers, woodpeckers, and vultures.

In addition to the Mansfield sandstone, named after the nearby town, the park's geology includes coal, which was mined there in the late 1800s and early 1900s. Seams are still evident in places.

Turkey Run boasts some of the most challenging hiking trails in the state, some with ladders ascending sheer rock faces. Steps are common.

While Turkey Run may not have been Indiana's first state park, an argument can be made that it is the most spectacular. Colonel Richard Lieber, also known as the Father of Indiana State Parks, wanted its canyon lands to be number one. But for logistical reasons, McCormick's Creek State Park claimed the honor.

Like McCormick's Creek, Turkey Run's first parcels were purchased in 1916 during the state's centennial. The name's origins aren't known for certain. One version holds that in winter wild turkeys would gather in the canyon's runs—its bottoms—because they found them warmer than the open landscape. Another says pioneer hunters would herd the birds through the runs for easier harvest. Others just say large numbers of turkeys lived in the area.

Among the park's attractions is the Colonel Richard Lieber Cabin, which commemorates his contributions to the state and nation. The largest of its kind in Indiana, the structure was

Rocky Hollow-Falls Canyon Nature Preserve,
Turkey Run State Park

constructed of virgin timber in the 1840s. The ashes of Richard and his wife, Emma, are buried amid a hemlock grove in the park.

As with many of Indiana's public lands, a number of Turkey Run's improvements—shelter houses, saddle barn, sandstone trail structures—were built by President Franklin D. Roosevelt's Civilian Conservation Corps, whose Camp 8 was stationed there in 1934–1935. Known as FDR's "tree army," these hearty lads were hired by the federal government to reclaim and improve vast natural areas of the Hoosier landscape during the Great Depression.

77b. Rocky Hollow-Falls Canyon Nature Preserve

The 1,609-acre Rocky Hollow-Falls Canyon Nature Preserve is a dedicated state nature preserve, with 391 acres recognized as a National Natural Landmark. According to the National Park Service, its landscape "contains forested areas of virgin beech-maple stands, steep sandstone gorges that harbor virgin boreal relict populations of the state endangered Canada yew, state watch-listed eastern hemlock, and some of the largest black walnut in the Midwest."

Among Rocky Hollow preserve's more fascinating sandstone formations, the Devil's Punchbowl is a pothole formed by glacial erratics—pieces of glacial Canadian bedrock—caught in swirling backwash. The narrow gorges of colorful, textured sandstone with small waterfalls over the bedrock are lined with ferns, hydrangeas, and the native hemlocks.

In addition to Canada yew and eastern hemlock, the preserve harbors a number of rare and unusual species, including the state rare Deam's mercury and wolf bluegrass and state watch-listed yellow buckeye, sparse-lobe grape-fern, and rose turtlehead.

The upland areas support old-growth mesophytic forest—an intermediate type that thrives in between wet floodplain and dry upland forests. The Sugar Creek terraces support old-growth floodplain forest. The flatter sections on the uplands have old fields in various stages of succession.

Rocky Hollow-Falls Canyon Nature Preserve

Activities

Hiking Trails: Eleven (0.5–2.0 miles), easy to very rugged.
Camping: 213 electric sites, youth tent areas, camp store, dumping station.
Other Activities: Cabins (inn operated); fishing; inn, with indoor pool, meeting and conference facilities, restaurant; picnic areas, playgrounds; interpretive naturalist services, nature center/planetarium; nature study; photography; saddle barn; shelters, tennis and other games; wildlife watching.

Directions

GPS coordinates: 39.882173, –87.201941
From I-70

- North on US 231, through Greencastle, to State Road 236, 22.9 miles
- West on State Road 236 to Main Street in Marshall, 15.8 miles
- North on Main Street, becoming Marshal Road, to State Road 47, 2.4 miles
- West on State Road 47 to park entrance, 0.9 mile

From I-74

- South on US 231 at Crawfordsville to East South Boulevard/ State Road 47, 3.9 miles
- Southwest on State Road 47 to park entrance, 21.8 miles

78a. Shades State Park

Owned by Indiana Department of Natural Resources,
Division of State Parks & Lakes

The 3,541-acre Shades State Park is among the least developed and most rugged of Indiana's state parks, sharing many natural characteristics with Turkey Run State Park about five miles down the Sugar Creek Valley: heavily wooded forests covering narrow ridgetops and creek-hollowed ravines exposing walls of sandstone and slate bedrock. Camping is primitive. Trails are rugged and often require walking through flowing, rocky-bottomed streams and climbing steps and/or ladders.

Spreading across Montgomery, Parke, and Fountain Counties, Shades is known for its beautiful cliffs that overlook five miles of the Sugar Creek, Clifty Creek, and Indian Creek Valleys and for its unique landforms left by glacial activity more than ten thousand years ago. Among the geologic marvels are backbones, a punchbowl, and a convex waterfall. Small waterfalls are common. Fossils are found on the sandbars.

Shades boasts Indiana's first dedicated state nature preserve (see the Pine Hills Nature Preserve entry below), which is arguably its most spectacular. The preserve is separated from the park by State Road 234 but *must* be accessed from a connector trail inside the park.

The park's sandstone bedrock formed some three hundred million years ago. The cliffs were carved by glacial meltwater from the Wisconsin glacier that covered most of Indiana until it began melting roughly 13,600 years ago. In places the drops are a sheer one hundred or more feet. Others feature spectacular honeycombs in the cliff faces.

The Shades forest is a mix of deciduous hardwoods—blue beech, sycamore, tulip poplar, dogwood, sugar maple, red oak,

Pine Hills Nature Preserve, Shades State Park

American elm—and evergreens, including native, state rare white pine and state watch-listed eastern hemlock. This mixture, rare this far south, once dominated this region and still thrives in Canada today.

Although rugged, unspoiled, and uncrowded—Shades is widely regarded as Turkey Run with fewer people—the park is not wilderness. Car and RV campers are allowed. An amphitheater sits near the campground. The three-thousand-foot-long and one-hundred-twenty-foot-wide Roscoe Turner Flight Strip, where visitors once landed their planes, is no longer used but still exists.

Shades was known in early settlement times as the "black forest"—visitors today recommend it for stargazing—and earned the name "Shades of Death." Various accounts say that darker moniker evolved from the land's eerie, deep-forest environment; an early settler's death at the hands of the Piankeshaw

Indians; or another settler's death at the axe-wielding hands of his wife.

Indiana was Miami Indian land when the European explorers and settlers arrived in the late seventeenth and early eighteenth centuries. According to legend, a large village of Piankeshaw, a branch of the Miami tribe, occupied the acreage that today is Shades State Park. Legend also says six hundred Native American warriors fought a decisive battle here.

The Miami ceded West Central Indiana to the Americans in the Treaty of St. Mary's in 1818, and settlers started arriving in the late 1820s. Due to shallow soils and forbidding topography, most of the Shades forest was left intact. Built around a series of natural springs in one of the ravines, a health resort and recreation area called the Shades was organized and developed in 1886 by the Garland Dells Mineral Springs Association. A year later, a forty-room inn was built near what is now the Devil's Punchbowl.

With an eye toward preservation, the "Father of Shades," Joseph W. Frisz, purchased enough Dells Mineral Springs stock between 1909 and 1916 to gain control. By the late 1930s, his holdings had grown to 2,200 acres, with a scenic inn amid a grove of mature oak trees, hiking trails, swimming, fishing, and natural spring water.

The Frisz family sold the property to a holding company in 1947, which held it until a subscription company called Save the Shades raised enough to purchase and give it to the state. Shades became Indiana's fifteenth state park that same year.

The park is open for day use only during the off-season, from November through March. Visitors must leave at dusk during this time, and no camping is available. Overnight camping is available at Turkey Run.

78b. Pine Hills Nature Preserve

The 480-acre Pine Hills Nature Preserve was purchased by The Nature Conservancy and deeded to the state in 1961 as Indiana's first dedicated state nature preserve. It is recognized by the National Park Service as a National Natural Landmark.

Pine Hills features deep ravines formed by glacial meltwater that, over the past thirteen thousand or so years, has carved Indian Creek, Clifty Creek, and Sugar Creek out of the region's Mansfield sandstone, so named for the nearby town. Situated roughly ten miles upstream from the Wabash River, the Pine Hills landscape is covered with an evergreen-hardwood mix that features relict stands of state endangered Canada yew, state rare eastern white pine, and state watch-listed eastern hemlock. Other rare and unusual plant species at Pine Hills include state rare longstalk sedge, roundleaf dogwood, wolf bluegrass, and softleaf arrow-wood; and state watch-listed American pinesap.

The water's erosive power left in its path four narrow ridges called backbones in Pine Hills that rise seventy to one hundred feet above the creeks. The most dramatic, Devil's Backbone, narrows to six feet in one spot. According to the National Park Service, Pine Hills Natural Area "is probably the most remarkable example of incised meanders in the Eastern United States."

Pine Hills rare mix of hardwoods and evergreens is separated from Shades by State Road 234 and must be accessed by trail from inside the park gate.

Activities

Hiking Trails: Eleven (0.5–2. 5 miles), easy to rugged.
Other Activities: Fishing, hiking, hunting, nature study, photography, wildlife watching.

Directions

GPS coordinates: 39.925233, –87.071819
From I-70
- North on US 231, through Greencastle, to State Road 234, 28.7 miles
- West on State Road 234 to park entrance, 10.6 miles

From I-74
- South on US 231 at Crawfordsville to State Road 234, 10.8 miles
- West on State Road 234 to park entrance, 10.6 miles

Pine Hills Nature Preserve, Shades State Park

79. Big Walnut Preserve

Owned by The Nature Conservancy

The National Park Service recognized the staggering creek valley that borders the 2,697-acre Big Walnut Preserve in Putnam County as a natural wonder a half century ago. Its 1968 designation of 502 acres as the Big Walnut Creek National Natural Landmark means the landforms support "outstanding biological and geological resources." Another 245 acres are also designated as a dedicated state nature preserve.

"The site contains one of the few stands in Indiana where American beech, sugar maple, and tulip poplar grow on alluvial Genesee soil and includes relict species of a postglacial forest that occupied the area 5,000 to 6,000 years ago," the National Park Service says on its website.

The Big Walnut Preserve surrounds Fortune Woods—a 120-acre stand of old-growth hardwood forest—and represents one of the few remaining stands of this type of climax forest in West Central Indiana. The ridges support oak and hickory, the bottomlands sycamore, eastern cottonwood, and red maple. Visible only from the water, Big Walnut's relict stands of state endangered Canada yew and state watch-listed eastern hemlock include some the state's largest known specimens of these trees.

In addition to the evergreens, an uncommon plant that flourishes in the Big Walnut Creek watershed is Goldie's fern. Wildflowers include spring beauties and anemones in the uplands and Virginia bluebells in the bottomlands.

Big Walnut Creek has been nominated as a National Audubon Society Important Bird Area. Birds that live in or pass through the Big Walnut's large, intact-forest ecosystem include cerulean warbler, worm-eating warbler, hooded warbler—all state species of special concern—and great blue herons.

Big Walnut Creek has carved its imprint into glacial till deposited some 13,600 years ago by the retreating Wisconsin glacier, the last ice sheet to cover Indiana. Its rugged topography spared its ancient woodlands from the settler axes that cleared the rest of West Central Indiana for agriculture in the thirty years after their arrival in the 1820s. A rock along the trail bears

Big Walnut Preserve

a 1914 inscription from C. J. Baker and says: "The Lost 40. Only God can make a tree."

The aquatic plants and animals the Big Walnut Preserve's clear water supports survived plans in the 1960s and 1970s to dredge the creek for a barge canal and associated development. In 1982, the Ralph and Eileen Hultz family sold a portion of their land to The Nature Conservancy. Ralph, who was born in an 1837 cabin that is preserved in the Big Walnut Creek area, refused to allow any timber harvesting, even though he worked in nearby sawmills. After Ralph's death, Eileen likewise conserved the land, selling the rest to The Nature Conservancy in 1993.

In the late 1990s, preservationists persuaded two developers with plans to build houses on nearly two hundred acres on two separate parcels instead to sell to The Nature Conservancy, which acquired the land as an addition to the Big Walnut Creek National Natural Landmark. The larger natural complex called the Big Walnut Natural Area has expanded to more than three thousand acres, including the 128-acre Hall Woods Nature Preserve a mile south and across US 36. (See Hall Woods entry below.) The Nature Conservancy manages surrounding farmlands under conservation easements as buffers between the preserve and surrounding land uses.

The one-mile-loop Tall Timbers Trail, with spur to the creek, is a moderate hike that is often wet and requires crossing a feeder creek. Parking is available at the trailhead.

Historic covered bridges still stand in and near the Big Walnut Preserve.

Activities
Hiking Trails: One (1.1 miles), steps and creek crossings.
Other Activities: Nature study, photography, wildlife watching.

Directions
GPS coordinates: 39.796760, −86.777449
From I-70
- North on US 231 through Greencastle to US 36, 16.6 miles
- East on US 36 to County Road 200E in Bainbridge, 4.0 miles
- North on County Road 200E to County Road 800N, 20.7 miles
- East on County Road 800N to County Road 250E, 0.5 mile
- North on County Road 250E to County Road 950N, 1.5 miles
- East on County Road 950N to preserve parking lot, 1.4 miles

From I-74
- South on US 231 at Metronet to State Road 236 15.9, miles
- East on State Road 236 to County Road 250E at Roachdale, 4.8 miles
- South on County Road 250E to County Road 950N, 3.4 miles
- East on County Road 950N to preserve parking lot, 1.4 miles

80. Hall Woods Nature Preserve
Owned by Indiana Department of Natural Resources,
Division of Nature Preserves
The 128-acre Hall Woods Nature Preserve in Putnam County borders the Big Walnut Creek about a mile south of the Big Walnut Preserve and features moist, upland and bottomland forests with stunning ravines and creek-side ecosystems—interspersed with stands of old growth. Ninety-four acres have been designated as a dedicated state nature preserve.

Hall Woods Nature Preserve

A loop trail follows a forested ridgetop past a mint-condition one-room log cabin to the Big Walnut Creek, a siltstone-bottomed waterway that, according to the Indiana Division of Nature Preserves, "has been identified as among the best quality stream segments in Indiana." The cabin's origins are unknown, though the odds are it was a "getaway cabin" built in the 1930s.

On its website, The Nature Conservancy says: "Hall Woods serves as a microcosm of the entire Big Walnut Natural Areas project: deep, rich woods filled with sweet-singing warblers, soft slopes covered in wildflowers, sparkling streams full of life and a human history that serves to inspire."

The moister upland areas support maple, hickory, ash, and cherry trees, with significant numbers of towering white oaks. The lush understory, which shows little signs of disturbance, supports sassafras, dogwood, and spicebush. Lowland species that thrive in the ravines include silver maple, sycamore, Ohio buckeye, and tulip poplar. Wildlife commonly seen in Hall Woods includes warblers, swallows, kingfishers, and dragonflies.

Along with the Big Walnut Preserve (see the Big Walnut Preserve entry above), Hall Woods, just east of Bainbridge, is one of more than three-dozen separate tracts—totaling more than three thousand acres—that comprise a larger natural complex known as the Big Walnut Natural Area. The tracts are owned by public, private, and nonprofit organizations, including The Nature Conservancy.

Activities
Hiking Trails: One, easy to moderate.
Other Activities: Nature study, photography, wildlife watching.

Directions
GPS coordinates: 39.755956, −86.787330
From I-70
- North on US 231 to US 36, 17.3 miles
- East on US 36, through Bainbridge, to County Road 300E, 4.9 miles
- Southeast on County Road 300E (becoming County Road 675N) to preserve, 0.5 mile

From I-74
- South on US 231 at Crawfordsville to US 36, 22.3 miles
- East on US 36, through Bainbridge, to County Road 300E (becoming 675N), 4.9 miles
- Southeast on County Road 300E (becoming County Road 675N) to preserve, 0.5 mile

81. Hemlock Ridge Nature Preserve
Owned by Central Indiana Land Trust
The thirty-nine-acre Hemlock Ridge Nature Preserve in Putnam County supports a rare stand of state watch-listed eastern hemlock overlooking the Big Walnut Creek, amid high-quality examples of moist floodplains, uplands, and ravine forests. Hemlock, which can live a thousand years and is more common much farther north, is a relict species that survives in the state on just a few steep, moist, north-facing slopes.

A self-guided trail at this remote dedicated state nature preserve traverses a field owned by a neighbor to the entrance. At the preserve marker, the trail passes through a meadow and into the hemlock stand, with views overlooking Big Walnut Creek, north and east of the Big Walnut Preserve.

The marker recognizes the late Central Indiana natural area stewardship leader Randy Lewis. A meadow within the preserve was reforested in 2006 and named in Lewis's honor.

Activities
Hiking, nature study, photography, wildlife watching.

Directions
GPS coordinates: 39.819908, −86.719810
From I-70
- North on US 231, through Greencastle, to US 36, 17.9 miles
- East on US 36 to County Line Road, 10.6 miles
- North on County Line Road to County Road 1100N, 4.1 miles
- West on County Road 1100N to North County Road 775E (confusing signage: after stop sign, gravel road, angles to right), 1.4 miles
- North on County Road 775E back to County Road 1100N, 0.2 mile
- West on County Road 1100N to preserve, 0.5 mile

From I-74
- South on US 231 at Crawfordsville, to US 36, 17.9 miles
- East on US 36 to County Line Road, 10.6 miles
- North on County Line Road to County Road 1100N, 4.1 miles
- West on County Road 1100N to North County Road 775E (confusing signage: after stop sign, gravel road, angles to right), 1.4 miles
- North on County Road 775E back to County Road 1100N, 0.2 mile
- West on County Road 1100N to preserve, 0.5 mile

82. Portland Arch Nature Preserve
Owned by Indiana Department of Natural Resources,
Division of Nature Preserves
The 435-acre Portland Arch Nature Preserve in Fountain County is named for the 7.5-foot-high natural bridge carved through a sandstone cliff by Spring Creek, a small tributary of Bear Creek. From this National Natural Landmark, Bear Creek meanders a half mile or so west and north to the Wabash River—through a

Portland Arch Nature Preserve

dramatic gorge that features concave cliffs, forests, occasional waterfalls, spring-seep wetlands, open prairies, and savannas.

Of Portland Arch, The Nature Conservancy observes on its website: "The abundance of cliff-dwelling plant communities, diversity of ferns and primitive non-flowering plants are stunning." With its towering, ninety-foot cliffs of Mansfield sandstone alternating from side to side, Bear Creek Canyon is as scenic as any in the state's rocky, rugged south, and by virtue of its National Nature Landmark definition holds "outstanding biological and geological resources."

Also a dedicated state nature preserve, Portland Arch's ecosystems support an abundance of unique plant species, including some relicts. State endangered Forbe's saxifrage, state threatened ledge spike-moss, and state watch-listed hay-scented fern, as well as marginal shield fern, are found on the cliffs. Flowering dogwood also shares the steep slopes with the oaks and hickories. The bottoms and ravines support American beech, basswood, sugar maple, and black walnut. The canyon's upper edges are home to wild sarsaparilla, witch hazel, partridgeberry, and wintergreen.

Other rare and unusual plants at Portland Arch include state endangered woodland strawberry and velvetleaf blueberry; state rare longstalk sedge; and state watch-listed butternut, shining clubmoss, and American pinesap.

Mosses, lichens, and scattered beds of blueberry, huckleberry, and wintergreen cover the preserve's floor. Spring wildflowers include Dutchman's breeches, dogtooth violet, blue-eyed Mary, wood (celandine) poppy, and Canada wood nettle. In addition the open oak woodlands support shooting star, New Jersey tea, American hazelnut, purple milkweed, showy goldenrod, and more savanna species.

Portland Arch is named for the nearby river town that is now called Fountain. Following a small economic boom fueled by the ill-fated Wabash and Erie Canal, the preserve became a resort in the late 1800s and then a Boy Scout camp in the 1930s. A few building foundations from previous eras are visible.

Activities
Hiking Trails: Two, with separate trailheads 0.25 miles apart; primary trail to arch, 1.4-mile loop, moderate to rugged.
Other Activities: Nature study, photography, wildlife watching.

Directions
GPS coordinates: 40.216426, –87.333121
From I-74
- North on US 41 to County Road 650N, 6.7 miles
- West on County Road 650N to Walnut Street in Fountain, 4.8 miles
- Southwest on Walnut Street to Clay/Scout Camp Road, 1 block
- Southeast on Clay/Scout Camp Road to parking lot, 0.3 mile

From I-65
- West on State Road 28, south of Lafayette, to State Road 341, 28.6 miles
- South on State Road 341 to State Road 55 (East Covered Bridge, County Road East 750N), 3.0 miles

- West on State Road 55 to US 41, 5.0 miles
- South on US 41 to County Road 650N, 1.0 mile
- West on County Road 650N to Walnut Street in Fountain, 4.8 miles
- Southwest on Walnut Street to Clay/Scout Camp Road, 1 block
- Southeast on Clay/Scout Camp Road to parking lot, 0.3 mile

83. Fall Creek Gorge Nature Preserve

Owned by The Nature Conservancy

The 163-acre Fall Creek Gorge Preserve in Warren County is better known as the Potholes for its most unique natural feature—circular openings in the creek beds formed since the last Ice Age by swirling, rock-laden water flowing through a narrow sandstone canyon. These small basins range from a foot or two to more than six feet across, with depths from a few inches to four to five feet.

"Modern art on an ancient canvas" is how *The Nature Conservancy's Guide to Nature Preserves* describes Fall Creek Gorge, which was carved by glacial meltwater through three-hundred-million-year-old Pennsylvanian Period sandstone. Thirty-seven of its acres are designated as a dedicated state nature preserve.

Water from Fall Creek and tributary Fall Branch, which converge inside the preserve, is so clean it has received an exceptional-use designation by the Indiana State Board of Health. A series of small waterfalls over ledges run even in times of drought. Below the pothole-riddled falls, a wide and placid Fall Creek slowly feeds Big Pine Creek just north of the preserve on its way to the Wabash River a few miles east at the town of Attica.

Cliff edges atop Fall Creek Valley's steep-walled canyon support some relict, state rare eastern white pine; in West Central Indiana the eastern white pine is at the southern edge of its range. Other unusual flowering plant species include the state rare forked aster, as well as snow trillium and grass-of-parnassus.

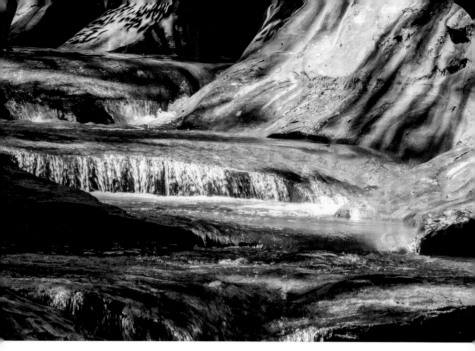

Fall Creek Gorge Nature Preserve

Oak-hickory forests dominate the ridges. Unusual liver-worts, lichens, mosses, and ferns are common among the rocky environs. Common spring wildflowers include bloodroot, spring beauty, and prairie trillium.

A wide variety of mammals, birds, amphibians, and reptiles thrive in Fall Creek Gorge Valley's forested-creek environment.

Historically, Warren County has been primarily farm country, with some coal mining. Several mines extracted the volatile rock on seams along Fall Creek west of the preserve boundary. As part of broader plans for flood control and recreational development in the 1960s, Congress authorized a dam on Big Pine Creek that would have flooded the Fall Creek Gorge. Like a similar scheme for Big Walnut Creek to the south and east, the Big Pine project was canceled in 1976.

Due to its rugged nature, the acreage that today comprises the Fall Creek Gorge Preserve survived in relatively pristine form. As a consequence, its stunning, physically challenging landscape has long been a popular destination for locals and nature lovers from Lafayette, Indianapolis, Chicago, and beyond.

Because of that popularity and resulting overuse, The Nature Conservancy and local officials actively control visitation. Parking is limited to a deliberately small parking lot. Potholes Road is marked off limits for parking, and county sheriffs enforce the ban. Illegally parked cars are towed.

Fall Creek Gorge is accessible by a rugged trail from the parking lot to the potholes and a sandbar at the junction of Fall Branch and Fall Creek. Across the stream and up a staircase, the path leads through the woods—with views of a horseshoe creek bend and the canyon below—to a broad, five-foot-high waterfall where Fall Creek, which has flowed for miles through glacial till, meets bedrock and flows over a ledge.

Fall Creek Gorge Preserve is open during the daylight hours.

Activities
Hiking, nature study, photography, wildlife watching.

Directions
GPS coordinates: 40.338228, –87.316493
From I-74
- North on US 41, through Attica, to Potholes Road, 16.1 miles
- North on Potholes Road to preserve entrance, 1.6 miles

From I-65
- West on State Road 28 south of Lafayette to US 41, 33.8 miles
- *Northwest on US 41, to Potholes Road, 4.6 miles*
- North on Potholes Road to preserve entrance, 1.5 miles

84. Weiler-Leopold Nature Preserve
Owned by NICHES Land Trust

The 179-acre Weiler-Leopold Nature Preserve in Warren County protects a biodiverse variety of native landscapes along the Wabash River and Little Pine Creek, including prairie, open oak savanna, floodplain forest, wooded slopes, and old fields. Combined with the adjacent Black Rock Barrens Nature Preserve, these properties protect nearly three hundred acres.

Weiler-Leopold Nature Preserve

One hundred acres of this dedicated state nature preserve's bottomlands have been returning to native forest habitat since May 2000, when thirty thousand trees were planted. A twelve-acre grassland area has been planted with native tall-grass prairie species and is periodically burned to enrich the soil and reduce competition from woody species and nonnative plants. Although the savanna—broken tree cover with prairie vegetation in the openings—is populated with white oaks, their crowns spread more because of the lack of competition for light.

Weiler-Leopold is named after its original co-owners Emanuel Weiler and A. Carl Leopold. Weiler was the founding dean of the Purdue University Krannert School of Management. Leopold, son of renowned naturalist Aldo Leopold, was an internationally known plant physiologist.

Glacial erratics, boulders left by retreating Wisconsin glacial ice sheets more than ten thousand years ago, are scattered along a loop trail that traverses the prairie (with some plants identified), follows the slope through the savanna, and returns to the prairie. A stone bench along the path is engraved with the biblical pronouncement "Hurt not the earth, neither the sea, nor the trees."

The Weiler-Leopold preserve shares a parking lot with the adjacent Black Oak Barrens Nature Preserve to the east.

Activities

Hiking, nature study, photography, wildlife watching.

Directions

GPS coordinates: 40.359270, −87.116068

From I-74

- North on State Road 25 to State Road 28, 11.8 miles
- West on State Road 28 to County Road 500E, 5.0 miles
- North on County Road 500E to Independence Road at Independence, 3.9 miles
- Northeast on Independence Road to preserve, 3.4 miles

From I-65

- West on State Road 28 south of Lafayette to County Road 500E, 29.6 miles
- North on County Road 500E to Independence Road at Independence, 3.9 miles
- Northeast on Independence Road to preserve, 3.4 miles

85. Black Rock Barrens Nature Preserve

Owned by NICHES Land Trust

The one-hundred-acre Black Rock Barrens Nature Preserve in Warren County features a siltstone barrens ecological community—rare in the Midwest—that may be the only habitat of this type in North Central Indiana. This dedicated state nature preserve is named for a dark sandstone outcropping a couple miles upstream on the Wabash River. (See the Black Rock Nature Preserve entry below.) Its thin soils support a narrow range of plants, some of which do not survive even a few miles away.

The upland barrens community runs south from the Black Rock preserve, along the river, through Black Rock Barrens, and into the adjacent Weiler-Leopold Nature Preserve. The landscape has been downcut by the river, carving deep ravines that in places drop more than one hundred feet. The underlying rock, known as Attica chert, is called Indiana Green for its color cast. Native Americans fashioned tools from it.

Black Rock Barrens Nature Preserve

Black Rock Barrens includes the forty-acre Birdfoot Barrens, which is named after the bird's-foot violets that thrive in its environs. It is adjacent to Weiler-Leopold Nature Preserve, which together total three hundred acres protected by the NICHES Land Trust along this section of the Wabash River Valley. Black Rock Barrens is 60 percent mature forest, with oaks and hickories dominating the uplands. The forty acres of bottomland woods were reforested 2001. Aside from the river, the preserve has no water supply.

Depending on the time of year, the preserve's diverse habitats support an equally diverse variety of woodland wildflowers, including harbinger-of-spring, sessile trillium, blue phlox, wild hyacinth, rue anemone, bird's-foot violet, yellow pimpernel, and prairie phlox, alongside goat's rue, little bluestem, lowbush blueberries, and yellow star grass.

The understory includes some unusual plants for this part of the continent, including state threatened ledge spike-moss, state rare glade mallow, and state watch-listed cream wild indigo.

Wildlife includes state endangered cerulean warblers and state species of special concern bald eagles.

Black Rock Barrens shares a parking lot and trail systems with Weiler-Leopold Nature Preserve.

Activities
Hiking Trails: One, loop trail, moderate to rugged.
Other Activities: Nature study, photography, wildlife watching.

Directions
GPS coordinates: 40.359270, –87.116068
From I-74
- North on State Road 25 to State Road 28, 11.8 miles
- West on State Road 28 to County Road 500E, 5.0 miles
- North on County Road 500E to Independence Road at Independence, 3.9 miles
- Northeast on Independence Road to preserve, 3.4 miles

From I-65
- West on State Road 28 south of Lafayette to County Road 500E, 29.6 miles
- North on County Road 500E to Independence Road at Independence, 3.9 miles
- Northeast on Independence Road to preserve, 3.4 miles

86. Black Rock Nature Preserve
Owned by NICHES Land Trust

The forty-five-acre Black Rock Nature Preserve in Warren County features a rare geologic formation called a black rock bluff that towers more than one hundred feet above the Wabash River. The preserve's landforms include high-quality oak woodlands, sandstone barrens, sandstone bedrock exposures, sandstone cliffs, and rock shelters. Thirty-two of its acres are recognized as a dedicated state nature preserve.

The Black Rock preserve's namesake bluff is a sandstone promontory with steep-sided shale ravines, sandstone cliffs, and seep springs that produce a variety of unusual habitats. No similar formations occur on the river within a hundred miles

Black Rock Nature Preserve

in either direction. The rock's dark color is from leaching manganese and iron oxides.

The barrens community stretches a few miles south and west along the river uplands to the Black Rock Barrens Nature Preserve and the adjacent Weiler-Leopold Nature Preserve. (See Black Rock Barrens and Weiler-Leopold sections above.) Trees and other vegetation grow slowly or not at all due to the site's southern exposure and the thin acidic soils.

Among the rare species of note at Black Rock Nature Preserve is the state threatened ledge spike-moss, which was recorded there in 1931 by Charles C. Deam, Indiana's first state forester and a botanist who authored four books on Indiana plants, including *Flora of Indiana* in 1940, the state's premier work on Indiana botany.

White oaks dominate the canopy, while prairie and other types of wildflowers share the forest floor with black huckleberry, goat's rue, and false smooth foxglove.

The Black Rock bluff is also an important historical site. Native Americans used it as a lookout over the Wabash, and in 1811, the Prophet—Shawnee Chief Tecumseh's brother Tenskwatawa—deployed warriors there to watch for General William Henry Harrison's advancing troops. Harrison, however, learned of the plan, rerouted his march, and surprised the Shawnee at the decisive Battle of Tippecanoe.

In 1838, a nearby site served as a campground on the Potawatomi Trail of Death, which was a 660-mile forced relocation of Native Americans from their Indiana homelands to Kansas.

The view of the valley from the Black Rock overlook is stunning, but it is obscured when the trees have leaves.

Activities
Hiking Trails: Short trail from the parking lot.
Other Activities: Hiking, nature study, photography, wildlife watching.

Directions
GPS coordinates: 40.366841, –87.100423
From I-74
- North on State Road 25 to State Road 28, 11.8 miles
- West on State Road 28 to County Road 500E, 5.0 miles
- North on County Road 500E to Independence Road at Independence, 3.9 miles
- Northeast on Independence Road to Indy Road, 3.2 miles
- East on Indy Road to County Road 1100E, 0.3 mile
- North on County Road 1100E to County Road 350N, 0.5 mile
- East on County Road 350N preserve, 1.1 miles

From I-65
- West on State Road 28 to County Road 500E, 29.6 miles
- North on County Road 500E to Independence Road at Independence, 3.9 miles
- Northeast on Independence Road to Indy Road, 3.2 miles
- East on Indy Road to County Road 1100E, 0.3 mile
- North on County Road 1100E to County Road 350N, 0.5 mile
- East on County Road 350N preserve, 1.1 miles

Granville Sand Barrens Nature Preserve

87. Granville Sand Barrens Nature Preserve

Owned by NICHES Land Trust

The forty-acre Granville Sand Barrens Nature Preserve in Tippecanoe County lies less than a mile south and east of the Wabash River and protects twenty-two acres of sand barrens, which are ecologically rare in Indiana and around the globe. This restored barrens-prairie-savanna complex's dry, windblown, sandy soils create a unique ecosystem that supports a diverse group of native plant and animal species.

A dedicated state nature preserve, Granville—along with the adjacent Roy Whistler Wildlife Area, another forty acres of sand barrens to the north that NICHES Land Trust also owns—preserves one of the best remaining examples of this long-vanished ecosystem that existed in pre-European settlement times.

Among the barrens' rare and unusual plants are the state endangered fringed puccoon and state rare forked bluecurl, along with hairy puccoon and leadplant. Native forbs and grasses have been planted on eighteen acres to help buffer the barrens.

Granville Sand Barrens is periodically burned to control woody species and promote native species growth. Birds at the preserve include the lark sparrow, yellow breasted chat, and orchard oriole.

The Roy Whistler Wildlife Area has no parking area and is best accessed from the Granville Sand Barrens parking lot.

Activities
Hiking (no trails, but an old road runs along the southern edge), nature study, photography, wildlife watching.

Directions
GPS coordinates: 40.395285, –87.059887
From I-74
- North on State Road 25 to County Road 700W north of West Point, 17.7 miles
- North on County Road 700W to County Road 200S, 2.8 miles
- West on County Road 200S to County Road 825W, 1.3 miles
- North on County Road 825W to preserve, 0.5 mile

From I-65
- West on South Street, becoming Columbia Street, to South Second Street/Wabash Avenue, 3.9 miles
- South on South Second Street/Wabash Avenue to Old Romney Road, miles 2.1 miles
- Southwest on Old Romney Road to Elston Road, 0.7 mile
- Southwest Elston Road to Lilly Road/County Road 200S to County Road 825W, 7.3 miles
- North on County Road 825W to preserve, 0.5 mile

88a. Prophetstown State Park / Prophetstown Fen Nature Preserve
Owned by Indiana Department of Natural Resources,
Division of State Parks & Lakes

The two-thousand-acre Prophetstown State Park in Tippecanoe County features more than nine hundred acres of restored prairie—at the merger of the Tippecanoe River and the Wabash River—reminiscent of Indiana's presettlement landscape.

Prophetstown State Park

Named after the Shawnee Indian village established there in 1808, the park stretches southwest along the Wabash, from the two rivers' confluence to Interstate 65 just northeast of Lafayette.

Up to two-thirds of Indiana's newest state park will be restored to grassland over time, with wetlands, fens, and savannas—native habitats that coexisted with the prairies—also being restored. Nonnative trees are being replaced with oaks and others that thrived along river bluffs and in the savannas.

Steep, narrow bluffs tower over the rivers, whose junction below creates a seasonal wetland that attracts shorebirds and waterfowl. The lowland trails are subject to flooding.

The rivers marked the presettlement edge of a vast, westward-reaching tallgrass prairie that dominated the land when the Shawnee Indians and their Native American ancestors ruled. Native prairie remnants survive today almost exclusively in cemeteries and along railroad tracks, where the soil was never disturbed.

The gently rolling prairies, which supported hundreds of wildflower species along with the grasses, thrived on the rich soils that formed atop the vast glacial deposits of gravel, sand, and large boulders. Fire, generally caused by lightning but sometimes by errant campfires, discouraged woody competitors and released nutrients that enriched the soil for the prairie vegetation. Among the replanted native grass species at Prophetstown State Park today are big bluestem, little bluestem, Indian grass, and side-oats grama.

The fen is a particularly uncommon postglacial feature. (See Prophetstown Fen Nature Preserve below.)

Surrounded by History

Prophetstown State Park is steeped as much in human history as it is in natural history. The Battle of Tippecanoe was fought in 1811 about a mile west of the park, a skirmish that blunted the swelling tide of Indian resistance being led by Shawnee Chief Tecumseh against European encroachment. Prophetstown is named after Tecumseh's brother Tenskwatawa, better known as the Prophet.

White expansion had displaced the Shawnee from their Southern Ohio, West Virginia, and Western Pennsylvania homelands, and Tecumseh believed an alliance of eastern tribes was the only way to stop the white man's advance. But while he was rallying tribes in the South, General William Henry Harrison moved 1,200 troops to the Tippecanoe River.

The general learned that the Prophet had stationed warriors at the Black Rock bluff just downriver as lookouts, and he instead marched his troops overland and surprised the Shawnee. The Prophet decided to attack before being attacked; after a two-hour battle, the Indians retreated to Wildcat Creek. Harrison burned the village.

Among the historic features at the park are the Museum at Prophetstown, a recreated eighteenth-century Woodland Indian village, and the Farm at Prophetstown, a recreated 1920s farm.

88b. Prophetstown Fen Nature Preserve

The 134-acre Prophetstown Fen Nature Preserve protects one of Central Indiana's largest and highest-quality fens. Characterized by their grasses, sedges, and wildflowers, fens are peat-forming wetlands that receive nutrients from sources other than precipitation. At this dedicated state nature preserve, the source is calcium-rich groundwater that seeps downhill from a slope. Fens are less acidic than bogs and have higher nutrient levels.

Other natural communities found within Prophetstown Fen include sedge meadow, wet prairie, and bluff dry upland forests. Noteworthy species include Riddell's goldenrod and obedient plant.

Harrison Creek, named after the territorial governor, is a permanent, high-quality, seepage-fed stream that runs through the preserve. The creek rises in the fen and snakes through a peatland scattered with glacial boulders.

The Prophetstown Fen preserve, which is not marked as such on the park map, is located along the Harrison Creek along the park's north-central border.

Activities

Hiking Trails: Four (1.9–3.5 miles), easy to moderate; one hiking/biking (3.2 miles), easy.

Camping: 110 sites, fifty-five with full electric, sewer, and water hookups; comfort station with modern restrooms and shower, including a family restroom; all are accessible.

Other Activities: Aquatic center, with bathhouse, showers, changing areas, restrooms, lockers (guest provides locks), and concession area; nature study; photography; picnicking; recreation building; shelters; wildlife watching.

Directions

GPS coordinates: 40.497613, –86.842110

From I-65

- South on State Road 43 (River Road) to Burnett's Road, 0.3 mile

- East on Burnett's Road to T at Ninth Street, 0.4 mile
- South on Ninth Street to Swisher Road, 0.4 mile
- North on Swisher Road to park, 1.6 miles

Tipton Till Plain Section

89a. Eagle Creek Park

Owned by Indy Parks and Recreation

The 5,300-acre Eagle Creek Park in Marion County, named after the creek and reservoir that bisect it, is ranked by Wikipedia as one of the top twenty largest urban parks in the nation. And while it is promoted as a place to "run, sail, bike and hike," the northwest Indianapolis park's dominant theme is preservation—especially the preservation of birdlife.

Eagle Creek's diverse habitats and large waterbody provide critical habitat for breeding, migrant, and overwintering bird species, including neotropical passerines, resting waterfowl and water birds, and, in years of low rainfall, migrant shorebirds.

The park has been designated as an Important Bird Area by the National Audubon Society, which says it plays "a critical locale in central Indiana for breeding, migrant, and overwintering bird populations." The park's large size and habitat diversity, along with the large waterbody, supports a variety of birds "that is unparalleled in other locations in Marion County and Central Indiana." Several state species of special concern breed in Eagle Creek Park, including the red-shouldered hawk, black-and-white warbler, and hooded warbler.

A broad chunk of the 1,400-acre reservoir's northern edge is set aside as a bird sanctuary with open water, wetlands, islands, and a physical barrier that keeps boats out. Rising above the reservoir's eastern shore, the Eagle Creek Ornithology Center features indoor and outdoor viewing areas. The trail to the Eagle's Crest preserve passes a raised boardwalk that leads to a lowland observation deck on the sixty-acre Scott Starling Nature Sanctuary, the site of several ecological restoration projects.

Nearly four thousand of Eagle Creek's 5,300 acres are forested, with minimal clearing for playgrounds and amenities.

East of the water lies the forty-two-acre Spring Pond Nature Preserve (see Spring Pond Nature Preserve below). Across the bay, the 297-acre Eagle's Crest Nature Preserve (see Eagle's Crest Nature Preserve entry below) occupies the park's northwest side. Campgrounds are nonexistent.

Woodland habitats include deciduous forest, coniferous woodlots, and riparian woods, which coexist with early successional areas, scrub-shrub, restored prairie, and emergent wetlands. Second-growth deciduous woodland is the most prevalent habitat type, supporting the state endangered cerulean warbler and several Audubon WatchList species, including willow flycatcher, wood thrush, blue-winged warbler, prairie warbler, prothonotary warbler, and Kentucky warbler.

The park east of the reservoir, which is oriented nearly perfectly north and south, is laced with nearly seventeen miles of hiking trails on five paths.

The development that does exist at Eagle Creek is limited to the east side of the park and consists of "treetop adventures," with thirty-nine tree crossings and five zip lines; a world-class rowing course built for the 1987 Pan American Games; playgrounds; shelters; swimming beach; and a marina with an outfitter.

Eagle Creek Park's preservation history began in 1934 with the purchase of twelve acres by J. K. Lilly, who served as board chair and president of Eli Lilly and Company, whose holdings had grown to more than two thousand acres when he donated them to Purdue University in 1958. Purdue sold the verdant landscape eight years later to the City of Indianapolis to dam the creek for flood control and create a park around it. Eagle Creek Park was dedicated in 1972.

89b. Spring Pond Nature Preserve

The forty-two-acre Spring Pond Nature Preserve represents a forest community that once covered the state's Central Till Plain, which spans a broad swath of Central Indiana from the Ohio to the Illinois state lines. Its namesake waterbody is located inside the park gate on the reservoir's east side.

Eagle Creek Park

This dedicated state nature preserve is primarily mature, second-growth forest on a relatively level, poorly drained upland site that is dominated by a wet-damp forest of American beech, sugar maple, sycamore, bur oak, and ash. Its flat topography supports many wet, poorly drained areas.

The preserve supports several rare and unusual plant species, including state endangered Montgomery hawthorn, state rare rushlike aster, and state watch-listed sparse-lobe grape-fern and thicket sedge.

Marked trails intersect within the Spring Pond boundary. An unmarked trail leads through the preserve to the marsh from Parkway East Drive just south of 62nd Street and south of the preserve sign.

89c. Eagle's Crest Nature Preserve

The Hoosier Hikers Council describes the 297-acre Eagle's Crest Nature Preserve as "an oasis of mature hardwood forest" for nature lovers seeking quiet, natural solitude in the Indianapolis urban environment.

"With dramatic overlooks of Eagle Creek Reservoir and rare examples of primitive forest, the Eagle's Crest Trail is full of variety and surprises," the Hikers Council says on its website of this dedicated state nature preserve. "The thoughtful preservation of these ancient forest areas allows the visitor a rare glimpse into the past to see the landscape much as it appeared to the Native Americans before European settlers arrived."

Located on the park's northwest side across the reservoir, Eagle's Crest supports a handful of rare and unusual plants, including state rare wolf bluegrass, and state watch-listed sparse-lobe grape-fern, thicket sedge, and orange coneflower.

The preserve's old, moist, second-growth upland forest communities were purchased by Lilly in the early days. Its shoreline is situated directly across from the ornithological center and offers prime habitat for birdwatching.

Dominated by red oak, sugar maple, American beech, white oak, and shagbark hickory, some of the preserve's trees are stunning in their height and breadth. Thick blooms of native

Eagle's Crest Nature Preserve.

wild leek illuminate the forest floor in late summer. Fall offers a kaleidoscope of color.

Eagle's Crest Nature Preserve, which doesn't require a park entry fee, is accessible only from the Scott Starling Nature Sanctuary parking area on Wilson Road. Follow the ridge trail to the Eagle's Crest rental house. The trailhead is due east of the house, where a 1.25-mile loop trail follows a ridge with vistas across the Eagle Creek Valley before descending to the water with expansive views of the bird sanctuary.

Activities
Hiking Trails: Five (1.25–6.75 miles), easy to difficult.
Other Activities (outside the nature preserves): Boat ramp (limit ten-mile-per-hour motors), canoeing, cross-country skiing, dog park, fishing, fitness course, marsh and bird sanctuary, nature centers, nature study, orienteering, Ornithology Center, photography, picnicking, pistol range, pontoon boating, rowing, sailing, shelters, swimming beach, treetop adventure, wildlife watching.

Directions
GPS coordinates: 39.852580, –86.292240
From I-74
- North on I-465 to 56st Street, 2.8 miles
- West on 56th Street to park entrance, 1.0 mile

From I-65
- West on 71st Street/Eagle Creek Parkway and park gate, 0.0 mile

Directions to Eagle's Crest Nature Preserve from 56th Street Park Gate
GPS coordinates: 39.886755, –86.308106
- West on 56th Street, across reservoir, to Raceway Drive, 1.9 miles
- North on Raceway Drive (becoming Fishback Road) to Wilson Street, 2.7 miles
- East on Wilson Street to Scott Starling Nature Sanctuary, 0.6 mile

90. Marott Park Woods Nature Preserve

Owned by Indy Parks and Recreation

The eighty-four-acre Marott Park Woods Nature Preserve in Marion County consists of upland forest, floodplain forest, and successional fields in an urban setting on Indianapolis's north side. Located in Marott Park just north of Broad Ripple, the preserve is bisected by Williams Creek from its northern boundary on East 75th Street to its southern boundary on the White River West Fork.

This dedicated state nature preserve's sixteen acres of second-growth forest are considered one of the best places in Indianapolis for viewing wildflowers and native plants, including the state endangered Montgomery hawthorn. Dedicated in 1987 as the first piece of today's refuge, this remnant offers a sense of how the area may have looked prior to European settlement in the 1820s.

Marott Park Woods supports a variety of wildflowers, including rue anemone, wild ginger, mayapple, sessile trillium,

Marott Park Woods Nature Preserve

cutleaf toothwort, and wood (celandine) poppy. Plant species such as staghorn sumac and Canada goldenrod also grow here.

Native trees growing on the preserve include young stands of moist floodplain species, such as sycamore and hackberry. Others of interest include Ohio buckeye, pawpaw, bur oak, chinquapin oak, and rough-leaved dogwood.

Much of the remainder of Marott Park was used for agriculture and is being restored from a weedy landscape to floodplain woodland with native species. These early successional areas, however, contain invasive shrubs and trees, such as Amur honeysuckle, Siberian elm, white mulberry, tree-of-heaven, and common privet.

Fording Williams Creek is the only way to get from the preserve's western section to its eastern section. The Monon Trail marks the preserve's eastern edge and offers informal access points.

The park and preserve are named for the George and Ella Marott family, which donated eighty-seven acres of land for a nature park. Other parcels were added for a total of 102 acres of parkland. The parking lot is across from the Park Tudor School.

Activities
Hiking, nature study, photography, wildlife watching.

Directions
GPS coordinates: 39.887070, −86.145498
From I-65
- North on Meridian Street in downtown Indianapolis to 71st Street, 6.9 miles
- East on 71st Street to College Avenue, 0.6 mile
- North on College Avenue to preserve, 0.3 mile

91. Ritchey Woods Nature Preserve
Owned by Fishers Park & Recreation

The fifty-five-acre Ritchey Woods Nature Preserve in Hamilton County consists primarily of moist upland forest with a small portion of wet-moist floodplain forest, surrounded by residential neighborhoods and the Indianapolis Metropolitan Airport. Located in the Town of Fishers, this dedicated state nature preserve is part of a larger, 127-acre natural area with restored wetlands, prairies, and forests.

The Ritchey preserve harbors several rare and unusual plant species, including the state endangered Montgomery hawthorn and state watch-listed butternut. The uplands are dominated by second-growth sugar maple and red oak and support common woodland wildflowers, such as phlox and waterleaf. The wet-moist floodplain forest along Cheeney Creek (pronounced *Chaney*) supports green ash, Ohio buckeye, and American elm.

Skunk cabbage, which flowers in February and assumes larger-than-life dimensions, dominates the wetland area, alongside a variety of plants and wildflowers, including wild bergamot.

Former agricultural land, the site also features examples of glacial erratics, which are boulders randomly deposited by retreating ice sheets more than ten thousand years ago. These rocks have been relocated by farmers who plowed the fields.

Ritchey Woods Nature Preserve

Beginning in 1997, the Indiana University–Purdue University Indianapolis Center for Earth and Environmental Science has converted 130 acres of the farmland to prairie and wetland ecological communities. Wet prairie, sedge meadow, and wetland habitats were restored by removing or plugging drainage tiles to allow the hydrology to approximate natural conditions. A successional prairie community was seeded with native plants. Native tree species were planted to restore the existing flatwoods.

The woods were donated by Dr. James O. Ritchey to The Nature Conservancy, which in turn gave them to the Children's Museum of Indianapolis, which gave them to the Town of Fishers.

Activities
Hiking, environmental education programs, nature study, photography, wildlife watching.

Directions
GPS coordinates: 39.938581, –86.033089
From I-69
- West on 96th Street on Indianapolis's northeast side, to Hague Road, 0.1 mile
- North on Hague Road to preserve, 0.8 mile

92a. Fort Harrison State Park

Owned by Indiana Department of Natural Resources,
Division of State Parks & Lakes

The 1,700-acre Fort Harrison State Park—also known as the "last forested corner left in Marion County," according to park literature—occupies a portion of the former Fort Benjamin Harrison on Indianapolis's northeast side. Undeveloped by the US Army from 1903 to 1996, the park features four nature preserves and the nine-acre Delaware Lake. It's a day-use-only facility, with no camping.

Bisected by Fall Creek, which runs for 3.5 miles inside the park, Fort Ben's ecosystem includes an unbroken stretch of bottomland and upland forests with gentle slopes, ravine forests, meadows, ponds, and a small area of till plain flatwoods. These natural environs support lichens, mosses, and an abundance of wildflowers and mushrooms amid a hardwood forest composed of beech, maple, sycamore, and ash.

Not only does Fort Harrison offer natural features unmatched in the city, but, according to the National Audubon Society, it's an Important Bird Area whose bird habitats are among the best in Central Indiana: "This Important Bird Area supports one of the richest and most abundant breeding bird communities within this region of Indiana. In fact, summer counts and surveys for breeding birds often exceed eighty species at this locale."

Among the bird species that live in or migrate through Fort Harrison are state endangered cerulean warbler. State species of special concern include hooded warbler and worm-eating warbler.

Through the years, Indiana Audubon has recorded several specialty species at Fort Ben, including brown creeper, Kentucky warbler, northern parula warbler, prothonotary warbler, summer tanager, and pileated woodpecker. Noteworthy species include palm warbler, Connecticut warbler, mourning warbler, orange-crowned warbler, and yellow-throated warbler.

Other bird species found at Fort Harrison State Park are Acadian flycatcher, American goldfinch, Baltimore oriole,

Fort Harrison State Park

belted kingfisher, Canada goose, Carolina chickadee, common yellowthroat, eastern bluebird, eastern wood-pewee, green heron, indigo bunting, Louisiana waterthrush, mallard, northern rough-winged swallow, orchard oriole, ovenbird, red-eyed vireo, scarlet tanager, song sparrow, eastern towhee, tufted titmouse, warbling vireo, white-eyed vireo, wood thrush, yellow-billed cuckoo, and yellow-throated vireo. Great blue herons are common, as they have a rookery on the north side of Fall Creek in the Chinquapin Nature Preserve, which is closed to the public. Beaver, deer, frogs, squirrels, and turtles are also present.

A Rich Natural and Human History

The Fort Harrison landscape was created by glacial activity that deposited fertile soils on the Central Indiana land surface when the last ice sheet began retreating some thirteen thousand years ago. Elk, bison, river otters, and black bears inhabited Fall Creek Valley in presettlement times.

Native Americans are first recorded in the region roughly eight thousand years ago, using the vast forest and lush waterways for hunting and fishing. The Delaware Indians ceded what is now Fort Harrison and Indianapolis to the Americans in the 1818 Treaty of St. Mary's. Settlers, migrating north and west from Kentucky and Ohio, established the first homesteads in the 1820s and began clearing the woodlands and replacing them with farms.

Fort Harrison was a US Army post established in 1906 and named after Indiana's only president. During a round of base closings in 1996, the army ceded the lands that are now Fort Harrison and Charlestown State Parks to the state for the twenty-second and twenty-third state parks.

The park and surrounding area's military past is enshrined by several facilities, including the Visitors Center, Museum of 20th Century Warfare, the Citizen's Military Training Camp that was once known as Camp Glenn, the preserved CCC Headquarters, and the World War II prisoner of war camp.

In addition to Warbler Woods and Lawrence Creek Nature Preserves, Fort Harrison State Park encompasses two other dedicated state nature preserves on the north side of Fall Creek that are closed to the public. The 115-acre Chinquapin protects the great blue heron rookery. The 135-acre Bluffs of Fall Creek Nature Preserve supports a riparian forest.

92b. Warbler Woods Nature Preserve

Warbler Woods Nature Preserve follows Fall Creek for a half mile or so and is lined with floodplain forests and dissected with gentle slopes. Wildflowers and other ephemeral plant life thrive on this dedicated state nature preserve's forest and floodplain floors.

Several bird species nest in Warbler Woods, including state endangered cerulean warbler and state species of special concern hooded warbler, along with Kentucky warbler, brown creeper, wood thrush, ovenbird, and Acadian flycatcher.

Two hiking trails pass through Warbler Woods. The 1.1-mile Fall Creek Trail follows the creek and features a sturdy walkway that traverses the steepest terrain and helps prevent hillside erosion.

Warbler Woods Nature Preserve,
Fort Harrison State Park

92c. Lawrence Creek Nature Preserve

Lawrence Creek Nature Preserve borders the Lawrence Creek and is likewise characterized by dissected slopes and ravine forests, along with a small area of till plain flatwoods. Like Warbler Woods, Lawrence Creek provides nesting habitat for migrant birds, including brown creeper, wood thrush, ovenbird, Acadian flycatcher, and several warblers—state endangered cerulean and state species of special concern hooded and Kentucky among them.

The park's longest and most difficult hiking path—the 3.6-mile Lawrence Creek Trail—loops through this dedicated state nature preserve and has two trailheads.

Activities

Hiking Trails: Six (1–3.6 miles), one multiuse, easy to difficult.
Other Activities: Dog park, fishing, golf course, horse trail, nature study, photography, picnic sites, shelters, sledding walking/jogging trails, wildlife watching.

Directions

GPS coordinates: 39.864870, –86.016163
From I-465

- East on 56th Street on Indianapolis east side to Post Road to park, 1.8 miles
- North on Post Road to Shafer Road, 0.5 mile
- West on Shafer Road to park, 0.3 mile

93. Shrader-Weaver Nature Preserve

Owned by Indiana Department of Natural Resources, Division of Nature Preserves

The ninety-six-acre Shrader-Weaver Nature Preserve in Fayette County supports old-growth, floodplain, and successional forests, along with a seep spring and an 1830s-era pioneer farmstead. Twenty-nine upland acres of old-growth forest have been designated as a National Natural Landmark for their "outstanding pre-settlement beech-maple forest" with "unusually large trees, such as a fifty-six-inch diameter burr oak and a thirty-four-inch diameter black maple."

Shrader-Weaver Nature Preserve

While beech and maple dominate the old-growth upland forest at this dedicated state nature preserve, they thrive alongside tulip poplar, black cherry, slippery elm, chinquapin oak, and bur oak. A grove of black walnut is recognized as one of the state's most magnificent and includes the largest specimen in Indiana.

Shrader-Weaver is widely recognized as having one of Indiana's most spectacular wildflower displays. The number of wildflower species, according to The Nature Conservancy's website, are "too many to count." In *The Nature Conservancy's Guide to Indiana Preserves*, the organization says: "Every year, pilgrimages are made from great distances to this living museum to witness the wildflower display."

A short list includes red trillium, skunk cabbage, golden ragwort, marsh marigold, jewelweed, blue-eyed Mary, Dutchman's breeches, spring beauty, blue phlox, doll's eyes, mayapple, wild geranium, and appendaged waterleaf.

Other rare and unusual plants at Shrader-Weaver include state endangered Montgomery hawthorn and state watch-listed butternut and bog bluegrass, as well as Michigan lily, swamp goldenrod, and cup plant.

The bottomland forest was cut and grazed in the past and is now in a successional stage. Large bur oak, red oak, green ash, and sycamore still survive. Golden ragworts blanket the trail in spring. The shrub layer includes pawpaw, Virginia creeper, and spicebush.

A variety of bird species live in or pass through Shrader-Weaver, including the state endangered cerulean warbler, along with barred owl, great-crested flycatcher, blue-gray gnatcatcher, ovenbird, scarlet tanager, Baltimore oriole, red-eyed vireo, wood thrush, titmouse, and Acadian flycatcher.

Williams Creek, which bisects the property near its western edge, originates a couple miles to the north and feeds the Whitewater River some ten miles to the south and east.

The farmstead is not marked and is accessible via a side path.

Piles of stones, called glacial erratics, offer evidence of the site's natural history. These rocks were erratically dropped on the till plain by glaciers that began retreating some thirteen thousand years ago and, ultimately, were piled at the sides of the field by farmers for easier plowing.

At the request of Laz and Edith Weaver, who donated the land, a caretaker lives on the property. The farmstead and barn were built from timber and clay from the property.

A memorial stone at the parking lot, placed there in 2016 by the Indiana Native American Indian Affairs Commission, honors "the indigenous tribes that lived on this land prior to Indiana becoming a state."

Activities

Hiking Trails: Two loop, self-guided; easy to moderate.
Other Activities: Nature study, photography, wildlife watching.

Directions

GPS coordinates: 39.720190, −85.222245
From I-70
- South on Wilbur Wright Road to US 40, 2.6 miles
- East on US 40 to Bentonville Road, 1.0 mile
- South on Bentonville Road to County Road 700N, 4.5 miles

- East on County Road 700N to County Road 450W, 4.5 miles
- South on County Road N450W to preserve, 1.7 miles

94. Wilbur Wright Fish & Wildlife Area

Owned by Indiana Department of Natural Resources, Division of Fish & Wildlife

The 1,070-acre Wilbur Wright Fish & Wildlife Area in Henry County consists of varied upland and river valley habitats along the Big Blue River and its tributary, the Little Blue River. The landscape features mature woodlands, old fields, prairie plantings, and scattered wetlands, with a diverse mix of wildlife habitats.

The Big Blue River marks Wilbur Wright's western boundary, with its floodplain occupying about a third of the wildlife area. The rest is uplands and the Little Blue River Valley.

Fish and wildlife areas are managed for hunting and fishing. Wilbur Wright's mix of ecosystems attracts more two hundred animal species and provides excellent songbird habitat.

Wright also manages another 896 acres on three nearby public lands that offer upland game, woodland, and waterfowl hunting: Province Pond Wetland Conservation Area, 210 acres, with a concrete boat ramp; Randolph County Wildlife Management Area, 508 acres; and Modoc Wildlife Management Area, 167 acres.

The area is named after famed aviation pioneer Wilbur Wright, who was born a few miles east near Hagerstown. It is located adjacent to the New Castle Correctional Facility.

Wilbur Wright does not have any marked trails, but service roads provide access for hiking.

Activities

Berry, mushroom, and nut gathering; fishing; hiking; hunting, accessible; nature study; photography; trapping; wildlife watching.

Directions

GPS coordinates: 39.964806, −85.352573

From I-69

- East on State Road 38 (West State Street) at Pendleton to US 36, 1.9 miles
- East on US 36 to State Road 103, 21.0 miles
- South on State Road 103 to wildlife area, 2.2 miles

From I-70

- North on State Road 3, through New Castle, to County Road 75N, 6.6 miles
- East on County Road 75N to State Road 103 (North 14th Street), 1.0 mile
- North on State Road 103 to wildlife area, 1.9 miles

95. Stout Woods Nature Preserve

Owned by Purdue University

The thirty-five-acre Stout Woods Nature Preserve in Henry County is a high-quality example of the Central Till Plain flatwoods forest type that was native to vast areas of Central Indiana in presettlement times. Little impacted by invasive species, this woodland with wetlands supports a rich diversity of plants and animals that include salamanders, sedges, white oaks, red oaks, bur oaks, and tulip poplars.

This dedicated state nature preserve, also known as the Stout Memorial Woods, was owned by the family and has been disturbed little since the mid-1800s. The timber that was removed was used as farm wood for the family's three farms. It has been the subject of a continuing forest inventory since the 1920s and today serves as a living laboratory example of what the Indiana landscape looked like at the time of settlement.

Park on County Road 350N and walk along a farm field to the forest. A trail with unraised boards leads into the woods.

Activities

Hiking, nature study, photography, wildlife watching.

Directions

GPS coordinates: 39.983004, –85.443052

Stout Woods Nature Preserve

From I-69
- South on State Road 109 (Scatterfield Road) at Anderson to US 36, 3.5 miles
- East on US 36 to North County Road 300W at Sulphur Springs, 11.7 miles
- South on County Road 300W to intersection with West County Road 350N and the preserve, 1.5 miles

From I-70
- North on State Road 3 to South County Road 500S, 0.6 mile
- West on South County Road 500S to South County Road 125W, 0.3 mile
- North on South County Road 125W (turns left at 1.9 miles) to West County Road 100S, 4.1 miles
- West on West County Road 100S to South Greensboro Pike, 0.3 mile
- North on South Greensboro Pike, becoming Sulphur Springs Road, to North County Road 300W, 4.9 miles
- North on North County Road 300W to intersection with West County Road 350N and the preserve, 0.2 mile

96a. Summit Lake State Park

Owned by Indiana Department of Natural Resources, Division of State Parks & Lakes

The 2,680-acre Summit Lake State Park in Henry County includes an eight-hundred-acre namesake lake surrounded by an array of natural habitats that support a diverse collection of plant and animal species, especially birds. Its open water, deciduous woodlands, open brush, old fields, thickets, mudflats, marshes, wetlands, and prairie restorations support an estimated one hundred bird species.

The Indiana Audubon Society says warblers, ducks, swans, geese, grebes, and shorebirds frequent Summit Lake. Some unusual species that have been observed include the state endangered least bittern, marsh wren, American bittern, osprey, and black tern, along with the bald eagle and great egret, both state species of special concern.

Summit Lake attracts the largest concentrations of migrating waterfowl in the Midwest outside of the Great Lakes. With the exceptions of loons and deep-diving ducks, most tend to concentrate in the nature area, which consists of the three marshes and a pond in the park's far northeastern reaches. The nature area is not accessible from inside the park but is by county road. Obtain permission to enter from the park office.

Birds frequent the entire park area, with rare ones usually choosing the lake's islands and surrounding marshes as resting areas during migration. Two islands can be viewed from Sunset Shelter inside the park. The three most important can be viewed only from Dam Access Road, which requires permission from the park manager to enter. Another small island is located within the nature area marsh.

Waterfowl remain at Summit Lake throughout the winter, provided open water is available. Ducks, geese, and other aquatic birds are most abundant October through early December and March through early April. November tends to be the peak. Shorebirds are most common mid-July through early November and again April through May. Woodland bird flights occur in May and again September through October.

Summit Lake State Park

Bass, sunfish, crappie, perch, and catfish abound in Summit Lake.

Three hiking trails offer views of the lake.

The half-mile-wide Big Blue River Valley was carved by glacial meltwaters more than ten thousand years ago. Fossils from mastodon, elk, and bison have been found in the area's peaty soils.

Summit Lake, which became Indiana's nineteenth state park in January 1988, has history that traces back to the 1950s, when Henry County residents began calling for a recreational facility close to home. By 1966, the Big Blue River Conservancy District had formed to establish the Big Blue River Recreation Area, with goals that included flood control and waterway improvement.

Construction of a dam at the Big Blue River headwaters began in the mid-1970s. In 1988, the recreation area was sold to the state of Indiana for Summit Lake State Park. The name is derived from the park's status as the highest elevation in the surrounding area—near the highest elevation in the state.

Summit Lake is accessible for the physically challenged.

96b. Zeigler Woods Nature Preserve

The 127-acre Zeigler Woods Nature Preserve features old-growth woodlands, rolling hills, and a scenic valley on the southwest side of Summit Lake State Park. Permission from the park office is required to park by and enter this dedicated state nature preserve.

With little evidence of human disturbance, the Zeigler preserve represents a high-quality example of the rolling, moist, upland hardwood forests and depressional wetlands that were native to East Central Indiana in presettlement times. Its wooded bluffs loom a hundred feet above the Big Blue River Valley below.

The landscape supports mature stands of white oak, red oak, white ash, shagbark hickory, sugar maple, and American elm on the rich slopes, with black oak, basswood, blue ash, slippery elm, and pignut hickory occupying the drier ridges and slopes. Ephemeral wetlands in the spring provide ideal habitats for smallmouth salamanders and wood frogs.

Established in 1991, the preserve was originally owned by Marjorie and Sherman Zeigler from Muncie, who donated it to The Nature Conservancy, which gave it to the state.

Ziegler Woods has no trail. You must receive permission from the park office to enter the Nature Area and Dam Access Road.

Activities

Camping: 125 Class A campsites, with flush toilets, hot water, and showers. Occupancy is limited to two weeks; reservations recommended.

Hiking Trails: Four (0.75–2 miles), moderate, one accessible.

Other Activities: Boating: privately owned boats may be launched, idle speed only; boat rentals: paddleboats, rowboats and canoes; rental cabin, ADA accessible; fishing; interpretive naturalist service; nature study; photography; picnic area; shelter houses; swimming beach: bathhouse, concession building, restrooms; volleyball; wildlife watching.

Directions

GPS coordinates: 40.018921, –85.302631

From I-69

- East on State Road 38, through Pendleton, to US 36, 2.0 miles
- East on US 36 to North Messick Road, 23.0 miles
- North on North Messick Road to park, 1.0 mile

From I-70

- North on State Road 3 to US 36, 11.0 miles
- East on US 36 North to Messick Road, 3.9 miles
- North on North Messick Road to park, 1.0 mile

97. Mounds State Park

Owned by Indiana Department of Natural Resources,
Division of State Parks & Lakes

The 290-acre Mounds State Park, located on the banks of the White River West Fork just east of the Anderson city limits, protects a diverse mix of landforms and ecosystems. But the third-smallest Indiana state park in Madison County is foremost a significant historic site. Featuring ten of the finest examples of prehistoric earthwork and mound building in Indiana, the park's centerpiece is the Great Mound, which was built by the prehistoric Adena-Hopewell people around 160 BC.

The Mounds State Park landforms include limestone bluffs, upland woods, floodplain woods, creek ravines, wet sedge meadows, fens, seeps, caves, and the river, all of which support a diverse collection of plant and animal life. The downcut terrain is rugged in places.

The woodlands produce phloxes, irises, anemones, and other wildflowers indicative of a high-quality woods in relatively undisturbed conditions.

The White River floodplain supports sugar maple, American elm, black walnut, tulip poplar, hackberry, red maple, and sycamore trees, along with Miami mist, Philadelphia fleabane, and other wildflowers. The understory features bladdernuts, dogwoods, and gooseberries.

White River West Fork, Mounds State Park

Several alkaline seeps have formed in Mounds State Park where water percolates through the bluffs and then seeps into and across the soil, picking up minerals from the glacial gravel deposits along its descent. Unique plant and animal communities survive in seeps.

The Mounds Fen Nature Preserve is an alkaline fen, likewise created by water filtering through the gravel, with exceptionally clean water and high biodiversity. It supports more than four-dozen plant species. The location of this dedicated state nature preserve is neither marked on maps nor shared with the public.

The park also protects a three-acre wet sedge meadow that is bordered by willows and red osier dogwoods. In addition to sedge species, the meadow supports blazing star, goldenrod, golden ragwort, and primrose.

In addition to common Central Indiana critters, the fauna of Mounds State Park includes the rare gray petaltail dragonfly—a state species of special concern that has inhabited the earth for 200 million years and is found at the fen and seeps. Also found at the fen, the clamp-tipped emerald dragonfly, with its metallic bronze with green eyes, is likewise rare in Indiana. The star-nosed mole is a state species of special concern that is generally found only in the northern counties.

Human History

The Adena-Hopewell people, Woodland Period hunter-gatherers who date to 1000 BC and who were among the area's first inhabitants, built the Mounds State Park earthworks—any structures made from earthen materials. Later cultures, most notably the Hopewell Indians, used some of them for burial purposes. But archaeologists believe they mostly served as gathering places for religious ceremonies, celebrations, and observations of solstices, equinoxes, and other stellar events.

More than three hundred earthworks have been recorded in Central Indiana. All three types of Native American earthworks—mounds, circular enclosures, and complexes—are preserved in Mounds State Park. They range from a few inches tall to several feet high. One has a sequence of clay platforms covered by layers of ash.

The Great Mound, a circular enclosure, is nearly a quarter-mile in circumference and has an internal ditch that is ten feet deep and sixty feet across. It has a nine-foot-tall embankment and is sixty-three feet wide at the base. The central platform is 138 feet across.

No one knows why the Adena and Hopewell cultures disappeared from the area.

Mounds State Park was settled in the early nineteenth century by a family of German immigrant farmers, who eventually leased part of it for an amusement park that operated from 1897 through 1929 but still featured the mounds as attractions. While the park included a roller coaster, skating rink, shooting gallery, carousel, and pavilion with a restaurant and dance hall, its owners also made the mounds a point of regional pride and as well as a destination.

During the Great Depression, the land sold to the Madison County Historical Society, which transferred it to the state for Mounds State Park, which was created in 1930.

Activities

Hiking Trails: Six (0.4–2.5 miles), easy to rugged.

Camping: Seventy-five electric sites, dumping station, flush toilets, hot water, showers, picnic tables, and grills; youth tent areas; primitive camping for church and other youth groups with adult supervision, with water and vault toilets.

Other Activities: Fishing on the White River; nature center/ visitor center with gift shop, interpretive naturalist services; picnicking/shelters (shelter reservations); playground; recreation building; nature study; open playfields; photography; swimming pool; wildlife watching.

Directions

GPS coordinates: 40.095639, –85.618491

From I-69

- West on County Road 67 at State Road 67 exit north of Anderson to County Road 100S, 3.1 miles
- West on County Road 100S to State Road 232 (Mounds Road), 0.2 mile
- North on State Road 232 to park, 0.5 mile

98. Red-tail Nature Preserve

Owned by Red-tail Land Conservancy

The 105-acre Red-tail Nature Preserve in Delaware County supports restored prairie and woodland on the south end of the City of Muncie's Prairie Creek Reservoir, a 1,275-acre lake surrounded on three sides by 750 acres of public land. The Red-tail preserve serves as a vital link between wildlife habitats and features an osprey nest platform.

Replanted native grasses and wildflowers in the Edgar H. and Lois C. Seward Memorial Prairie reach heights of eight feet in late summer. These colorful plants attract butterflies and birds and are viewable from an amphitheater and a loop trail that traverses the site.

The Red-tail preserve connects to the Cardinal Greenway rail trail via a paved trail, which continues across a county road to

Red-tail Nature Preserve

a network of multiuse park trails. Cardinal is the state's longest rail trail and stretches sixty-two miles from Marion to Richmond.

Created as an outdoor educational facility and situated between the rail trail and the reservoir, Red-tail was the first preserve acquired by the Muncie-based Red-tail Land Conservancy.

Activities
Hiking Trails: One (0.5 mile), loop, easy.
Other Activities: Amphitheater, hiking, nature study, observation plaza, photography, wildlife watching.

Directions
GPS coordinates: 40.099101, –85.299948
From I-69
- East on State Road 67 south of Muncie to US 35, 12.8 miles
- East on US 35 to County Road 650S, 4.8 miles
- East on County Road 650S to County Road 461E, 0.8 mile
- North on County Road 461E to preserve, 200 feet
From I-70
- North on State Road 3 to County Road 700S, 16.9 miles

- East on County Road 700S to US 35, 3.2 miles
- North on US 35 to County Road 650S, 0.7 mile
- East on County Road 650S to County Road 461E, 0.8 mile
- North on County Road 461E to preserve, 200 feet

Bluffton Till Plain Section

99. Hughes Nature Preserve

Owned by City of Muncie

The seven-acre Hughes Nature Preserve protects an area of hardwood forest on the White River West Fork on Muncie's industrial-urban east side, across the water from the John M. Craddock Wetland Nature Preserve (below). The preserve connects to the Cardinal Greenway rail trail and provides access to the river and opportunities for birdwatching in Delaware County. The Red-tail Land Conservancy manages the preserve.

Today's woods were the site of a variety of factories from the late nineteenth to the mid-twentieth centuries, which produced shoes, clay pots for the glass industry, and collectible pottery. Fire destroyed the buildings in 1968, and the site began a long road to restoration. The last owner, Robert L. Hughes, left the woodlot to the City of Muncie with a permanent conservation easement that guaranteed it would remain forever natural.

The site, however, had been invaded by invasive plants, especially bush honeysuckle. Volunteers from a variety of groups and organizations cleared the honeysuckle from the preserve and nearby properties and then replanted a thousand native trees and grasses and wildflowers.

Aside from a paved spur off the Cardinal Greenway that leads to a river overlook, the Hughes Preserve has paths but no marked trails. The Cardinal Greenway is the state's longest rail trail, stretching sixty-two miles from Marion to Richmond.

Activities

Other Activities: Hiking (no trails), nature study, photography, wildlife watching.

GPS coordinates: 40.196125, −85.369751

From I-69

- East on State Road 332 to MLK Jr. Boulevard, 10.0 miles
- South on MLK Jr. Boulevard to Hackley Street, 1.6 miles
- South on Hackley Street to Washington Street, 0.2 mile
- East on Washington Street to Brady Street, 0.4 mile
- North on Brady Street to preserve, 0.2 mile

From I-70

- North on State Road 3 (Macedonia Avenue at State Road 67) to Ohio Avenue in Muncie, 23.7 miles
- Northwest on Ohio Avenue to Lincoln Street, 0.1 mile
- North on Lincoln Street to Main Street, 0.3 mile
- West on Main Street to Brady Street, 300 feet
- North on Brady Street to preserve, 0.2 mile

100. John M. Craddock Wetland Nature Preserve

Owned by Cardinal Greenway Inc.

The twenty-seven-acre John M. Craddock Wetland Nature Preserve in Delaware County occupies a bend in the White River West Fork in an urban-industrial area on Muncie's near-east side, just across the water from the Hughes Nature Preserve (above). The preserve is managed by the Red-tail Land Conservancy.

Home to an osprey nest platform, the wetland preserve provides a stopover for migrating birds and a home for other wildlife. The dominant wetland habitat is scrub-shrub, which supports short, woody species like shrubs, young trees, and trees whose growth has been stunted. A sedge meadow occupies the saturated soils that lie in the Craddock preserve's core.

After undergoing a decade and a half of intensive stewardship—removing invasive species and replanting native plant species—the preserve is succeeding in reaching a more natural state. As of 2015, more than 220 plant and animal species had been documented on the site, which, due to its floodplain location, was never successfully farmed or developed.

John M. Craddock Wetland Nature Preserve

More than fifty bird species have been recorded on the Craddock preserve, including cardinal, downy woodpecker, northern flicker, red-tailed hawk, and red-winged blackbird. Tree species include chinquapin oak, sugar maple, silver maple, green ash, eastern redbud, sycamore, eastern red cedar, honey locust, and boxelder maple. Mammals that frequent the site include white-tailed deer, coyotes, raccoons, cottontail rabbits, chipmunks, red foxes, and opossums.

Work is ongoing at the Craddock wetlands to restore the emergent wetlands, moist prairies, and upland wooded areas and provide a place for contemplation. In addition to invasive species control, the preserve is subjected to controlled burns to discourage the growth of unwanted species.

The Craddock wetlands preserve serves as a self-guided, outdoor laboratory for conservation education and features illustrated, interpretive signs on stewardship, wetlands, upland woods, prairie, and birds. Classes at Ball State University use it for educational purposes.

Initially a gift to the city of Muncie, the preserve is named for John M. Craddock, a local water-quality specialist who devoted his life to restoring aquatic habitats and riparian wildlife corridors along the White River and other waterways. He created and led the city's Bureau of Water Quality from 1972 to 2003.

Activities
Hiking Trails: One (0.3 mile), with boardwalk, ADA accessible.
Other Activities: Access to White River Greenway, overlook pavilion with green roof, nature study, photography, river overlook, wildlife watching.

Directions
GPS coordinates: 40.194547, −85.363723
From I-69
- East on State Road 332 to MLK Jr. Boulevard, 10.0 miles
- South on MLK Jr. Boulevard to Bunch Boulevard, 1.4 miles
- East on Bunch Boulevard to preserve at Gavin Street, 0.9 mile
From I-70
- North on State Road 3, becoming Macedonia Avenue at State Road 67, to Ohio Avenue in Muncie, 23.7 miles
- Northwest on Ohio Street to Lincoln Street, five hundred feet
- North on Lincoln Street to Jackson Street (State Road 32), 0.2 mile
- East on Jackson Street to Bunch Boulevard, 0.3 mile
- North on Bunch Boulevard to preserve at Gavin Street, 0.1 mile

101. Davis-Purdue Agricultural Center Forest
Owned by Purdue University
The 703-acre Davis-Purdue Agricultural Center Forest in Randolph and Jay Counties includes a fifty-two-acre National Natural Landmark that represents "the best old growth oak-hickory forest on the Till Plain and possibly one of the finest such forests in the eastern United States," according to the National Park Service. Located northeast of Muncie, the Davis-Purdue site is mostly tillable agricultural land with 126 acres of forest in four separate plots.

Davis-Purdue Agricultural Center Forest

The landmark forest on the Elkhorn Creek is open to the public, but it has no marked trails, and the trails it does have get overgrown quickly and are hard to follow. Late fall through early spring are the best times to explore Davis-Purdue.

Contributing to the Davis-Purdue's national landmark recognition is the fact that it was originally mapped in 1926 by Purdue forestry professor Burr N. Prentice and is the largest and oldest temperate deciduous forest mapped in North America. The woods support exceptionally large specimens of red oak, white oak, swamp white oak, bur oak, ash, and a variety of walnuts, as well as basswood and sugar maple.

Martha F. Davis donated the property to Purdue in 1917 in her son's memory.

Activities
Hiking, nature study, photography, wildlife watching.

Directions
GPS coordinates: 40.253193, −85.147740
From I-69
- East on State Road 28 (US 35) through Albany, to State Road 1, 22.1 miles
- South on State Road 1 to preserve, 2.9 miles

From I-70

- North on State Road 1 to preserve, 29.6 miles

102. Mississinewa Lake

Owned by Indiana Department of Natural Resources,
Division of State Parks & Lakes

The 14,386-acre Mississinewa Lake property in Miami County features a 3,210-acre namesake lake surrounded by forest, prairie, and farmland that attracts a wide variety of wildlife and offers viewing opportunities and scenic beauty for hikers, bicyclists, and motorists. More than nine thousand acres are managed for wildlife.

One of the largest natural area complexes in Northern Indiana, this recreation area is located southeast of Peru on the Mississinewa River and spans Wabash, Miami, and Grant Counties. Four State Recreation Areas (SRAs)—Miami SRA, Frances Slocum SRA, Red Bridge SRA, and Pearson Mill SRA—each with concrete boat ramps, are located around the lake. Miami and Frances Slocum are the most used. The Frances Slocum State Forest lies just north of the dam.

Mississinewa Lake's surface covers five square miles and is surrounded by moderate terrain that features mature woods with spring wildflowers, open meadows, creek habitats, and scenic views of the lake and dam.

Among the area's natural attractions are limestone formations known as Cliffs of the Seven Pillars that formed over thousands of years as the rushing waters of the Mississinewa—named after the Miami *Mischis-in-wah*, for river on a slope—washed away the riverbank's soft bedrock. The Miamis had a trading post on the cliffs and used them for council meetings and social events. According to legend, gold coins are buried in one of the caves, but it is guarded by a nest of snakes.

The pillars are viewable from the riverbank on the Frances Slocum Trail. The best view is from across the river at a public site on County Road 400E just west of the dam.

Mississinewa is the largest of three Upper Wabash River flood-control reservoirs and operates as a unit with nearby

Mississinewa Lake

J. Edward Roush Lake and Salamonie Lake to reduce Upper Wabash flooding. It also coordinates with downstream lakes to reduce Lower Wabash and Ohio River flooding. Trails and roads, including Mississinewa Road, can be underwater during wet seasons.

The Lost Sister Trail is named for Frances Slocum, the white pioneer woman who, in 1778, at age five, was taken from her Pennsylvania Quaker home at Wilkes-Barre by the Delaware Indians. She was later named Ma-con-a-quah—Little Bear Woman—and married War Chief Shepoconnah. After he went deaf, they established a successful trading post—called Deaf Man's Village—near Peru.

Slocum was identified by a relative in 1837 but chose to continue her life among the Delaware. She died in 1847 and is buried in the Francis Slocum Cemetery in Waltz, about two miles east of the Lost Sister's namesake state recreation area.

Peoria, just downstream from the dam, was originally the heart of the Great Miami Reserve and was known just as the Reserve. In October 1849, the Reserve was divided into thirty-six lots with four streets and named Peoria.

Activities

Hiking Trails: Five (0.4–2.5 miles), easy to moderate.

Camping: Miami SRA—modern campgrounds; electric and non-electric; hot showers; flush toilets; sewage, water and electric hookups; playgrounds; horseshoe pits; volleyball court; basketball court; and eighteen-hole disc golf course; mooring area for boats, not adjacent to the campsites.

Other Activities: Fishing, piers available in Miami SRA from May into October; hunting, in season; interpretive naturalist service; nature study; photography; picnicking; shelter houses; swimming beach, with showers, changing area, restrooms and concession; volleyball courts; wildlife watching.

Directions

GPS coordinates: 40.696194, –85.954465

From US 31

- East on County Road 500S southeast of Logansport to County Road 625E, 9.1 miles
- North on County Road 625E, to lake office, 0.2 mile

From I-69

- West on State Road 218 to State Road 15, 11.8 miles
- Northwest on State Road 15 to State Road 124, 6.3 miles
- West on State Road 124 to County Road 675E, 7.9 miles
- South on County Road 675E to County Road 380S, 1.1 miles
- West on County Road 380S to County Road 550E, 1.5 miles
- South on County Road 550E to County Road 500S, 1.1 miles
- East on County Road 500S to County Road 625E, 0.8 mile
- North on County Road 625E to lake office, 0.2 mile

103. Asherwood Nature Preserve

Owned by ACRES Land Trust

The 160-sixty-acre Asherwood Nature Preserve straddles the Asher Creek southwest of Wabash and features narrow ridgetops with deep ravines, open areas, and a small amount of floodplain forest. Supporting more than three hundred plant species and 145 bird species in Wabash County, Asherwood includes a sixty-acre dedicated state nature preserve.

Asherwood Nature Preserve

Asherwood lies about three miles east of the Frances Slocum State Forest. Among the unusual plant species there are state watch-listed shining clubmoss and pretty sedge.

American beech and sugar maple dominate the moist upland forest ridgetops, while oak and hickory command the dry-moist uplands. Deep, moist ravines separate the ridges. Asher Creek, which feeds the Wabash River a couple miles to the north, winds through the bottomlands, which support wetlands, small seep springs, and three diverse ponds, some with small piers and shelters.

The site was formerly owned by the Marion Community Schools and, known as Asherwood Environmental Learning Center, features an aviary with rescued raptors like red-tailed hawk, barred owl, turkey vulture, and bald eagle, which is a state species of special concern. A memorial stone declares the aviary is dedicated to Evelyn I. Gottschalk, a "Mississinewa Audubon Club member who inspired many people with her love for birds, wildflowers, and our natural world."

Activities

Hiking Trails: Network (2.6 miles).

Other Activities: Nature study, photography, wildlife watching.

Directions

GPS coordinates: 40.737411, –85.931126

From US 31

- East on US 24 west of Logansport to North Broadway at Peru, 57.2 miles
- South on North Broadway to State Road 124, 1.7 miles
- East on State Road 124 to the preserve, 8.0 miles

From I-69

- North on State Road 5 to State Road 124, 1.5 miles
- West on State Road 124 to preserve, 25.5 miles

104. Hathaway Preserve at Ross Run

Owned by ACRES Land Trust

The seventy-two-acre Hathaway Preserve at Ross Run in Wabash County protects a spectacular, deeply incised bedrock gorge with waterfalls, riffles, flumes, reef fossils, exposed bedrock, and fifty- to seventy-five-foot cliffs. Its combination of geologic features—four-hundred-million-year-old Silurian Age limestone and dolomite—is rare in Northern Indiana.

The dedicated state nature preserve includes much of Ross Run, a Wabash River tributary, and supports moist-upland forest, dry upland forest, floodplain forest, a pine planting, and limestone cliff natural communities.

Among the rare and unusual plant species at Hathaway are state endangered thinleaf sedge and fineberry hawthorn, and state threatened northeastern smartweed.

The woods feature mature oaks with trunks that exceed four feet in diameter and a diverse understory with a spectacular spring wildflower display. Firepink and other wildflowers provide color through the summer.

Activities

Hiking Trails: One (2.0 miles), moderate.

Hathaway Preserve at Ross Run

Other Activities: Hiking, nature study, photography, wildlife watching.

Directions

GPS coordinates: 40.808114, −85.758113

From US 31

- East on US 24 west of Logansport to Alt US 24 (Stitt Street) in Wabash, 15.0 miles
- East on Alt US 24 to Bond Street, 0.6 mile
- South on Bond Street to Mill Street, 0.3 mile
- Southeast on Mill Street to Canal Street, 0.7 mile
- East on Canal Street to Huntington Street, 0.6 mile
- South on Huntington Street, across the Wabash River, to Waterworks Road, 0.5 mile
- Northeast on Waterworks Road to Meridian Road, 1.2 miles
- North on Meridian Road to Baumbauer Road, 0.3 mile
- East on Baumbauer Road to preserve, 2.1 miles

From I-69

- West on US 224 at Markle to State Road 5, 6.4 miles

- South on State Road 5 to Division Road, 2.5 miles
- West on Division Road, via to County Road 500E, 12.2 miles
- North on County Road 500E to Hanging Rock Road, 0.2 mile
- West on Hanging Rock Road to State Road 524, 1.5 miles
- South on State Road 524 to Baumbauer Road, 0.8 mile
- West on Baumbauer Road to preserve, 2.2 miles

105. Salamonie River State Forest

Owned by Indiana Department of Natural Resources,
Division of Forestry

The 850-acre Salamonie River State Forest lines the west bank of the Salamonie River in Wabash County. It features more than twenty-three miles of hiking and horse trails along rocky waterfall gorges, hills and bluffs, and a small lake. Salamonie includes some high-quality natural communities that support a wide diversity of plant species, including some that live on the edge of their natural ranges and are rare in the state.

Lying north of the Salamonie River Dam, the state forest is one piece of a larger natural area that includes Kokiwanee Nature Preserve across the river and Salamonie Lake south of the dam. Other natural features include ravines, river overlooks, open fields, stands of hardwood and pine trees, as well as hardwood plantations used for research.

The four-acre Hominy Ridge Lake and the Salamonie River support a variety of fish species, including largemouth bass, bluegill, redear sunfish, and walleye pike. Game species include deer, turkey, squirrel, fox, and raccoon.

The state forest is also managed for timber, wildlife, and watershed protection. A six-acre walnut plantation was established in 1963 and is still tested annually to learn how well various seeds grow in the region. Red oak and white oak plantations were planted in 1983 and are managed to produce quality trees in less time.

The region's natural areas are named after the Native American word *o-sah-mo-nee*, which means "yellow paint." Miami and Osage Indians made yellow paint from the bloodroot plant that grew along the river.

Salamonie State Forest's twenty-first-century natural character has its most recent roots in the 1930s, when the community rallied to save the badly eroded riverside farmlands, and the Civilian Conservation Corps (CCC) restored the site as a demonstration project for managing eroded land. Working under the Roosevelt-era Works Progress Administration, which provided jobs to unemployed workers during the Great Depression, the two-hundred-member CCC unit planned and replanted the forest, built the lake and recreation facilities, and opened a stone quarry.

The Hominy Ridge Shelter House is listed on the National Register of Historic Places.

Activities
Hiking Trails: One (0.33 miles); 9 miles of fire trails.
Horse Trails: Four (1.8–8.0 miles).
Cross-country Skiing: All trails.
Camping: One primitive campground; one family campground, twenty-one campsites; horseman's camp, fifteen sites. Campsites are available on a first come, first serve basis. Pit toilets and drinking water available.
Other Activities: Boat launch, electric trolling motors only; fishing; hunting; nature study; photography; wildlife watching.

Directions
GPS coordinates: 40.812516, –85.717176
From US 31
- East on US 24 west of to State Road 524 (America Road) at Lagro, 20.7 miles
- East on State Road 524, becoming Davis Street and America Road, to State Forest, 3.6 miles

From I-69
- West on US 224 at Markle to State Road 5, 6.4 miles
- South on State Road 5 to Division Road, 2.5 miles
- West on Division Road to County Road 500E, 12.2 miles
- North on County Road 500E to Hanging Rock Road, 0.2 mile
- West on Hanging Rock Road to State Road 524, 1.5 miles
- South on State Road 524 to State Forest, 1.2 miles

Salamonie Lake

106. Salamonie Lake

Owned by Indiana Department of Natural Resources,
Division of State Parks & Lakes

The 12,554-acre Salamonie Lake property in Wabash and Huntington Counties includes the 2,665-acre Salamonie Reservoir and five State Recreation Areas, along with marshes, wetlands, and forty ponds. Recreational opportunities run the gamut, from hiking and camping to wildlife watching, boating, hunting, and fishing.

Salamonie Lake lies three miles downstream from the Wabash River and forms a broader natural complex with the Salamonie State Forest and Kokiwanee Nature Preserve, which border the river to the north. The property is situated between the cities of Wabash and Huntington and its two sister state reservoirs: Mississinewa Lake and J. Edward Roush Lake, also known as Huntington Lake.

The Salamonie Reservoir is created by a 133-foot-tall, 6,100-foot-long dam on the Salamonie River, whose name comes from the Native American word *o-sah-mo-nee*, which translates as "yellow paint." The region's Miami and Osage Indian tribes made yellow paint from the bloodroot plants that grew along the river banks.

Salamonie Lake is one of the three Upper Wabash Valley lakes built in the late 1960s for flood control in the Wabash River Basin. Together, Mississinewa, Salamonie, and Roush Lakes operate largely as a unit.

Three small towns were flooded for the reservoir, including Monument City, which was platted in 1876 and named after its first structure—a Civil War monument engraved with the names of twenty-seven local men who died in the war. The monument and town cemetery were relocated just north of the lake.

The SRAs include the following:

- Lost Bridge West State Recreation Area: modern, primitive and horse camping; boat ramp; marina; beach; youth campground; nature center; fish cleaning station; accessible fishing pier; playgrounds; wildlife viewing areas; picnic areas; trails; shelter house
- Lost Bridge East State Recreation Area: boat ramp, trails, picnic areas, shelter house
- Mount Etna State Recreation Area: boat ramp, shelter house, trails
- Dora-New Holland State Recreation Area: boat ramp, shelter house, trails
- Mount Hope State Recreation Area: boat ramp

The reservoir is managed by the US Army Corps of Engineers, which operates Observation Mound and Tailwater Recreation Areas. Observation Mound offers picnicking, shelter house, playground, fishing, nature/hiking trail, and public restrooms.

Activities
Hiking Trails: Five (0.4–13.0 miles), easy to moderate.
Snowmobile Trail: One (40 miles).
Cross-Country Skiing Trail: One (12 miles), one-way.

Camping: Electric, Lost Bridge West; primitive, Lost Bridge West, Apple Orchard, Salamonie River State Forest; primitive, horse camp, Lost Bridge West, Salamonie River State Forest; primitive, youth group, Lost Bridge West.

Other Activities: Basketball and volleyball courts; boating, ramps and marina; fishing; hiking; horseshoe pits; hunting; interpretive, cultural, and recreational programming; nature study; photography; picnicking, tables, grills, toilet facilities, mobility accessible picnic tables; playgrounds; shelters; swimming beach; wildlife watching.

Directions
GPS coordinates: 40.764886, −85.625709
From US 31
- East on US 24 west of Logansport to State Road 524, at Lagro, 22.3 miles
- South on State Road 524 (becoming County Road 500E/ America Road) to Lincolnville Road, 6.9 miles
- East on Lincolnville Road to County Road 800E, 3.6 miles
- North on County Road 800E to Lost Bridge Road, 0.3 mile
- Northeast on Lost Bridge Road to Lake, 0.9 mile

From I-69
- North on State Road 5 south of Huntington to State Road 124, 1.5 miles
- West on State Road 124 to Chapel Road, 7.5 miles
- Northwest on Chapel Road (becoming County Road 500S) to County Road 900W, 2.2 miles
- North on County Road 900W to Lost Bridge Road, 0.7 mile
- West on Lost Bridge Road to Lake, 0.3 mile

107. Kokiwanee Nature Preserve
Owned by ACRES Land Trust
The 139.5-acre Kokiwanee Nature Preserve in Wabash County protects a biologically diverse ecosystem across the Salamonie River from the Salamonie State Forest. This dedicated state nature preserve supports old-growth forests, natural springs, streams, and a lake.

Kokiwanee Nature Preserve

The undeveloped land is managed as a refuge for plants and animals, including snow trillium, wood ducks, and great blue herons. Multiple waterfalls—with names like Daisy Low, Kissing, and Frog Falls—tumble fifty feet or so along bluffs and cliffs to the river below.

For forty years Kokiwanee operated as a Girl Scout camp and still features remnants from that time, including foundations and old structures such as privies and shelter houses. It features an elaborate trail system, with multiple unmarked interconnectors.

Activities

Hiking Trails: One (2.7 mile), loop, moderate. Dogs must be on leash.

Other Activities: Fishing, nature study, photography, wildlife watching.

Directions

GPS coordinates: 40.819470, –85.683014

From US 31

- West on US 24 west of Logansport to State Road 524 at Lagro, 22.1 miles
- East on State Road 524 to Hanging Rock Road, 2.3 miles
- East on Hanging Rock Road to County Road 500E, 1.2 miles
- South on County Road 500E to County Road 50S, 0.6 mile
- East on County Road 50S to preserve, 0.8 mile

From I-69

- West on US 224 at Markle to State Road 5, 6.4 miles
- South on State Road 5 to Division Road, 2.5 miles
- West on Division Road to Stone Road, 11.2 miles
- South on Stone Road to County Road 50S, 0.5 mile
- West on County Road 50S to preserve, 0.2 mile

108. Hanging Rock National Natural Landmark

Owned by ACRES Land Trust

The five-acre Hanging Rock National Natural Landmark (NNL) in Wabash County on the south bank of the Wabash River protects natural exposures of fossilized Silurian coral reef. It is also known as Hanging Rock and Wabash Reef. The Silurian Age limestone is characteristic of the Midwest, but it is mostly exposed in quarries and rarely as a rock formation.

"Hanging Rock is an impressive natural exposure of an exhumed reef that rises seventy-five feet above the Wabash River," the National Park Service says on its NNL website. "Wabash Reef, one of the best-known fossil reefs in the world, has been the subject of numerous studies responsible for the development of modern reef theory."

The reef formed more than three hundred million years ago when Indiana and much of the Midwest was covered by a vast, shallow, equatorial sea. Since the Wisconsin glacial ice began its retreat some thirteen thousand years ago, the Wabash River has undercut the rock, leaving the top overhanging its base above the water, offering stunning views of the river valley. Native Americans used Hanging Rock as both an overlook and a landmark.

Hanging Rock National Natural Landmark

While paths lead to the top of Hanging Rock, they are not part of the preserve's official trail.

Activities
Hiking Trails: One (0.3 mile).
Other Activities: Nature study, photography, wildlife watching.

Directions
GPS coordinates: 40.829692, –85.708424
From US 31
- West on US 24 west of Logansport to State Road 524 at Lagro, 22.1 miles
- East on State Road 524 to County Road 500E
- East Hanging Rock Road, 2.3 miles
- East on Hanging Rock Road to landmark, 0.7 mile

From I-69
- West on US 224 at Markle to State Road 5, 6.4 miles
- South on State Road 5 to Division Road, 2.5 miles
- West on Division Road to County Road 500E, 12.2 miles

- North on County Road 500E to Hanging Rock Road, 0.2 mile
- West on Hanging Rock Road to landmark, 0.5 mile

109. J. E. Roush Fish & Wildlife Area

Owned by Indiana Department of Natural Resources,
Division of Fish & Wildlife

The 7,347-acre J. E. Roush Fish & Wildlife Area in Huntington County stretches in a long, narrow band along fifteen miles of the Wabash River. Dedicated to hunting and fishing, the state-owned property includes 350 acres of impoundments and the nine-hundred-acre J. Edward Roush Lake, also known as Huntington Reservoir.

The lake's undeveloped shoreline is surrounded by mixed woodlands that provide habitat for numerous animals—game and nongame. Game animals include deer, fox, coyote, squirrel, rabbit, turkey, dove, and pheasant. During migrating seasons, the site is frequented by loons, cormorants, eagles, gulls, and terns.

Fish species in the wetlands, lake, and river include channel catfish, crappie, largemouth bass, smallmouth bass, white bass, walleye, redear sunfish, and bluegill.

Roush Lake, formed by a dam on the river, is one of the three Upper Wabash Valley lakes built in the late 1960s for flood control in the Wabash River Basin. Together, Roush, Mississinewa Lake, and Salamonie Lakes operate largely as a unit.

The Indiana Division of Reservoirs operated Roush Lake until 1998; the Division of State Parks & Reservoirs did so until 2010. Since then it has been run by the Division of Fish & Wildlife. The former Little Turtle State Recreation Area and Kilso-quah State Recreation Area are open to the public but are no longer operational. Swimming is not allowed.

Activities

Camping: Forty-one electric sites, fourteen primitive sites, with fire rings, picnic tables, water fountains, pit toilets.

Other Activities: Boating, motorized on Roush Lake, nonmotorized and electric motors only on impoundments; dog training;

J. E. Roush Lake

fishing; hiking; hunting, accessible; mushroom hunting; nature study; photography; picnicking at Kil-So-Quah boat ramp; shooting range; trapping; wildlife watching.

Directions

GPS coordinates: 40.835804, −85.465409

From US 31

- East on US 24 west of Logansport to State Road 9 at Huntington, 33.7 miles
- South on State Road 9 to Division Road, 2.4 miles
- East on 100N to Fish and State Road 5, 3.4 miles
- South on State Road 5 to Fish & Wildlife Area, 0.3 mile

From I-69

- West on US 224 at Markle to State Road 5 before Huntington, 6.7 miles
- South on State Road 5 to Fish & Wildlife Area, 2.1 miles

110. Anna Brand Hammer Reserve

Owned by ACRES Land Trust

The forty-acre Anna Brand Hammer Reserve in Wells County includes a twenty-acre dedicated state nature preserve that protects fourteen acres of moist upland forest with a high concentration of hickory trees. Other common trees include sugar maple, American beech, black cherry, red oak, and hop hornbeam, with smaller numbers of white oak, black walnut, and sycamore.

A small, seasonal stream winds through the forest. The remainder of the Hammer Preserve is former farmland, where trees have been planted on six adjacent acres to augment the forest cover.

This natural area's varied habitats support a range of wildflowers, including spring beauty, purple cress, cut-leaved toothwort, trout lily, Dutchman's breeches, blue phlox, squirrel corn, firepink, and mayapple.

Activities

Hiking Trails: One (0.5 mile), easy.

Other Activities: Nature study, photography, wildlife watching.

Anna Brand Hammer Reserve

Wabash River, Acres Along the Wabash Nature Preserve

Directions

GPS coordinates: 40.859406, −85.230645

From I-69

- East on US 224 at Markle to County Road 100W at Uniondale, 5.9 miles
- North on County Road 100W to County Road 800N, 2.0 miles
- East on County Road 800N to preserve, 0.6 mile

From I-70

- North on State Road 1 at Cambridge City to US 224, 69.3 miles
- West on US 224 to County Road 100W at Uniondale, 39.9 miles
- North on County Road 100W to County Road 800N, 2.0 miles
- East on County Road 800N to preserve, 0.6 mile

111. Acres Along the Wabash Nature Preserve

Owned by ACRES Land Trust

The eighty-seven-acre Acres Along the Wabash Nature Preserve in Wells County lines the north bank of the Wabash River for three-quarters of a mile and offers peaceful, scenic views of the river while protecting a twenty-seven-acre dedicated state nature preserve.

The tree-lined bluffs on the preserve's west portion support a mixed-hardwood stand that is dominated by sugar maple, black maple, and slippery elm. Mature red oaks, bur oaks, and sycamores thrive along the riverbank, sharing the bottomlands with hackberries, silver maples, cottonwoods, black willows, and boxelder maples.

Among the notable plant species at Acres Along the Wabash are the state rare grove meadow grass and state watch-listed pretty sedge. The site produces spectacular wildflower displays, supporting species such as shooting star and wild hyacinth. Warblers and other migrating birds inhabit the woods in spring. Wood thrushes, red-eyed vireos, and other species nest in summer. Common wildlife at Acres Along the Wabash includes foxes, squirrels, chipmunks, groundhogs, raccoons, and muskrats.

Activities

Hiking Trails: One (2.3 miles), moderate.
Other Activities: Nature study, photography, wildlife watching.

Directions

GPS coordinates: 40.802578, –85.218971
From I-69

- East on US 224 at Markle to State Road 116 (Morse Street), 0.1 mile
- Southeast on State Road 116 to preserve, 7.3 miles

From I-70

- North on State Road 1 at Cambridge City to State Road 116 north of Bluffton, 62.2 miles
- North on State Road 116, through Murray, to preserve, 6.0 miles

112. Ouabache State Park

Owned by Indiana Department of Natural Resources,
Division of State Parks & Lakes

The 1,104-acre Ouabache State Park borders the Wabash River in Wells County and supports a variety of natural habitats, including magnificent oak-hickory forest, woodland marsh, pine plantations, and twenty-five-acre Kunkel Lake.

Ouabache State Park

The park provides habitat for deer, foxes, squirrels, and other wildlife. It features a wildlife exhibit with American bison and a one-hundred-foot fire tower with stunning views of the park and surrounding farmland.

Ouabache, pronounced like the river, is the French spelling of the Miami Indian word *waapaahsiiki*, which means "it shines white," "pure white," or "water over white stones." The region was Miami territory in pre-European times. After the Indians were forcibly relocated to Kansas and Oklahoma in the 1830s and 1840s, white settlers cleared the parkland for agriculture.

A century later, in the early 1930s, the landscape that is today's Ouabache State Park was severely eroded and set aside as the Wells County State Forest and Game Preserve. Through reforestation and land management programs implemented by the Roosevelt-era Civilian Conservation Corps (CCC), the land returned to a natural state. In addition to reclaiming the land, the CCC constructed buildings and shelters of native stone that remain today.

During the game preserve era, the site produced the most pheasant and quail chicks in the United States and was known as the nation's "Greatest Wildlife Laboratory." Some of the old pens are still visible. Rabbits and raccoons were also raised for release.

By the time the property was designated as the Ouabache State Recreation Area in 1962, the game-raising program had been phased out. In 1983, the state recreation area became the state park.

The bison exhibit at Ouabache is the latest in a tradition of wildlife exhibits on the parkland. Previous subjects have included bear, eagle, coyote, fox, and badger.

The American bison, North America's largest land mammal, once roamed Indiana from the state's northwest prairies, where they grazed, to its southern woodlands, where they blazed trails called traces to salt licks. The plains bison in the lower forty-eight states are smaller than the woods bison of Northern Canada and Alaska.

Also called American buffalo or just buffalo, the bison were driven from Indiana by the early 1800s and slaughtered nationwide for decades. Within a century, only one free-roaming herd survived in the United States—in Yellowstone National Park—and the buffalo were on the brink of extinction.

Conservation efforts nationwide have established herds at preserves like Ouabache, where six to eight live in a twenty-acre pen across from the fire tower. In 2016, The Nature Conservancy relocated twenty-three bison from South Dakota to the Kankakee Sands in Newton County, where they now roam free on more than a thousand acres, the first to do so in two centuries. (See the Kankakee Sands entry above.)

A paved ten-foot-wide asphalt trail connects Ouabache State Park to the Rivergreenway Trail, which follows the Wabash for roughly three miles to the east edge of Bluffton.

Activities

Hiking Trails: Five (1–6 miles), easy to moderate.
Bicycle Trail: One (2.75 miles), paved.
Camping: Electric and primitive youth tent for approved groups only, dumping station, flush toilets, hot water, showers.
Other Activities: Basketball courts; boating—electric trolling motors only, no more than twelve-volt batteries, paddleboats; fishing; lodge; nature center, with interpretive seasonal naturalist services; nature study; photography; picnicking; playgrounds; shelter houses; swimming pool; tennis courts; volleyball court; wildlife watching.

Directions

GPS coordinates: 40.725318, –85.122870
From I-69

- East on US 224 at Markle to State Road 116 (Morse Street), 0.1 mile
- South on State Road 116 to State Road 124, 11.2 miles
- East on State Road 124 to State Road 201, 3.6 miles
- South on State Road 201 to park, 1.6 miles

Baltzell-Lenhart Woods Nature Preserve

From I-70
- North on State Road 1 to State Road 116 at Bluffton, 64.9 miles
- East on State Road 116 to County Road 450E, 1.7 miles
- North on County Road 450E to State Road 201, 0.7 mile
- Southeast on State Road 201 to park, 0.5 mile

113. Baltzell-Lenhart Woods Nature Preserve
Owned by Indiana Department of Natural Resources, Division of Nature Preserves

The thirty-seven-acre Baltzell-Lenhart Woods Nature Preserve in Adams County supports moist and wet-moist flatwoods that are dominated by oaks and hickories, with bur oak, swamp white oak, pin oak, red maple, sycamore, and cottonwood thriving in the moister areas.

Although this dedicated state nature preserve's woodland is typical of this natural region, its previous owners cut few trees, and it features an old-growth component. Wildflowers include prairie trillium, mayapple, wild geranium, and false Solomon's seal. The understory is thick in summer. Poison ivy is common.

Victor Baltzell donated the preserve property in memory of his wife, Alice Lenhart-Baltzell.

Activities
Hiking, nature study, photography, wildlife watching.

Directions
GPS coordinates: 40.774247, –84.925627
From I-69
- North on State Road 5 at Warren to State Road 124, 1.4 miles
- East on State Road 124, through Bluffton, to US 27 at Monroe, 25.9 miles
- North on US 27 to County Road 200N, 2.4 miles
- East on County Road 200N to preserve, 0.6 mile

From I-70
- North on State Road 3 at New Castle, to State Road 67 on the north side of Muncie, 27.9 miles
- Northeast on State Road 67 to US 27 at Portland, 27.2 miles
- North on US 27 to County Road 200N, 24.0 miles
- East on County Road 200N to preserve, 0.6 mile

114. Fogwell Forest Nature Preserve
Owned by ACRES Land Trust

The 61.5-acre Fogwell Forest Nature Preserve in Allen County protects a mature, second-growth forest in a lowland area with poorly drained depressions. Twenty-eight of its acres have been designated as a dedicated state nature preserve. The site supports an especially diverse mix of fern and woodland sedge species.

Situated at the end of a cul-de-sac within earshot of Fort Wayne's Airport Expressway, Fogwell Forest's gently undulating landforms produce tree compositions that change significantly with slight differences in elevation. Sugar maple, American beech, white oak, and red oak thrive on the drier sites; bur oak, red maple, swamp white oak, green ash, and buttonbush dominate the wetter sites.

Fogwell Forest Nature Preserve

The preserve harbors three rare plant species, including state endangered finely nerved sedge, state threatened straw sedge, and state watch-listed pretty sedge. Flowering dogwood, spicebush, pawpaw, and maple-leaved viburnum thrive in the understory, with large-flowered trillium, Dutchman's breeches, trout lily, wild geranium, wild ginger, jack-in-the-pulpit, and various violet species common on the forest floor.

Shallow vernal pools fill with water in the spring and dry out through the summer. Tall, straight swamp white oaks grow near the pools. Plant growth is dominated by sedges and ferns, such as sensitive fern and lady fern. Squirrels, raccoons, owls, and a variety of other wildlife live year-round in the preserve.

The Fogwell family owned and farmed the property for three generations. After the first generation sold some timber in the 1920s, Indiana's first state forester, Charles C. Deam, persuaded the family to enroll the remaining woods in Indiana's Classified Forest Program for protection.

A sign just inside the forest declares it a classified forest and private property, but the woods are part of the Fogwell preserve and are open to the public.

Activities
Hiking Trails: One (1.9 miles), easy.
Other Activities: Nature study, photography, wildlife watching.

Directions
GPS coordinates: 40.999855, −85.238544
From I-69
- East on Lower Huntington Road on Fort Wayne's south side to Whippoorwill Drive, 1.6 miles
- Southeast on Whippoorwill Drive to preserve, 0.4 mile

115. Fox Island Nature Preserve
Owned by Allen County Parks Board
The 270-acre Fox Island Nature Preserve in Allen County protects marshes and swamps that border a glacial sand dune created when the last ice sheets receded from Northeast Indiana

Fox Island Nature Preserve

more than ten thousand years ago. The diversity of landscapes on this dedicated state nature preserve, along with its relatively natural conditions, supports hundreds of plants and animals.

The Fox Island preserve is part of a larger natural complex in the Little River Watershed. It comprises nearly half of the 605-acre Allen County park of the same name and is located directly south, across a railroad track, from the Eagle Marsh nature preserve. The park, which is bordered on its southern side by the Little River and bisected on its western end by Interstate 69, supports the largest chunk of unbroken forest in Allen County.

Fox Island features a diversity of habitats, including marsh, seasonal ponds, wooded sand dunes, mature woodlands, wetland forest, brushy fields, bushy thickets, pine plantations, restored prairie, and a borrow pit lake.

More than two hundred bird species have been identified at the park, which the Indiana Audubon Society calls "the best spot in Northeast Indiana for migrant woodland songbirds." Fox Island is especially known for woodland songbirds, including warblers, vireos, thrushes, and flycatchers, as well as sparrows, woodpeckers, hawks, owls, marsh birds, and waterfowl. Bird species recorded at Fox Island include the state endangered American bittern and least bittern, and state species of special concern worm-eating warbler, along with olive-sided flycatcher, alder flycatcher, yellow-bellied flycatcher, little blue heron, common moorhen, northern saw-whet owl, long-eared owl, Bell's vireo, summer tanager, LeConte's sparrow, red crossbill, and common redpoll.

More than 180 wildflowers and more than forty tree species have been recorded at Fox Island. Black oak predominates on the higher, drier dunes; white oak, black walnut, and black cherry on the moist slopes; and willow, cottonwood, and sycamore on the low mucky soils.

The preserve's northwestern portion features wetlands with open water surrounded by emergent vegetation. Old fields in various stages of succession are also part of the landscape.

Situated near the western outlet of Glacial Lake Maumee, Lake Erie's predecessor, Fox Island's forty-foot-high sand dune stretches the length of the park. The sand and marsh are remnants of a glacial sluice formed when the Wisconsin glacier's receding meltwaters formed the St. Joseph and St. Marys Rivers. During low water flow in winter, winds piled large drifts of fine sands around the area. Fox Island's dune is the best remaining example of this landform in the entire Midwest.

The marsh, which features an elevated observation deck, is inhabited by deer, muskrat, beaver, and waterfowl. An elevated boardwalk makes close observation of aquatic life possible during the wet seasons. The marsh occasionally dries up.

The twenty-five-foot-deep lake at the park's west end was created when its soil was "borrowed" to build overpasses for Interstate 69. The lake's clear, clean water comes from springs; it is stocked with bass, bluegill, catfish, and crappie.

In presettlement days Fox Island was part of the portage between the Maumee and Wabash Rivers that was used by the Indians, French, and English to connect the Great Lakes with the Mississippi River.

Before it was purchased as Allen County's first park and nature preserve in 1971, Fox Island's timber had been cleared for a family farm. The pine plantation is left over from a Christmas tree farm.

Much of the park is accessible; parts are wheelchair accessible.

Activities
Hiking Trails: Six miles of marked trails.
Other Activities: Fishing, nature study, photography, wildlife watching.

Directions
GPS coordinates: 41.016375, −85.238754
From I-69
- Southwest on US 24 on Fort Wayne's southeast side to Liberty Mills Road, 0.3 mile
- East on Liberty Mills Road to Ellison Road, 0.2 mile
- South on Ellison Road to Yohne Road, 1.1 miles
- East on Yohne Road to park / preserve, 0.7 mile

116. Eagle Marsh
Owned by Little River Wetlands Project
Eagle Marsh is a 716-acre wetland nature preserve in Allen County that protects a variety of lowland habitats in the Little River Watershed, including shallow-water wetland, sedge meadow, prairie, mature forest, and young forest. The marsh is drained by the Graham McCulloch Ditch, which feeds the Little River about three miles to the west.

Together with the adjacent Fox Island County Park and other private lands, the Eagle Marsh preserve is one piece of a nearly two-square-mile natural complex southwest of Fort Wayne that is managed primarily for wildlife. Among the fauna that frequent the site are twenty-eight bird and two amphibian species that are endangered or of special concern in Indiana.

Eagle Marsh

More than 220 bird species have been identified at Eagle Marsh, which abuts I-69 to the west. Among them are bald eagles and peregrine falcons, both state species of special concern, and common loons, great horned owls, and red-tailed hawks.

Eagle Marsh is one of the largest wetland restorations in Indiana. Work began in 2005 when the nonprofit Little River Wetlands Project broke drain tiles, removed pumps, and dug shallow areas deeper so the land would hold water in ways that it would naturally. More than forty-five thousand native trees and shrubs were planted. More than five hundred acres were seeded with native rushes, grasses, and wildflowers. Another forty acres of mature forested wetland were acquired between 2007 and 2010, providing habitat for wildlife that requires large trees, sandy soil, or leaf litter for their life cycles.

Eagle Marsh is situated on the St. Lawrence Continental Divide between the Great Lakes and Mississippi River drainage basin. In 2014 and 2015, an existing berm on the Graham McCulloch Ditch was expanded, and other changes were made to the hydrology to prevent the invasive Asian carp in the Wabash River from reaching the marsh during major flood events. In effect, the divide was moved to Eagle Marsh.

Activities
Hiking Trails: Nine (1–2 miles), easy, some wet.
Other Activities: Nature study, photography, wildlife watching.

Directions to trail
GPS coordinates: 41.029417, –85.251142
From I-69
- Northeast on US 24 (Jefferson Boulevard) on Fort Wayne's southeast side to Olde Canal Place, 0.4 mile
- Southwest on Olde Canal Place to preserve, 0.7 mile

Directions to Continental Divide
GPS coordinates: 41.042503, –85.230347
From I-69
- Northeast on US 24 (Jefferson Boulevard) to Engle Road, 1.1 miles
- East on Engle Road to divide, 0.5 mile

117. Lindenwood Nature Preserve
Owned by Fort Wayne Parks & Recreation

The 110-acre Lindenwood Nature Preserve in Allen County protects a high-quality, mature oak-hickory forest in the Fort Wayne city limits that is dominated by white oaks, red oaks, and shagbark hickories. The bulk of the city park—eighty-six acres—is a dedicated state nature preserve.

The Lindenwood preserve features a pond and supports a diverse wildflower population, especially in spring, that includes wild geranium, wild ginger, bloodroot, spring beauty, jack-in-the-pulpit, and three varieties of trillium. Squirrels, rabbits, and deer are common in the woods.

Lindenwood Park was established in 1987. In 1994 it was designated as a state nature preserve with a mission to protect

Lindenwood Nature Preserve

the preserve's natural habitat, provide programs and events that promote environmental education and cultural enrichment, and foster awareness that nature enhances quality of life through artistic inspiration, spiritual connection, physical fitness, and exploration.

Activities

Hiking Trails: Four (0.25–1.0 mile), easy. One wheelchair and stroller accessible.

Other Activities: Nature study, photography, picnicking, pavilion, wildlife watching.

Directions

GPS coordinates: 41.079143, –85.179485
From I-69

- East on US 24 (Jefferson Boulevard) to Lindenwood Avenue, 4.7 miles
- North on Lindenwood Avenue to preserve, 0.4 mile

Mengerson Nature Rreserve

118. Mengerson Nature Reserve
Owned by ACRES Land Trust

The thirty-six-acre Mengerson Nature Reserve in Allen County supports three stages of forest succession: open meadow, early stage, and mature. This dedicated state nature preserve is surrounded by suburban housing and development on Fort Wayne's northeast side; it is flat with small wet spots and is divided by a couple ditches.

The grassy meadow forest supports hawthorn and dogwood trees; the early-stage forest supports various elms, oaks, hickories, and maples; the mature forest supports beech-maple. The understory includes spicebush and blue beech.

The Mengerson preserve's diverse habitats attract a variety of wildlife and wildflowers, including spring beauty, mayapple, green dragon, jack-in-the-pulpit, and prairie trillium.

The trails feature boardwalks to prevent damage to the ecosystem.

The preserve, whose parking lot is connected to a private driveway, was donated by Carl and Ursula Mengerson to be entrusted as public land. A sign just inside the preserve memorializes "Carl's red oak, quercus rubra, planted: 1987."

Activities
Hiking Trails: One (1.2 miles), easy.
Other Activities: Nature study, photography, wildlife watching.

Directions
GPS coordinates: 41.120274, –85.067598
From I-69
- South on Coldwater Road on Fort Wayne's north side to Washington Center Road, 0.2 mile
- East on Washington Center Road to Reed Road, 2.8 miles
- South on Reed Road to Stellhorn Road, 1.0 mile
- East on Stellhorn Road to preserve (road divider requires turning around in the Maple Crest Shopping Center), 0.6 mile

119. Meno-aki Nature Preserve
Owned by Allen County Parks Board

The 120-acre Meno-aki Nature Preserve in Allen County supports a diversity of natural communities on the scenic Cedar Creek, including a rare hill prairie, along with dry-moist forest, moist upland forest, and floodplain forest. The hill prairie, which features prairie vegetation along south-facing bluffs overlooking the creek, is especially rare this far east.

The dedicated state nature preserve occupies a portion of Fort Wayne's 250-acre Metea Park between the city and Leo-Cedarville. Cedar Creek, one of only three State Natural, Scenic, and Recreational Rivers in Indiana, bisects the park into north and south sections. The Meno-aki preserve includes acreage on both sides of the water.

Steep, wooded ravines carve the landscape from the bluff tops to the floodplain. Oak-hickory forest dominates the ecosystem past the prairie plants and away from the bluffs.

The park is named for Potawatomi Indian Chief Metea, whose Muskwawsepeotan village was situated near the mouth of the

Meno-aki Nature Preserve

Cedar Creek just downstream from the park boundary. The village name means "town on the old red wood creek." Meno-aki means good or blessed land.

The southeasternmost Potawatomi village in Indiana, Muskwawsepeotan was settled after the Potawatomis began moving from the St. Joseph River near South Bend in 1795.

The northern portion of Metea Park can be accessed off Hursh Road between Puff and Halter Roads.

Activities
Hiking, nature study, photography, wildlife watching.

Directions
GPS coordinates: 41.201551, −85.035905
From I-69
- East on Union Chapel Road north of Fort Wayne to park, 3.2 miles

Bicentennial Woods Nature Preserve

120. Bicentennial Woods Nature Preserve
Owned by ACRES Land Trust

The seventy-nine-acre Bicentennial Woods Nature Preserve pro-tects what is believed to be the last remaining virgin timber in Allen County, including several oaks estimated at two hundred years old. Willow Creek, a tributary of Cedar Creek, bisects the preserve, which also contains small bluffs, a buttonbush wet-land, a pond, and an upland field.

The old growth—known as the Cathedral Oaks south and west of the creek and the Arnold Oaks north and west of the creek—share the hilly terrain with massive, old-growth syc-amores. In addition, this dedicated state nature preserve sup-ports an unusual variety of tree species, including bur oak, swamp white oak, shagbark hickory, bitternut hickory, sugar maple, black walnut, basswood, black cherry, sassafras, slippery elm, and flowering dogwood.

Woodland wildflowers include blue phlox, wild geranium, jack-in-the-pulpit, rue anemone, Dutchman's breeches, appendaged waterleaf, mayapple, drooping trillium, prairie trillium, spring beauty, firepink, and cardinal flower. Among the bird species that nest in and pass through Bicentennial Woods are yellow-throated vireo, indigo bunting, pileated woodpecker, great-crested flycatcher, and American goldfinch. The wetland and creek provide habitat for salamanders and frogs.

The preserve was acquired in 1994 to honor the Fort Wayne bicentennial.

Activities
Hiking Trails: 2.6-mile network, easy to moderate.
Other Activities: Nature study, photography, wildlife watching.

Directions
GPS coordinates: 41.250597, –85.139525
From I-69
- West on Union Chapel Road to Coldwater Road, 1.4 miles
- North on Coldwater Road to Shoaff Road, 3.5 miles
- West on Shoaff Road to preserve, 0.25 mile

121. Little Cedar Creek Wildlife Sanctuary Nature Preserve
Owned by ACRES Land Trust
The eighteen-acre Little Cedar Creek Wildlife Sanctuary Nature Preserve in Allen County is a floodplain forest with hills that support large oaks, sycamore, and tulip trees along the Little Cedar Creek. The dedicated state nature preserve was temporarily closed in 2016 to protect it from invasive Japanese stiltgrass.

The Little Cedar Creek preserve's lowlands feature stream meanders, are wet except in times of drought, and support marsh marigolds and skunk cabbage. The unusual green dragon wildflower grows here, along with trout lily, large-flowered trillium, jack-in-the-pulpit, and blue phlox.

Pileated woodpeckers, wood ducks, and great blue herons are common.

This Little Cedar Creek preserve was a gift from Jerry and Molly Mackel.

Activities
Hiking Trails: One (0.8 mile), easy.
Other Activities: Nature study, photography, wildlife watching.

Directions
GPS coordinates: 41.259091, –85.142858
From I-69
- West on Union Chapel Road just north of Fort Wayne to Coldwater Road, 1.5 miles
- North on Coldwater Road to Fitch Road, 4.2 miles
- West on Fitch Road to Sunlight Lane, 0.5 mile
- South on Sunlight Lane to preserve, 0.2 mile

122. Tom and Jane Dustin, Robert C. and Rosella C. Johnson, and Whitehurst Nature Preserves
Owned by ACRES Land Trust

The Tom and Jane Dustin Nature Preserve in Allen County consists primarily of high-quality forest—upland, ravine, and floodplain—with steep bluffs along the Cedar Creek's north bank. This eighty-eight-acre dedicated state nature preserve's landforms also include meadows and a wetland that supports an impressive display of state threatened horned bladderwort in spring.

The Dustin preserve adjoins the Robert C. and Rosella C. Johnson Nature Preserve and Whitehurst Nature Preserve to form a contiguous eighty-eight-acre natural area near Huntertown that is protected by ACRES Land Trust.

The Cedar Creek, which forms the Dustin preserve's southern boundary, is one of only three Indiana waterways designated as Indiana Natural, Scenic, and Recreational Rivers. Wildcat Creek in Tippecanoe and Carroll Counties and the Blue River in Harrison, Crawford, and Washington Counties are the others.

The Dustin preserve is named after legendary Indiana environmentalist activists Tom and Jane Dustin, whose former

Tom and Jane Dustin Nature Preserve

home houses the ACRES Land Trust headquarters and whose property forms the bulk of the combined preserves. The Dustins, founding members of the nonprofit conservation organization, played key roles in passing many of Indiana's most significant pieces of conservation legislation, including the Natural and Scenic Rivers Act and the Nature Preserves Act.

Incorporated in 1960, ACRES is Indiana's second-oldest land trust. The organization received its first donated property—the Spurgeon Woodland Reserve—the next year.

Activities
Hiking Trails: One (1.8 miles), moderate.
Other Activities: Nature study, photography, wildlife watching.

Directions
GPS coordinates: 41.250722, –85.120329

Vandolah Nature Preserve

From I-69
- West on Union Chapel Road north of Fort Wayne to Coldwater Road, 1.4 miles
- North on Coldwater Road to Chapman Road, 3.5 miles
- East on Chapman Road to preserve, 0.7 mile

123. Vandolah Nature Preserve
Owned by ACRES Land Trust
The forty-five-acre Vandolah Nature Preserve in Allen County contains wet-moist floodplain forest and moist upland forest communities on the Cedar Creek. Bisected by Interstate 69 just north of Fort Wayne, this dedicated state nature preserve features steep ravines, old fields, a marsh, and a stunning creek view from an eighty-foot escarpment.

In spring, the Vandolah preserve supports an explosion of wildflowers on the hills, including twinleaf, wild ginger, hepatica, jack-in-the-pulpit, Dutchman's breeches, bloodroot, rue anemone, and several varieties of trillium.

The marsh attracts waterfowl, such as great blue herons, green herons, hooded mergansers, and wood ducks. Pileated woodpeckers have been reported in the woods. Wildlife includes deer, raccoons, beavers, minks, and foxes.

A trail that follows Cedar Creek under I-69 connects the preserve's two sides. Cedar Creek is one of only three Indiana Natural, Scenic, and Recreational Rivers.

Activities
Hiking Trails: Two-mile trail system.
Other Activities: Nature study, photography, wildlife watching.

Directions
GPS coordinates: 41.234819, −85.092484
From I-69
- West on Union Chapel Road on Fort Wayne's north side to Auburn Road, 0.4 mile
- North on Auburn Road to Vandolah Road, 3.0 miles
- East on Vandolah Road to Tother Road, 0.2 mile
- South on Tother Road to preserve, 0.1 mile

124. McNabb-Walter Nature Preserve
Owned by ACRES Land Trust
The 192-acre McNabb-Walter Nature Preserve in Allen County protects mostly moist upland forest and features a picturesque high bank on the St. Joseph River and deep ravines along Davis Fisher Creek. A portion of the preserve, which includes a forty-one-acre dedicated state nature preserve, supports old-growth forest that is dominated by sugar maples and tulip poplars.

The largest nature preserve in Allen County, McNabb-Walter also supports red oak, white oak, American beech, and sycamore. A small floodplain forest lines the banks of the river and

St. Joseph River, McNabb-Walter Nature Preserve

the creek, which converge on the preserve. Wildflowers—spring beauty, large-flowered trillium, cut-leaved toothwort, rue anemone, harbinger-of-spring, and others—thrive on the forest floor with rich variety and quality.

Remnants of a maple sugar camp that operated on the McNabb-Walter site remain, including an old sleigh that was used to haul the sap.

McNabb-Walter spans Davis Road and has two parking lots. The westernmost lot and trail lead a short distance to the riverbank. The river view is mostly obscured when the foliage is full. The easternmost lot and trail lead through the woods and along the creek.

Activities
Hiking Trails: One (1.4 miles), easy.
Other Activities: Nature study, photography, wildlife watching.

Directions

**GPS coordinates: Western lot, 41.260498, –84.940620;
Eastern lot, 41.262130, –84.937741**

From I-69

- East on State Road 1 north of Fort Wayne to Roth Road,
  10.7 miles
- South on Roth Road to Hurshtown Road, 0.8 mile
- East on Hurshtown Road to Cuba Road, 1.0 mile
- North on Cuba Road to Davis Road, 1.4 miles
- Northeast on Davis Road to preserve eastern lot, 0.2 mile, to
  western lot, 0.4 mile

Maumee River, Blue Cast Springs Nature Preserve

BLACK SWAMP
NATURAL REGION

BLACK SWAMP NATURAL REGION

125. Blue Cast Springs Nature Preserve

Owned by ACRES Land Trust

The eighty-eight-acre Blue Cast Springs Nature Preserve protects 3,150 feet of the Maumee River and features primarily riparian topography with upland forest, floodplain forest, thirty-foot bluffs, a natural spring, and numerous ravines. Fifty-four acres are designated as the only dedicated state nature preserve in Indiana's Black Swamp Natural Region, which lies east of Fort Wayne near the Indiana-Ohio border.

Blue Cast Springs' high-quality, oak-dominated flatwoods forest and other natural communities support many hydro-sensitive species and help maintain their regional populations. Great blue herons nest on the preserve.

The bluffs offer vistas of the Maumee River and one of its islands, though trees mostly obscure the views in summer. Ravines run through the upland forest and feed the river.

The preserve's name draws from the natural spring, whose bluish-tinged waters were once thought to have healing properties and were pumped, bottled, and marketed internationally as tonic water from 1902 through 1955.

The Blue Cast Springs preserve borders the historic Wabash and Erie Canal for 960 feet.

Activities
Hiking Trails: One (1.1 miles), easy.
Other Activities: Nature study, photography, wildlife watching.

Directions
GPS coordinates: 41.153966, –84.862694
From I-69

- East on I-469 just south of Fort Wayne to Webster Road, 23.9 miles
- North on Webster Road to Old US 24, 0.7 mile to Blue Cast Road, 3.9 miles
- East on Blue Cast Road to preserve, 200 feet